Palgrave Macmillan Studies in Family and Ii

Series Editors: **David Morgan**, Universi
University of Edinburgh, UK and **Grahai**

Carmen Lau Clayton
BRITISH CHINESE FAMILIES
Parenting, Relationships and Childhoods

Lara McKenzie
AGE-DISSIMILAR COUPLES AND ROMANTIC RELATIONSHIPS
Ageless Love?

David Morgan
RETHINKING FAMILY PRACTICES

Petra Nordqvist, Carol Smart
RELATIVE STRANGERS
Family Life, Genes and Donor Conception

Julie M. Parsons
GENDER, CLASS AND FOOD
Families, Bodies and Health

Róisín Ryan-Flood
LESBIAN MOTHERHOOD
Gender, Families and Sexual Citizenship

Sally Sales
ADOPTION, FAMILY AND THE PARADOX OF ORIGINS
A Foucauldian History

Tam Sanger
TRANS PEOPLE'S PARTNERSHIPS
Towards an Ethics of Intimacy

Tam Sanger and Yvette Taylor (*editors*)
MAPPING INTIMACIES
Relations, Exchanges, Affects

Lisa Smyth
THE DEMANDS OF MOTHERHOOD
Agents, Roles and Recognitions

Vilna Bashi Treitler (*editor*)
RACE IN TRANSNATIONAL AND TRANSRACIAL ADOPTION

Katherine Twamley
LOVE, MARRIAGE AND INTIMACY AMONG GUJARATI INDIANS
A Suitable Match

Palgrave Macmillan Studies in Family and Intimate Life
Series Standing Order ISBN
HBK 978–0–230–51748–6
PBK 978–0–230–24924–0 (*outside North America only*)

You can receive future titles in this series as they are published by placing a standing order. Please contact your bookseller or, in case of difficulty, write to us at the address below with your name and address, the title of the series and one of the ISBNs quoted above.

Customer Services Department, Macmillan Distribution Ltd, Houndmills, Basingstoke, Hampshire RG21 6XS, England

Gender, Class and Food

Families, Bodies and Health

Julie M. Parsons
Plymouth University, UK

Softcover reprint of the hardcover 1st edition 2015 978-1-137-47640-1

First published 2015 by
PALGRAVE MACMILLAN

Palgrave Macmillan in the UK is an imprint of Macmillan Publishers
Limited, registered in England, company number 785998, of Houndmills,
Basingstoke, Hampshire RG21 6XS.

Palgrave Macmillan in the US is a division of St Martin's Press LLC,
175 Fifth Avenue, New York, NY 10010.

Palgrave Macmillan is the global academic imprint of the above companies
and has companies and representatives throughout the world.

Palgrave® and Macmillan® are registered trademarks in the United States,
the United Kingdom, Europe and other countries.

ISBN 978-1-349-56162-9   ISBN 978-1-137-47641-8 (eBook)
DOI 10.1057/9781137476418

This book is printed on paper suitable for recycling and made from fully
managed and sustained forest sources. Logging, pulping and manufacturing
processes are expected to conform to the environmental regulations of
the country of origin.

A catalogue record for this book is available from the British Library.

Library of Congress Cataloging-in-Publication Data
Parsons, Julie M., 1964–
Gender, class and food : families, bodies and health / Julie M. Parsons,
Plymouth University, UK.
pages cm — (Palgrave Macmillian studies in family and intimate life)

1. Food habits—Social aspects.   2. Food—Social
aspects.   3. Nutrition—Social aspects.   I. Title.
GT2855.P37 2015
394.1'2—dc23   2015015589

Typeset by MPS Limited, Chennai, India.

For Chris, because food is love

Contents

Acknowledgements

This book would not have been possible without the input from respondents and I am extremely grateful to each and every one of them for the time and effort they put into their food stories. I adopted an auto/biographical approach after attending my first British Sociological Association Auto/Biography study group winter conference, where an informal chat with Gayle Letherby led me to consider this relevant to the study of food. Indeed, Gayle's unwavering support over the years has been invaluable, as has the help and guidance I received from Alison Anderson and latterly Kay Inckle. Thank you all. Taking an auto/biographical route has not been an easy path and I am therefore indebted to those openly supportive of it, notably David Morgan. In preparing this book I thank everyone at Palgrave Macmillan, especially Harriet Barker and Amelia Derkatsch. I would also like to thank Susie David for her excellent proofreading skills. Finally, my husband Chris and children Finlay and Lilly, thank you for not being too critical of my everyday foodways.

1
Introduction

In a twenty first century neo-liberal era, *everyday foodways* are a powerful means of drawing boundaries between social groups, distinguishing the 'self' from the 'other', defining who we are and where we belong. Throughout this book I draw upon data and analysis of 75 auto/biographical food narratives that formed the basis of my doctoral study: 'Ourfoodstories@e-mail.com; an auto/biographical study of relationships with food'. My research leads me to argue that everyday foodways enable individuals to present themselves as responsible neo-liberal citizens, so that eating healthily for example demonstrates an engagement with public and medical discourses that positions the self as responsible for her or his own health and well-being (responsible individualism). In this book, I emphasise the power of everyday foodways in maintaining and reinforcing social divisions along the lines of gender and class. Indeed, everyday foodways have become a potent means of 'doing gender' (West and Zimmerman 1987) and performing a middle class habitus (Bourdieu 1984).

Throughout, I use the term foodways. This usually refers to the production and distribution of food at a macro level; it is also used in anthropology when exploring food cultures or shared common beliefs, behaviours and practices relating to the production and consumption of food (Counihan 1999). Here I also consider foodways at a micro level, to reflect the multiplicity of ways of 'doing' food that incorporates all aspects of everyday food practices, from acquiring food, growing it, or shopping for it, preparing, cooking, sharing and eating (in/outside the domestic sphere), to the consumption of food media. This incorporates the notion of foodways as an essential aspect of an individual's cultural habitus (Bourdieu 1984), which is cultivated and inculcated over time. Indeed, foodways are narratives of relational affectation, or how we learn to know food, with our food preferences embedded, produced and maintained through the practice of doing 'tastes', over and over again (Carolan 2011: 6). Thus, foodways are 'affective practices' (Wetherell 2012: 96), because they are ongoing emotional, socially constructed, embodied, situated performances infused with sedimented social and personal history. This sedimentation is like lime scale fixing itself to the inside a kettle, it becomes part of the material body of the kettle, naturalised.

Further, 'foodways' has multiple meanings; it highlights the significance of modes of practice or ways of 'doing' food, as well as movement and direction across time (history) and space (culture). Consequently, foodways connect the individual with the social through everyday practices (action/habit). The significance of foodways or ways of doing food is reminiscent of West and Zimmerman's (1987) notion of 'doing' gender, Butler's (1999) conceptualisation of gender as performance, and Morgan's (1996) theories on 'family practices' as significant in distinguishing between what families 'are' and what families 'do', in contrast to the institution of 'the' family (Morgan 2011). A focus on foodways therefore emphasises the embodied, affective, everyday food performances; interactions and temporal ways of doing food that connect past, present and future.

It is notable therefore that foodways (like gender and class) work within three interconnecting domains: (1) on an 'individual' level, through socialisation, internalisation, identity work and the construction of the self; (2) through interactional 'cultural' expectations and 'othering' of practices; and (3) via 'institutions' that control access to resources, as well as ideologies and discourses (Risman 2004). Thus, performances of everyday foodways are validated, constrained and facilitated by reference to wider institutional contexts that may include gender (patriarchy), class (economics), culture (capital) and 'the' family (discourse). Accordingly, everyday foodways inculcate a cultural habitus (Bourdieu 1984) through the repetition, reproduction and reinforcement of values and tastes. Hence, in an era of heightened anxiety about obesity, everyday foodways continue to be morally loaded activities that have the power to consolidate cultural boundaries. Similarly, public health discourses reinforce divisions between appropriate and inappropriate foodways, with 'healthy' everyday foodways associated with 'good' food and therefore being good.

Gender and class

A focus on gender and class raises obvious questions about why and how these forms of stratification still matter. Indeed, the impact of class and gender on foodways seems to belong to a former era and have more in common with research carried out across the UK in the early 1980s (Murcott 1982, 1983, Charles and Kerr 1988). In these studies gender roles within the home were clearly demarcated and economic social class directly related to household expenditure on food. Today gender and class positions are considered fluid and less easy to discern. Instead, there are cultural codes and symbols that individual consumers choose to buy into, such as 'healthy' eating or 'authentic' cuisine and these give the impression that we are free from patriarchal constraints and economic determinism. Of course this belies the reality for many, especially in terms of everyday foodways, that what we eat, with whom, how, where and when, are heavily influenced by cultural values inculcated within the family over time, and although this does not seem to relate directly to patriarchy (Walby 1990) or economic capital (Bourdieu 1984), 'time' is money, with those in control of it still mostly male.

When discussing gender throughout this book I will be referring to performances of femininities and masculinities (Butler 1999), or 'doing gender' (West and Zimmerman 1987). Although I identify as a feminist scholar, I will not be providing analysis of the range of possible feminist perspectives, as these are well rehearsed elsewhere (Cairns and Johnston, in press). Suffice to note that I agree with the Fawcett Society's (2010) mission statement in supporting 'a vision of society in which women and men enjoy equality at work, at home and in public life'. For me, being, doing or becoming a feminist is a political act. It signifies an alignment with egalitarian values. In the context of gender identities, everyday foodways are routinised repetitions, performances and affective practices that give the impression of a stable self; these become part of the 'performativity' of heteronormative gender practices 'that creates the illusion of an inner essence or psychic gender core' (Butler 1999: 28). However, whilst gender is socially, culturally and discursively produced, it is also experienced through the division of labour at work and in the home. Indeed, everyday foodways are a powerful means of reproducing and reinforcing difference (individually and culturally), and the lived experience of 'doing gender' cuts across individual, cultural and structural domains, especially in relation to the micro-politics of gender; as Whitehead (2002: 14) notes, 'to be gendered is to be political'. It is also relational, for example men resort to hegemonic masculinities to distance themselves from emphasised femininities (Connell 1995:183). There is no single form of masculinity or femininity, instead men and women position themselves in terms of gender relations, 'so that to be a man is to be not like a woman [and] to be a woman is to be not like a man' (Bradley 2007:48). This has obvious implications when considering foodways over the life course.

In terms of social class I utilise Bradley's (2014: 434) class schema that builds upon a Marxo-Weberian tradition that includes three or possibly four classes, the elite, the middle class, the working class and the labour surplus class or most disadvantaged fraction of the working class. Further, Bradley (1996: 19) notes:

Class is a social category, which refers to lived relations surrounding social arrangements of production, exchange, distribution and consumption. While these may narrowly be conceived as economic relationships, to do with money, wealth and property ... class should be seen as referring to a much broader web of social relationships including, for example, lifestyle, educational experience and patterns of residence.

Thus, like gender, social class is relational and following Bourdieu's (1984) model of cultural capital and the Great British Class Survey (GBCS) 'class operate[s] symbolically and culturally through forms of stigmatisation and marking of personhood and value' (Savage et al. 2013: 222). In addition, cultural hostility or 'aversion to different lifestyles is perhaps one of the strongest barriers between the classes' (Bourdieu 1984: 56). This centres on a contested relationship with the legitimate or high cultural capital of the dominant classes and assumes a level of cultural hostility (strong dislike) towards the illegitimate or low/'vulgar' cultural forms of capital associated with the working class (and vice versa) (Bourdieu 1984, Warde 2011). Hence, in analysing contemporary foodways, it is pertinent to utilise

Bourdieu's (1984, 1996) forms of capital: economic capital (wealth and income), cultural capital (embodied, objectified, institutionalised), social capital (networks and relationships) and symbolic capital (the conversion and legitimisation of other forms of capital), as these are important resources in the boundary work and demarcation of moral hierarchies when considering what counts as legitimate/illegitimate taste (Bourdieu 1996).

Further, the manner of presenting, serving and eating food, or everyday foodways fulfils the social function of legitimising social difference (Bourdieu 1984: 6) and these cultural practices are gendered; as Skeggs (1997: 98) notes, 'the sign of femininity is always classed'. Indeed, Bourdieu (1986: 105) identifies mothers as significant in transforming economic capital into symbolic and cultural capital for their children; they are what Skeggs (2004a: 22) refers to as 'sign bearing' carriers of taste. For example, 'future oriented' middle classed food 'choices' become part of a reshaping of patriarchy that draws on the success of 'new' femininities, whilst simultaneously reaffirming a 'domesticated femininity from the past' (Taylor 2012: 16). Thus, respondents negotiate classed as well as gendered aspirations when reflecting upon transformations and improvements in their everyday foodways over the life course. In terms of contemporary constructions of new femininities, women today have to negotiate the twin poles of traditional femininity whilst embracing neo-liberal values of the autonomous self (Budgeon 2014).

Hence, 'doing gender to meet others expectations over time helps to construct our gendered selves' (Risman 2004: 431). Thus, when considering the intersectionalities of gender and class, firstly, everyday foodways reinforce classed feminine and masculine identities; as Morgan (1996: 158) argues, 'the micro-politics of food revolve around gender' and families tend to be 'mothered rather than gendered' (1996: 82). Today, for example working mums preparing healthy 'home-cooked' meals from scratch is a means of reproducing an idealised new feminine identity (Parsons 2014a, 2014b). Secondly, these everyday foodways reinforce middle class cultural norms and values regarding what is appropriate (middle class) mothering, with responsible mothers acting as guardians of health, as well as 'moral guardians of family eating' (McIntosh and Zey 1989, James et al. 2009b: 8).

Indeed, when exploring everyday foodways, the intersectionalities of gender and class remain vital in maintaining and drawing boundaries between appropriate and inappropriate foodways. A commitment to particular gendered and classed foodways protects individuals from association with 'other' ways of doing food. It ensures an association with a kind of food hegemony that insulates individuals from the stigmatising impact of improper foodways (Johansson et al. 2013). In an obesogenic environment with high profile public health discourses and mass media campaigns around 'proper' foodways it is hardly surprising that the anxious middle classes want to be seen to be doing the right thing. In 2002, Ruppel-Shell argued that the 'worried weighty' represented the biggest marketing opportunity in history for products that could alleviate the battle with weight watching. Over a decade later, this group is still negotiating the shifting boundaries between acceptable and unacceptable foodways.

However, in contemporary westernised neo-liberal societies, being worried about weight and health-consciousness are coded as feminine. Despite arguments regarding culinary capital and the value of sustainability, health and dietary restraint amongst elite groups in the Unites States (Naccarato and LeBesco 2012), men and elite men especially are not constrained by such discourses. Indeed, elite men are able to play freely within culinary fields. Further, in a culinary field high cultural capital is also measured in terms of cultural omnivorousness or a liking for high and low cultural forms (Peterson and Kern 1996). Warde (2011: 345) argues that this omnivore debate is significant as it not only draws symbolic boundaries within the dominant class, but also has the potential to mute cultural hostility towards working class forms of capital and this is developed and explored throughout the book.

Overall I focus on how identity is articulated, formed and reformulated through the social categories of gender and class, which are played out within a theatre of everyday foodways. This is not to dismiss the significance of other major/minor categories of gender intersections, such as (in no particular order) nation, (dis)ability, sexuality, age, religion, faith and migration. Indeed intersectionality is pertinent in discussions of identity, gender and power (Davis 2008, Nash 2008, Ratna 2013) and whilst it is more often used with reference to the intersectionalities of gender and race (Puwar 2004), in considering the intersectionalities of gender and class in the field of everyday foodways, it is notable that social, cultural, economic and symbolic capitals (Bourdieu 1986), become gendered resources in boundary work and the demarcation of moral hierarchies. These forms of capital intersect with gender and enable individuals to present themselves as responsible neo-liberal citizens engaged in 'appropriate' middle class and gendered foodways.

Therefore I examine how and why individuals position themselves as they do, which is primarily about their need to locate themselves as 'good' responsible citizens and the power of hegemonic forms of everyday foodways to delineate the moral boundaries between 'good' and 'bad'. The persistence of Cartesian dualism (Levi-Strauss 1969) and dichotomous thinking (Oakley 1992) alongside absolutist discourses regarding appropriate foodways contributes to the cultural milieu in which individuals are forced to negotiate their subjective positions. There is a dominant gendered division of food that espouses a masculine/feminine food dichotomy within mainstream westernised foodways (Adams 1990, Nath 2011). In developed capitalist consumer societies that draw upon neo-liberal discourses of responsible individualism, the notion of consumer choice and the moral imperative to make the 'right' choice is paramount. Further, making the 'right' choice assumes an engagement with a contemporary foodscape and current discourses on what might be considered 'appropriate' foodways.

Hence, respondents use individual foodways as 'narratives of becoming' responsible neo-liberal citizens (Deleuze and Guattari 1998) and these can be positioned within wider public discourses relating to issues of family, health and the body. Indeed, these common vocabularies (Mills 1959) of transformation demonstrate the ways in which everyday foodways reify traditional forms of gender, class, family, health and the body. Despite the notion of foodways as marginal to individual identity (Warde 1997), or identity work, respondents draw on recognisable socio-historical narratives from an imagined past that valorise their engagement with contemporary individualised identities, whilst simultaneously identifying themselves as belonging to positions that continued to be influenced by 'old' representations of gender and class.

This book is different in its scope to similar texts on food. The most recent, *Food and Femininities* (Cairns and Johnston, in press), centres on interviews and focus groups with women and a few men (USA/Canada), but essentially positions individuals as consumers, interested in food shopping and consumption. In *Culinary Capital*

(Naccarato and LeBesco 2012), the authors discuss food as a means of drawing boundaries and distinctions between elites in the USA mostly through analysis of popular American television programmes and advertising. In both there is a focus on food scenes or trends in the cultural consumption of food (real and symbolic), so that shifts in everyday foodways become an issue of consumer choice and identity formation. The authors from both books here and elsewhere (Johnston and Baumann 2010) focus on sustainability (environmentalism, ethics, localism, slow foods, farmers markets), health and dietary restraint as a means of distinguishing between consumer tribes. Following Bourdieu's (1984) conceptualisation of cultural capital, Naccarato and LeBesco (2012: 2) argue that there is a kind of culinary capital at work, in which 'food and food practices become markers of social status'. Cairns and Johnston (in press: 3) focus on femininity, how food is embedded in hetero-normative cultural conceptualisations of 'how to be and act feminine'. Neither fully acknowledges the power of the intersectionalities of gender and class on everyday foodways. In this book I therefore focus on femininities and masculinities, especially how they intersect with formations of class (Skeggs 1997). I highlight the power of everyday foodways in marking what is 'appropriate' or legitimate in terms of gender, class, food, families, embodiment and health.

Families, bodies and health

The subtitle to this book is 'families, bodies and health' and this represents the concerns of those participating in the study. These themes link public issues with private troubles (Mills 1959), as public health policies locate solutions to the 'problem of obesity', for example, within families. These are powerful ideological domains that impact upon the construction of a responsible neo-liberal self. Hence, everyday foodways become a means of demonstrating a commitment to health, whereby eating healthily signals a healthy body (mind) and a healthy family. Conversely if individuals are not considered to be complying with cultural expectations associated with health foodways, they are prone to be 'othered', demonised and stigmatised. Of course this is related to power, those with high status are less likely to be stigmatised; as Bergman (2009) notes, a big male body is more likely to be associated with power than a big female one.

Indeed, the everyday foodways of the dominant group can be used to inflate cultural hostility and reinforce legitimate forms of social, symbolic and cultural capital. For example, the media furore around Jamie Oliver's comments in a *Radio Times* interview (that coincided with a TV series and book launch) in which he said:

You might remember that scene in [a previous series] of Ministry of Food, with the mum and the kid eating chips and cheese out of Styrofoam containers, and behind them is a massive f****** TV.

(Deans 2013)

In this vignette, unauthorised foodways are clearly associated with 'take-away' food, marked as unorthodox and 'other'. It is notable that it is mum (not dad) that is implicated and Oliver uses cultural markers of class status to highlight how 'mum' is breaking the rules associated with legitimate class based maternal foodways. There is a lack of high cultural capital in this scene, it lacks a table, knife and fork, healthy vegetables, care, sociability and this is juxtaposed with excess in terms of a 'massive f****** TV'. These are powerful cultural markers that commit acts of condescension and symbolic violence, defined by Bourdieu and Wacquant (2002: 167) as 'the violence, which is exercised upon a social agent with his or her complicity'. Thus, cultural hostility, moral judgment and approbation are conferred because these are considered contentious foodways. This highlights the extent to which class status is embedded in everyday family practices (Morgan 1996, 2011). Indeed, foodways are 'saturated with class connotations' (Seymour 2013: un-paginated) and become part of a politics of aspiration (Andreou 2013) or dis-identification. Indeed, 'good taste' continues to create, mark and consolidate social divisions' (Bennett et al. 2009: 259). Indeed, 'culture' is not a matter of indifference for the powerful and for some sections of the middle class it remains critical and a source of ontological security (Dawson 2012: 311). I therefore utilise Bourdieu's (1984, 1986) theoretical framework in the context of analysing my data, in common with many 'feminists [who] have appropriated [his framework] in order to examine the relationship between gender and class' (Huppatz 2009: 45).

Thus, in westernised neo-liberal nations across the globe, in an era of arguably 'moral panic' (Cohen 2011) regarding obesity, everyday foodways more than ever have the power to define who we are and where we belong. The moral discourses concerning legitimate food-ways and appropriate ways of purchasing, preparing and consuming food, when, where and with whom, impact upon the presentation of the self in everyday life (Goffman 1959). In order to be considered a responsible neo-liberal citizen requires careful negotiation of the moral boundaries that distinguish 'good' from 'bad' foodways. It has been argued that in a post-modern, post-feminist epoch notions of gender and class are empty signifiers devoid of power. Yet, when respondents were asked to describe their lives around food, how their tastes and habits had developed over time, they resorted to rigid cultural scripts that were heavily coded, gendered and classed. These were living, breathing fully formed narratives and not the living dead 'zombie' categories that might have been expected (Slater and Ritzer 2001). Instead everyday foodways continue to be saturated with gender and class, the desire to distance oneself from 'other' foodways, whether this is because they are feminising or culturally contaminating, is strong. The narratives drawn upon throughout this book therefore highlight the power of everyday foodways to display what is legitimate in terms of families, bodies and health and these are presented, located and/or performed in terms of gender and class. Hence, the complex interplay of power and desire in everyday lives continues to be played out within a theatre of food.

Public/private issues

This book incorporates respondents' voices, values and issues of importance to them. I utilise an auto/biographical approach to everyday foodways because it highlights the interconnectedness of the individual and the social, the autobiographical and biographi-cal, the micro and the macro, the private and the public (Morgan 1998). This enables an exploration of the private troubles and public issues around everyday foodways (Mills 1959), whilst demonstrating the inter-textuality of auto/biographical accounts. Thus, there are two interrelated purposes of the study, firstly to explore the food memories of others, and secondly to critically examine the social and cultural milieu in which these are articulated. In keeping with Mills' (1959) argument in favour of the 'sociological imagination' personal troubles and public issues are interconnected. Indeed, food memories have been used by food researchers as this method illustrates the extent to which our memories of the everyday are socially constructed and simultaneously part of a shared socio-cultural history (Lupton 1996, Belasco 2008).

Originally, the primary aim of the research was to investigate the relationship between individuals and their food 'choice' using an auto/biographical research approach. However, once the research started I shifted my focus away from notions of choice in order to distance myself from the neo-liberal assertion that *all* individuals are free to choose their identities outside of social, cultural and/or financial constraints. This is because everyday foodways continue to be constrained by the intersectionalities of gender and class. A focus on food choice implies a wholly conscious engagement with highly individualised consumer identities and identity politics, when food consumption can be unconscious or mindless and constrained by more structural factors, such as class, gender, ethnicity, age, (dis) ability. The concept of 'choice' is politically and morally loaded, especially when choices are made from a limited set of options that are constrained by economics, and/or cultural norms and values. It fits with a notion of food choice as part of a Foucauldian (1979) disciplinary regime, the means by which individuals control or regulate their bodies in the process of creating themselves. In contemporary neo-liberal Western societies a high value is attached to individualism and the ability to make rational self-reflexive choices for one's self. What Foucault (1988: 18) refers to as technologies of the self that:

> *permit individuals to effect their own means or with the help of others a certain number of operations on their own bodies and souls, thoughts, conducts and way of being, so as to transform themselves in order to attain a certain state of happiness, purity, wisdom, perfection or immortality.*

This is not to suggest that individuals are never active agents in their everyday foodways, it is just that an emphasis on individualism belies the role of social ties, interaction cues, relationality and the embeddedness of individuals in family and/or kin relations (Jallinoja and Widmer 2011: 5). Brillat-Savarin's declaration (1970: 13) 'tell me what you eat and I'll tell you what you are' is indicative of the extent to which food is embedded within the cultural norms and values of an epoch. Hence, food and foodways are both individual and social. The individual is the carrier of these practices through routinised ways of knowing and understanding, but these conventionalised mental activities are not qualities of the individual (Reckwitz 2002: 249) but culturally specific. Hence, the focus on an auto/biographical approach is significant as it underlines the extent to which the individual and the social, the autobiographical and the biographical are interconnected (Morgan 1998).

Further, 'our food stories' are simultaneously individual and collective. They demonstrate 'social network affects' (Christakis and Fowler 2007) or how people are embedded in social webs of behaviour that spread across a range of social ties. It is a kind of social contagion or mimesis; for example, the significance of our relationships with others in the spread of 'obesity' in a population (Christakis and Fowler 2007), or the take up of a particular diet or exercise fad (Kolata 2007), reveals how social connections matter. Thus, foodways and other practices or routinised types of behaviour consist of several elements, things and their uses, as well as background knowledge. Indeed, there is a relationship between these things and the body; everyday foodways are about embodiment and the senses. It is how respondents understand these relationships, how these develop over time and impact on everyday lives that I consider. Specifically how these relationships and practices continue to be influenced by the intersectionalities of gender and class, despite arguments that gender, class and family are 'zombie' categories 'that no longer capture the contemporary milieu' (Beck, interviewed by Slater and Ritzer 2001: 262). An individualist perspective makes no allowance for the fact that some individuals have always been able to act outside of the structural constraints of gender and class (especially white men) whilst others are wholly constrained by them, even now. Indeed, the connection between what Mills (1959) refers to as private troubles and public issues and the development of a common vocabulary of motives persists.

Thus, public discourses form a repertoire of available stories that respondents can draw upon in the telling of themselves. For example, at the time of the research the UK government announced that most of the major food manufacturers had agreed to comply with standardised food labelling on their products by the summer of 2013. The Minister for Public Health, Anna Soubry, said that this development 'will help us all choose healthier options' (Hickman

2012: un-paginated). The Chairman of the British Dietetic Association (BDA), Helen Davidson, claimed 'consumers need a quick understanding of the relative healthiness of a product' (Hickman 2012: un-paginated). These claims make significant assumptions about individual agency, notably that individuals make deliberate wholly conscious decisions about what to eat. They ignore the social context in which foodways are performed and practiced and the extent to which these decisions are related to routinised habitus (Bourdieu 1984) and emotional responses or affective practices (Wetherell 2012). They assume that 'healthier' and 'healthiness' are objective standards of measurement, again ignoring the social and emotional context in which these terms are embedded. Also, that 'healthiness' is achievable and/or a desirable universal goal in everyday life for everyone.

Feeding time and Bourdieu

One route to exploring relationships with food is through memory (Sutton 2001), what Arendt (1996: 15) refers to as 'the storehouse of time'. The significance of time is also pertinent for Bourdieu (1984: 6) in terms of cultural capital and habitus; the disposition and embodiment of taste is inculcated or sediments over time. This includes what he refers to as a disposition for considering the future rather than living in the present that acknowledges a 'temporal power' (Bourdieu 1984: 315), or what Adkins (2011: 349) refers to as 'trading the future'. Hence, as Bourdieu (1986: 214–58) claims, the best measure of cultural capital is the amount of time devoted to acquiring it, because the 'transformation of economic capital into cultural [social and symbolic] capital presupposes an expenditure of time that is made possible by possession of economic capital'. In Bourdieu's thesis there is no innate aesthetic or pure taste, there is only 'taste' inculcated over time. Thus Bourdieu argues against a Kantian 'taste of sense' in favour of a 'taste of reflection' (Bourdieu 1984: 6). Indeed, following Bourdieu (1984) instant gratification, hedonism and 'lack' of time/investment in the future are associated with being in the present and a working class habitus. On the other hand, investing in the future, abstaining from having a good time is associated with a middle class disposition.

Indeed, as Morgan (1996: 166) explains 'food represents a particularly strong form of anchorage in the past [and] serves as one of the links between historical time, individual time and household time'. Thus, everyday foodways are so 'embedded in the domestic cultures of everyday life that they come to be regarded as natural' (Scott 2009: 106), part of the doxic order of things. Here *doxa* according to Bourdieu means 'the immediate belief in the facticity of the world that makes us take it for granted' (Bourdieu and Wacquant 1992: 73). Further:

> *The doxa comprises our naturalised understandings of how a particular field functions and which resources or types of capital are valuable within it. It is through doxic knowledge that agents make sense of the world and engage in meaningful patterns of behaviour, that is, practices*
> (Senn and Elhardt 2014: 320–1)

Thus, everyday foodways are everyday *doxa*, they are embedded and embodied habits, knowledge and practices learnt and sedimented over time. In a culinary field everyday foodways draw upon wider hegemonic discourses in a doxic battle over legitimacy. Therefore, auto/biographical memories are temporal reflections on the times in which they are written and imbued with 'romanticised representations and rememberings' (Taylor 2012: 16) of gender, class, food and family, past and present. There is a persistent tension between 'knowing' oneself and the creation of memory. For Deleuze and Guattari (1998) memory is the membrane that allows for the correspondence between the 'sheets of the past and the layers of reality'; it is a block of becoming. As Clough (2007: 29) notes, 'we write not with childhood memories but through blocs of childhood that are [always part of] becoming the child of the present'. We move backwards and forwards to locate a 'self', one that is, 'an autobiographical-techno-ontological writing block' (Clough 2007: 15). In creating an auto/biographical account, the presentation of the self in everyday life, one's narrative, continues to be a performance with front and backstage processes at work/play (Goffman 1963). It is mutable, temporal and in a continual process of becoming (Deleuze and Guattari 1998).

In keeping with an auto/biographical approach I write in the first person and draw upon my experiences (if and when appropriate). Everyday foodways are after all exactly that, and therefore experienced by researcher, respondent and reader. For example, when I began the research that forms the basis of this book, I assumed from my training as a sociologist, following the individualisation thesis from Beck (1992, 2002) and Giddens (1991), that the social, political and economic changes of late modernity had weakened the structural constraints of class and gender. Hence, as Adkins (2004: 192) argues, 'the axes of (socially organised) difference, such as class, gender and sexuality are more a matter of individual decision making in the act of creating the self as an individual'. It was with this in mind that I set out to explore 'individual' food histories from a convenience sample of women and men, rather than interviewing couples and/or families (Murcott 1983, Charles and Kerr 1988, Lupton 1996, 2000, 2005, Jackson 2009, James et al. 2009b).

Consequently, when asking respondents to consider their individualised auto/biographies in relation to food I expected reflections on changes in attitudes towards everyday foodways over the life course, a blurring of the boundaries between the genders in relation to both family foodways and body regimes (weight management), and perhaps an acknowledgement of the influence of health discourses (Foucault 1988, 1991). I assumed that if changes in the workplace had been matched in the private sphere, there would be more equality regarding domestic work and family foodways. I anticipated, due to public and media discourses on perceived health risks associated with obesity, that men would engage more in body regulation, self-care and 'fat talk' (Ambjörnsson 2005). I had not considered the extent to which respondents would assert their class positions in relation to foodways, nor how gendered these practices continue to be. Nor, despite the medicalisation of everyday life (Crawford 1980), that healthy eating would still be considered as part of a cultural script of normative (middle classed) femininity. In addition, neo-liberal politics that emphasise individual responsibility, active citizenship and economic independence are constructed as particularly white middle class values. In hindsight it seems unreasonable to assume that respondents would not be engaged with these values, particularly when family foodways are represented as part of a problem of obesity.

Methodological approach of the study

I invited potential participants to write their own auto/biographical food narratives through a series of asynchronous in-depth online

interviews, which is a form of computer-mediated communication (CMC) (Kozinets 2010). This entailed a series of written e-mail
exchanges with respondents similar to correspondence techniques
(Letherby and Zdrodowski 1995), from an e-mail account created
specifically for the study ourfoodstories@email.com. I purposely
chose to conduct the research through CMC because it represents
an emancipatory, non-hierarchical approach to research that enables
respondents to participate on their own terms in line with early feminist critiques of positivist approaches to research (Oakley 1981, Finch
1984). Hence, respondents can revise their narratives before sending
them and as Letherby (2003: 93) highlights, the act of writing can
be a political and enabling act, as respondents decide what they do
and do not wish to disclose. CMC can be spontaneous, quick and
fleeting, but also has some of the temporal qualities of traditional
letter writing – the frustration of waiting for the postman to deliver
a letter is not dissimilar to waiting for correspondence to be e-mailed
into an inbox. Similarly, there are traces of past epistolary traditions
in some of the narratives, as well as more modern touches such as
emoticons.

I received full ethical approval from the University ethics committee with the condition that I include an exclusion clause, 'that
strongly advised' potential respondents 'not to participate if they
had suffered from an eating disorder'. I used snowball sampling from
my own social network, which is common in food research (Lupton
2000, 2005), and sent out 190 invitations over nine months, roughly
10 per week. Once respondents agreed to participate, they chose or I
assigned a pseudonym and replied:

*What I'm really after is your 'food story'. Perhaps, this will include
your earliest food memories, favourite foods, memorable food occasions,
whether your eating habits have changed over time and why this may
be. Also, absolutely anything food related that you'd like to share.*

Respondents therefore formed part of a self-selecting group in that
the invitation appealed to those confident that they had 'something'
to contribute to research about everyday foodways. I also devised a
series of general, open questions that centred on eating and cooking,
that I sent out on request. I did not question respondents specifically
about any particular foodways and did not incorporate questions

relating to any fixed or clearly defined food related issues. I did ask if they had changed their eating habits at all and why this might be. It was very much an open invitation for them to tell their stories in their words and on their terms. It was the common vocabularies (Mills 1959) across the narratives that I was looking to discover, rather than directing them in any particular way.

Half of those invited to participate agreed to be involved, which resulted in 75 narratives by a self-imposed deadline. In terms of respondent demographics, one third were male, most were UK born, middle class (as identified by current or last occupational status), although the majority of the men were from social class 1. Respondents ages ranged from 27 to 85 years, with the majority born in the 1950s and 1960s (please refer to the demographics table in the appendix). The scope of food memories therefore spans the 1930s to the present day. Two thirds were parents at different stages in the life course, from those new to parenting to grandparents, and there was a range of family types including lone parents, co-habiting and married couples with children (and step-children).

The methodology followed a constructivist grounded theory approach; it was iterative with themes developing as the project progressed, so data collection and analysis were concurrent (Charmaz 2006). The analysis of respondents' texts was rigorous and centred on wider cultural narratives and symbols used in the telling of the self (Charmaz 2006). This highlights the inter-textuality of auto/biographical accounts and the extent to which written texts are social products, not unproblematic reflections of reality, and how individuals continue to be constrained by structural influences beyond their own free will (Stanley and Morgan 1993).

Therefore, the food stories at the heart of this book are co-created within a particular time and space. They reflect the socio-historical, political and cultural concerns of the time they were written. Indeed, respondents presented their food histories as a type of transformation narrative, expressing a shift in consciousness from unknowing child to all knowing adult with the memories of childhood explored through a modern day lens. Thus, respondents became 'health conscious', 'body conscious', and/or 'food conscious' over time. Hence, respondents' narratives are simultaneously highly individualised expressions of taste and/or distaste, and interpretations of wider social and cultural norms and values regarding 'good'/'bad', legitimate/unauthorised foodways. After several levels of analysis running concurrently with data collection, I identified five broad themes: (i) family relationships (foodways as reproducing family and family socialisation) (ii) maternal identities (foodways as representative of good/bad mothering), (iii) concerns about health (foodways as a means to achieving or practicing 'good' health and food as Complementary and Alternative Medicine), (iv) embodiment (issues related to weight management) and (v) the views and practices of mostly male gourmets (who used epicurean foodways as a means of expressing high cultural status and elite taste).

In a neo-liberal era I expected gender, class and family structures to be less significant due to the pervasive ideologies of individualism (Giddens 1991, Beck and Beck-Gernsheim 2002). Yet when locating themselves within their food narratives these 'zombie' (Slater and Ritzer 2001) categories remain significant if not vital for ontological security (Dawson 2012). The focus is therefore on the intersectionalities of gender and class expressed through everyday foodways. In these, individuals distanced themselves from 'other' food practices and created a hegemony of 'appropriate' foodways based on heteronormative middle class cultural norms. Thus, far from an 'anything goes' approach to everyday foodways there are rigid cultural scripts to negotiate and these are outlined and developed throughout the book.

However, it is notable that whilst the majority of female respondents conformed rigidly to these, the men did not. Indeed, there were those who blatantly and fearlessly transcended the boundaries of what might be considered appropriate foodways *some* of the time. Of course, this is a means of distancing the self from contamination from activities usually coded feminine and displaying hegemonic masculinities (Connell 2005), which are:

> *The [set of] qualities defined as manly that establish and legitimate a hierarchical and complementary relationship to femininity that, by doing so, guarantee the dominant position of men and the subordination of women.*
>
> (Schippers 2007: 94)

It also demonstrates how individuals with high cultural capital are able to *choose* to play by the rules of the game or not. Indeed, by not conforming to healthy dietary guidelines, for example, one is positioning the self outside of the moral discourses that stigmatise and blame. In a patriarchal society, some of the rules of the game within a culinary field just do not apply to men.

Subject positions/notes on the author

I am a feminist, sociologist, social researcher, lecturer, wife, mother, with a 'normal' body size and a part-time interest in epicurean foodways. In conducting my research I follow what I consider to be a feminist approach, which attempts to address the power relationships inherent in research and give 'voice' to respondents. I employ Butler's (1999) and West and Zimmerman's (1987) concept of gender as interaction/performance, Morgan's (1996) concept of family practices and Bourdieu's (1984) conceptualisation of cultural capital to position my work. My approach is therefore grounded in theories of gender/class/family/foodways as social constructions and performances rather than universal norms (Bourdieu 1984, West and Zimmerman 1987, 2009, Morgan 1996, 2011, Butler 1999). I do not focus on feminism or feminisms; instead I am interested in how gender and class intersect in the construction of a life around food. I use the first person and do not comply with the 'canons of writing practices from the nineteenth century that we should not be present in our texts and that the "I" should be suppressed' (Richardson 1997: 2–3).

So why study food? Partly it is about embodiment and a feminised subjectivity that considers foodways and 'fat talk' (Ambjörnsson 2005) as part of a gendered affective practice of self-surveillance and body management instilled from childhood. A protestant ethic that considered eating too much as sinful (from my father), whilst simultaneously having to contemplate the Biblical contention that one should 'eat, drink and be merry' (Luke 2013, 12: 19) (from my mother). Hence, I set out to explore the cultural capital associated with the 'thin ideal' (Germov and Williams 2004) or the tyranny of slenderness (Chernin 1981, LeBesco 2001) or the 'ethic of sobriety for the sake of slimness' (Bourdieu 1984: 175), as an enduring cultural symbol of contemporary femininity.

I locate my personal troubles (Mills 1959) in the context of tensions between maternal (family) and gourmet identities or issues of gender and high cultural capital (class). Hence, my interest in foodways is also a response to legitimations of elite forms of cultural capital that have the power to exclude and stigmatise. I started university in the autumn of 1991 when my son was almost a year old. It was there that I learned within the context of exploring second wave feminism that 'motherhood was a socially constructed patriarchal institution' (O'Brien Hallstein 2010: 132) and distinct from the act of mothering (Rich 1986). I considered that if it was the rigidity of gender roles that was keeping women confined to the domestic sphere, then a dis-identification with the institution of motherhood might ensure equality. However, I encountered a kind of 'matrophobia', a fear of becoming like one's own mother that Lawler (2000) takes from Rich (1986) and identifies as being embedded in classed processes of social mobility. Lawler (2000) pitches her argument against the individualisation thesis espoused by Beck (1992) and Giddens (1991, 1992) to highlight how upwardly mobile women as autonomous, individualised selves, secure middle class positions and then dis-identify with their working class mothers.

Today, there is a glorification of feminine domesticity and retreatism from the public sphere (Negra 2009: 130), as well as a fetishisation of the maternal that is also thoroughly classed (Littler 2013: 233). Further, O'Brien Hallstein (2010: 108) suggests that women now have to negotiate a 'split subjectivity between old and new gender expectations', whereby women need to be both 'successful at work and successful as mothers' (Douglas and Michaels 2004: 12). This works on the assumption that mothers engage in forms of 'intensive mothering', which is 'child centred, expert guided, emotionally absorbing, labour intensive and financially expensive' (Hays 1996: 8). Therefore, 'intensive mothering' is a legitimate 'ideology of contemporary mothering for women, across race and class lines, even if not all women actually practice it' (Hays 1996: 86).

Similarly, when considering epicurean foodways and a gourmet identity, I have clear recollections of early 'fine dining' experiences, with my father at a French Restaurant in Little Clarendon Street, Oxford, in 1982 (I recall eating frogs legs and *escargot* for the first and last time). However, despite a long-standing interest in the culinary arts, the emotional capital required for feeding the family, is as Reay (2004) identifies more about investing in others rather than the self and this works against the formation of a gourmet identity. Also:

To be a foodie requires self-absorption, self-love, self-delusion, self-confidence; in other words selfishness to a degree unsurpassed in modern times.
(Simmonds 1990: 130–1, cited by Ashley et al. 2004: 149)

This therefore excludes those engaged in 'intensive mothering' (Hays 1996) or contemporary maternal foodways. Thus, stratifications of gender and class continue to determine inequalities on many levels (Marmot and Bell 2012). Women are excluded from elite cultural positions and identities (Adkins and Lury 1999, Adkins and Jokinen 2008). The rigidity of these gendered and classed positions has implications for men who cook and women who do not. It is still mainly men who are able to play in a culinary field.

Throughout this book I make a contribution to the field of cultural food studies through a focus on gender, cultural capital (class) and foodways. I argue that specific middle class strategies of 'feeding the family' (DeVault 1991), have become a way of establishing elite status for women (Bourdieu 1984). Further, I contend that this form of elite cultural capital, like others, both excludes and valorises all those involved in 'feeding the family' on a number of levels. It excludes, because 'feeding the family' is located within a feminised domestic sphere in which men are rewarded for developing affective caring skills. This is similar to the feminisation of economic work in the public sphere, where Adkins and Jokinen (2008) note, men are rewarded for skills that are naturalised and considered part of a feminine habitus. Femininity on the other hand rarely carries status or capital. This reinforces the doxic order that caring is part of a natural feminine habitus.

Thus, there are contemporary cultural scripts of legitimate ways of feeding the family (DeVault 1991), notably the emphasis on healthy home-cooked food prepared from scratch, which carries high social, cultural and symbolic capital (Parsons 2014a, 2014b). On the other hand a 'gourmet' identity is a means of accruing social, cultural and symbolic capital in the field of foodways that centres on a leisurely pursuit and acquisition of skills that sediment over time. In the field of culinary arts, the 'gourmet' also inhabits a particular gendered habitus that is predominantly masculine because of the links with high cultural capital, elite status and leisure time. In both cases high cultural capital is accrued through an investment of time and/or money.

Indeed, the persistent distinctions between food play and food work contributes to the naturalising of women's work within the home. Hence, 'feeding the family' is conceptualised as hurried, low skilled, mundane and routinised (DeVault 1991) unlike the artistry of the epicurean, which is not 'work' at all. In a contemporary food-scape there is the additional pressure of preparing healthy 'home-cooked' meals prepared from scratch (Pollan 2013). This is a reaction against the impact of commercial/convenience foodways, but also a means of drawing boundaries between classes. Further, in an era of moral approbation regarding bodies out of control, feeding the family healthy 'home-cooked' meals prepared from scratch is a means of acquiring social, symbolic and cultural capital, with mothers in particular positioned as responsible for both the health and size of their own and other bodies (Parsons 2014a, 2014b). A focus on maternal identity does not exclude women who are not mothers as it has implications for contemporary conceptualisations of femininity and class that reach beyond the actual activity of mothering.

I draw heavily on the work of Bourdieu (1984, 1996) and material-ist feminist scholars such as Adkins and Skeggs (2004), Lawler (2008), McRobbie (2008), Reay (2004), and Skeggs (2004b). I position my study within a contemporary foodscape that considers gendered and classed aspects of everyday foodways significant. A central aspect of understanding how cultural capital works relates to notions of time and lack and these are referred to throughout the book. Thus, having time to play in a culinary field is a significant aspect of epicurean foodways, and time to prepare healthy home-cooked meals from scratch important for maternal foodways. Further, a lack of time is indicative of a lack of care and access to resources (money).

It should be noted that throughout the book I am unable to use all respondents' narratives (in terms of complete narratives and all responses), because the 'selection of some [letters] entails the de-selection of many more' (Stanley 2004: 205). Instead I present 'biographical assemblage[s] that remain open and incomplete, as a constant reminder of the forced coherences and closures of the bio-graphical discourse' (Tamboukou 2010: 10). Further, there is a limit to the range of recognisable cultural scripts available and positioning the self as a responsible neo-liberal citizen continues to be bound by issues of gender and class. Indeed Doucet (2009: 112) clearly articulates this dilemma in that:

> *Men's and women's lives as carers and earners are cut with deeply felt, moral and social scripts about what women and men should do within and outside of household life.*

Although there has been movement around these moral dilemmas (Duncan and Edwards 1999, Gerson 2002), they nevertheless exist as strong ideological scripts to mothering, fathering and everyday foodways. Overall, throughout the book I highlight how respondents' everyday foodways are like a 'prism, which absorbs and reflects a host of cultural phenomena' (Counihan 1999: 6). Thus, specific middle class strategies of 'appropriate' everyday foodways, whether these relate to families, health, embodiment or epicurean pleasures, have become ways of establishing status and/or legitimising social difference (Bourdieu 1984). Hence, everyday foodways continue to be powerful ways of 'doing' gender and class.

2
Family Foodways

Family foodways, despite the rise of a neo-liberal individualism that values autonomy, self-governance and self-control, remain significant in drawing boundaries and reinforcing legitimate ways of doing food *and* family. Individuals learn to 'do' gender and class through family foodways and consequently family foodways reinforce legitimate ways of doing gender/ class/ food/ family. Thus, family foodways are vital for inculcating class tastes (Bourdieu 1984) and table manners (Visser 1991). Further, because family represents a theatre for the civilising of appetites (Elias 1978, Mennell 1985), if appropriate family foodways have not been instilled it has implications for identity.

I use the term 'family' in its broadest sense, acknowledging the fluidity in the idea of family and not 'the' institution or ideological family (Morgan 2011: 34). In Morgan's (1996: 193–4) work the family is 'a facet of social life, not a social institution, it represents a quality rather than a thing' and 'it is an adjective rather than a noun', further Morgan (1996: 13) notes:

> *Family life can be considered through a variety of different lenses and from different perspectives. Thus, family practices may also be gender practices, age practices and so on. This point is made in order to stress that family life is never simply family life and that it is always continuous with other areas of existence. The points of overlap and connection are often more important than the separate entities, understood as work, family politics and so on.*

Therefore, Morgan's (2011: 65) approach highlights the extent to which family practices are relational, fluid and different from traditional relatively static models of 'the' family. Hence, 'the relationships between food, memories, emotions and family practices remain very strong' (Morgan 2011: 118). I assumed that gender, class and family would have less power due to the progress of individualisation and therefore respondents would document more of a 'negotiated family model' (Beck and Beck-Gernsheim 2002: xxi). However, this is not the model respondents wrote about. Instead, family foodways as socio-historical artefacts follow food trends in the UK, from the influx of ambient ready meals and TV dinners (convenience food) to the expansion of foreign travel (food creolisation), to more contemporary influences from the food scene (for example a commitment to authentic cuisine and/or cultural omnivorousness) and public discourses (for example healthism and responsible individualism).

In this chapter I focus specifically on how respondents position themselves as belonging to a particular class schema that draws on recognisable cultural codes and symbols. Notably that respondents' early memories of family foodways reflect contemporary issues within a culinary foodscape that values individualism and cultural omnivorousness or the appreciation of high *and* low culture (Peterson and Kern 1996). Warde et al. (2007: 146) define cultural omnivorousness as a 'breadth of cultural involvements', in three areas, 'taste, knowledge and participation'. However, Warde et al. (2007) measure this in terms of 'taste' in music, literature, television, film, painting and sport, they do not explore omnivorousness in relation to foodways. This could be because foodways, especially in the domestic sphere are conceptualised as feminine, and elite patterns of consumption are usually associated with male activities. So when measuring cultural omnivorousness as a sign of cultural distinction amongst privileged groups for example, an interest in sport (masculinity) is seen as a dimension of cultural omnivorousness, whilst foodways (femininity) is not. Cultural omnivorousness therefore tends to relate to activities outside of the domestic sphere, as markers of distinction and elite status. However, cultural omnivorousness is recognised by Naccarato and LeBesco (2012) as a significant aspect of culinary capital and I consider it a relevant marker of status and class within respondents' foodways.

Thus, it is through the recreation of childhood memories of family foodways that respondents express both individuality and compliance with dominant or legitimate forms of cultural capital. Indeed, the power of cultural representations of appropriate family foodways impacts upon how individuals represent their families, gender and class positions. The social and cultural milieu is reflected in their accounts and they demonstrate how particular cultural forms of middle class family foodways persist despite government and media discourses regarding the decline of family meals (Jackson 2009, James 2009b) and cooking skills (Meah and Watson 2011). Hence elite family foodways continue to be significant in terms of maintaining status and drawing boundaries within culinary fields.

Overall, respondents distinguish between experiences of family foodways past and present, both infused with cultural markers of taste and distinction. Two thirds of respondents are parents and conformed to a range of family 'types' including lone parents, cohabiting and married couples with children (and step-children). These families are at different stages in the life course, some respondents are new to parenting; for example, two unconnected respondents (Otaline, Tom) had just had their first child, some had young children (Drew, Kevin, Simon, Larry, Ollie, Lex, Faith, Faye, Imogen, Jocelyn, Laura, Lola, Molly, Noreen, Regan, Steph, Zoe), others are living with teenagers (Ed, Ophelia, Katrina, Melissa, Ruth, Valerie, Mark, Nick), for some their children had recently left the family home (Hannah, Ida, Gaby, Willow), or had adult children no longer living with them (Celia, Daisy, Harriet, Linda, Vera, James, Paul, Richard, Stephen, Walt). There are those like myself, who are living with some children but had others who had left the family home (Annie, Beth, Chloe, Edith, Helen, Paula, Ursula, Ian, Jake). There are temporary or intermittent family compositions as well, like Henry's whose stepchildren lived with him and his wife only part of the time. And Sam, whose work took him away from the family home for extensive periods of time, so ostensibly he was not living in a family environment on a full-time basis. Two respondents are in long-term non-heterosexual relationships at the time of the study. One of these couples had adult children from a previous relationship, not living with them at the time of the study.

Respondents' family foodways rely on familiar cultural scripts, with cultural artefacts and common brand names providing temporal markers. From 75 individual narratives there is one story that documents change over time and across legitimate middle class tastes. This narrative involves a distancing from convenience/ready meals, a commitment to 'healthy' family meals and snacks 'home-cooked from scratch' (Pollan 2013: 9), commensality (Fischler 1980, 2011) or the sharing of food, mostly (though not always) around a table from the Latin 'cum mensa' (in the company of a meal/table) and the development of cultural omnivorousness (Peterson and Kern 1996). It is notable that respondents adhered to this model of 'appropriate' middle class family foodways regardless of whether they could be positioned as middle class or not. Indeed, the power of what might be considered legitimate or dominant cultural expectations of 'appropriate' family foodways is such that working class mothers especially demonstrated a commitment to these markers in order to put a floor on their disadvantaged position (Skeggs 1997).

Commensality and cultural omnivorousness

Family foodways are embedded in family practices (Morgan 1996, 2011), or put another way foodways are the means by which families perform and reproduce socio-cultural norms everyday. They are simultaneously individual, social and relational and can be used as cultural symbols and markers of class position. These relational aspects of family foodways are not unlike Fischler's (1980, 1988, 2011) conceptualisation of commensality. This is the notion of food as representative of inclusion and exclusion, as a shared and sharing experience usually around a table, as a type of table fellowship (Coveney 2006). Further, Grignon (2001: 23–36) identifies a typology of commensality that includes 'domestic' commensality linked to private and family life as opposed to the 'institutional' commensality of the public sphere, an 'everyday' commensality related to the nuclear family and/or the usual circle of colleagues as opposed to an 'exceptional' commensality, which is evident at stressful times in the annual calendar or life cycle. He also identifies a 'segretive' or the 'we and not we' and a 'transgressive' or ambivalent commensality. Overall, his analysis emphasises the significance of foodways in drawing people together, creating bonds and/or excluding 'others'; it is essentially about social connections and sociability. Indeed commensality implies a degree of dependence and/or reciprocity and implies equal or hierarchical relationships depending on whether food is shared around a circular table or in a hierarchical manner, with someone presiding at the head.

Generally, family foodways are an important theatre for inculcating a cultural habitus that recognises and reproduces social, symbolic and cultural markers of value. It is the investment of time in developing 'a taste of reflection' (Bourdieu 1984: 6) and 'the total, early, imperceptible learning performed in the family from the earliest days of life' (Bourdieu 1984: 59) that is significant. Indeed, Friedman (2011) following Bourdieu (1984) argues that cultural capital is a modality of practice, it is not just about consuming something but the manner in which the consumption is expressed. In Friedman's study of comedy taste, he makes clear distinctions between the tastes of those with high cultural capital (HCC) who take time and work hard to appreciate their comedy, and those with low cultural capital (LCC) who passively enjoyed a cheap laugh. In Friedman's (2011) study he identifies 'family socialisation' as a means of measuring cultural capital, alongside qualifications and occupational status.

Family socialisation refers to the class position of respondents' parents, the assumption being that this impacts on the inculcation of future cultural appreciation practices and taste. I did not set out to gather this kind of data from respondents and cannot give them a cultural capital score, high or low. However, respondents did infer class positions and family socialisations within their narratives. Either they identified themselves as middle class from childhood, or reflected upon working class origins from a contemporary middle class position. Those with middle class socialisations include Nick (a 51-year-old consultant, married with two children) who 'does not really cook for me' but 'loves' food as 'it is all part of the sensual experience of life, like music, paintings, sex etc'. He notes:

My father worked all over the world during his working life, especially in Western Europe. We lived in County with quite a big garden and a decent vegetable patch and fruit bushes, fruit trees etc. ... Both my Mum and my Dad were brought up in houses with cooks so it was only really after WW2 that this kind of life ended and they had to start cooking for them selves. In fact my Non UK granny kept just one lady on till she died who did all the cooking and washing and cleaning. She was called

*Margit and was very affectionate to me as she had virtually brought my
Mother up as well ...*

Here the markers of elite cultural capital can be understood in
terms of references to staff (cooks), a big garden and a lot of foreign
travel, which would have been unusual in the time this narrative
took place, before the boom in cheap air travel in the UK from the
late 1970s. This vignette includes more contemporary indicators
of elite culinary capital such as a 'decent vegetable patch and fruit
bushes and fruit trees'. There has been a shift in attitudes in favour of
'home-grown' food and against highly commercialised, mass indus-
trial food production (Pollan 2013). On one level this relates to issues
of sustainability (Johnston and Bauman 2010); on another admitting
to having a vegetable patch or allotment in the past might have indicated a low income, whereas now it is more likely to be associated
with high cultural capital and having time to grow your own food.
Nick continues to explain that his mother was not from England and
this influenced the range of culinary experiences he had as a child:

*Everyday stuff probably wasn't that different to other middle class
English people. Sunday roasts, big breakfasts on Sundays made by my
Dad with bacon, eggs, tomatoes, mushrooms and fried bread eaten out
on the terrace in summer looking out over the garden. He put an outdoor
plug socket on the wall so we could take the toaster out there. It looked
like something off a battleship with a big circular screw thread cap on
a chain, to keep the rain out. My Mum made marmalade and jam and
all sorts of Non UK things too such as 'kerezet' – cream cheese with
chives and paprika and another thing with cucumber, dill, vinegar and
sugar – not sure what that's called. When I took packed lunch to school
for a few years, my lunch box was no different to anyone else's really;
sandwich, Jacob's club biscuit, and packet of crisps, tangerine but often
something else like a chunk of salami or Swiss cheese.*

Hence Nick is clearly positioning himself as a middle class English
man, reinforced by reference to what might be considered traditional British food, with a nod to cultural omnivorousness (Peterson
and Kern 1996), so whilst he had a typical lunch box with a *Jacob's*
club biscuit he also had the addition of 'something else'. Again,

cultural omnivorousness has high cultural value in a contemporary foodscape (Naccarato and LeBesco 2012). Nick's parents conform to traditional gender roles, with a contemporary twist; his mother has responsibility for 'feeding the family' (DeVault 1991) but 'cooks from scratch' (Pollan 2013) including home-made jam etc., whilst his father cooks for pleasure at the weekend and these are certainly issues of concern within a contemporary foodscape (Cairns et al. 2010, Parsons 2014b).

Simon (a 55-year-old married chef with one child) writes:

I was fortunate that my family lived in places like Hong Kong and Malaysia where our senses were constantly open to new sights, smells and flavours, where the Army tradition of curry lunches was still practiced and pineapples grew at the end of our garden ... So cardamom, ginger, lemongrass and sambals was as much a part of growing up as stew and boiled vegetables; peanuts were not only used as a spread for toast, but mixed with garlic, coconut and cumin to eat with skewers of marinated beef.

Hence, Simon is reflecting upon his family foodways from the past through a modern day lens that celebrates cultural omnivorousness (Peterson and Kern 1996) and authentic cuisine (Johnson and Baumann 2010, Naccarato and LeBesco 2012). His childhood family foodways originated in countries other than the UK, but are steeped in Army traditions and references to what might be considered traditional British fare such as 'stew and boiled vegetables'. Similarly, Charlie (a 49-year-old self-employed consultant, living with his partner) wrote about family foodways and socialisation across cultures:

Granma's homemade orange marmalade with wasps buzzing lazily around her thick forearms in the kitchen and stored in the cupboard under the stairs when finished along with dried stuff and cakes. Peppermints made in the same kitchen: icing sugar, peppermint flavouring formed into small thick 2p bite-sized treats for when we came back. The same recipe coming out in sweets appearing as treats, half covered with chocolate, at home wherever that was at the time. Chocolate covered orange peel sticks, put out in small bowls with the same peppermints on coffee tables with strict admonitions not to eat them all before lunch at Christmas.

Again, as in Nick's account, for Charlie there is an association between 'homemade' and made with care, this time it is his grandmother making sweet treats for him at Christmas or for when they 'came back'. This he contrasts with:

> *The smell of rice cooking and peanut sauce and basic South East Asian curry and fish paste really hits me right in the taste buds every time: open market stalls in the town, regimental curry lunches on the beach and the satay seller on the top of the arrival terminal at Subang airport in Malaysia as a seven and eight year old. Durian, the sweet sewer smell rising up to the third floor window from the street market in a 1967 Singapore and the lazy thwack of the ceiling fan in the hotel bedroom.*

Hence, Charlie's early family socialisation encompasses contrasting tastes, flavours, experiences and this inculcates a cultural omnivorousness that in contemporary culinary fields carries high cultural capital (Naccarato and LeBesco 2012). Ed (a 55-year-old carpenter, living with his partner and her daughter) writes about his early family foodways:

> *My earliest food memories are the spicy dishes and fruit of the Caribbean, where I grew up ... Watching Dad gutting freshly speared fish, and throwing them on the grill to cook, and him revelling in the hunter/gatherer role. Enormous crayfish, oysters, yellow fin tuna, stingray, grilled over a wood fire and then dressed with nothing more than squeezed lime and paprika. Crab stew. There always seemed to be a lot of people at these meals – we all were in and out of the neighbour's houses every day ...*

Ed is referring to the origins of his cultural omnivorousness, which as identified has high cultural capital (Naccarato and LeBesco 2012). These early family foodways also include his father in a traditional 'hunter/gather role' and cooking over a wood fire. Ed negotiates the contaminating associations between 'feeding the family' (DeVault 1991) and a traditionally feminine domesticity by reference to forms of hegemonic masculinities (Connell 2005) that stress masculine attributes that could relate to violence such as 'gutting', 'spearing' and lack of care when throwing food on to the grill. Yet, when considering this scene through a contemporary gaze, it is reminiscent of other displays of masculinity within a culinary field (Hollows 2003, Hollows et al. 2010) as well as elite culinary practices that favour a more sustainable approach (Johnston and Bauman 2010).

Early family foodways for Ralph (a 55-year-old single writer) have a different flavour; he notes that his first food memory was at:

> *8/9 years old – mustard-and-cress crisp sandwiches with white bread, served every Saturday night when 'Man in a Suitcase' came on the telly. Traveling to the 'Scottish Pie Shop' on the bus to Streatham to buy said pies and black puddings – my parents were from Glasgow – hence the diet.*

Ralph's narrative is full of working class references, 'crisp sandwiches', watching the TV, travelling on the bus, and white bread, which has shifted from an aspirational food in the early twentieth century to one associated with a 'lack' of taste (Mennell 1985). However, this is also about Ralph's parents' nationality; a kind of banal nationalism (Billig 1995) is at work and easily expressed through everyday foodways. However, Ralph continues:

> *I have a thing about lumps in mashed potatoes, which relates to a family trauma, and on the other hand, my father actually had very epicurean tastes – he had his side of the fridge. As I got older I used to dip into it more. Finding out that I liked olive oil at the around the age of 12 was a definite turning point.*

Firstly, he is noting that he prefers to have food prepared with care and is therefore more discerning in his tastes. Secondly, that his father also had refined tastes which Ralph began to appreciate himself from the age of 12. Indeed 'olive oil' and other Mediterranean foodways are persistent markers of 'good' taste within respondent narratives. It demonstrates engagement with wider cultural influences and hints at the development of cultural omnivorousness (Peterson and Kern 1996, Warde et al. 2007). Ralph's identification with his father in becoming an epicurean protects him from any feminine associations with refinement or fussiness around not eating lumpy mashed potatoes.

Fred (a 39-year-old single solicitor, foodie and former vegetarian) describes his early food experiences:

Going to my Nan's every Saturday and she had one of those huge cater-
ing margarine plastic boxes full of chocolate biscuits. She always kept it
in the fridge (she lived in a caravan and had the fire on all year round).
I'm sure plastic would melt so biscuits would have had no chance hence
the fridge. I can remember to this day the taste and texture of a chilled
Kit Kat. Oh and on the odd occasion I stayed she would make me that
roast beef from Birds-Eye, which came in a foil tray and had slices of
beef and gravy, a very distinctive taste. It's odd that I remember two
early experiences with my Nan, as we never really got on – she was a
difficult woman. Other early memories – Findus mince beef pancakes
and my first pizzas (frozen French bread ones, again I think from
Findus) ... I remember beef Monster Munch and the pickled onion ones
too. I used to drink nothing but full fat Coke when I was about 8 or 9
I suppose. Now I don't touch fizzy drinks. (or really anything other than
booze, peppermint tea or water and fruit and veg smoothies/ juices)

Here Fred's past and present merge and he peppers his narrative
with familiar brand names from the 1970s that locate his story
within a particular time and space. These foods from the past are
positioned in stark contrast to the diet he refers to today – references
to fruit and vegetable smoothies and 'not touching' fizzy drinks
infer an interest in 'good' food and healthy eating, which are values
relevant within a contemporary foodscape (Pollan 2013). Later he
claims 'I don't really like ready meals', but then again when referring
to a taste of home:

My Nan always used to serve me that Findus Roast Beef for one. It came
in a foil tin and had about two slices of beef and weird metallic gravy.
I loved it. Never ate it anywhere else.

On the one hand he eschews convenience foods and on the other
associates the taste of a classic TV dinner with the comfort and
familiarity of home. Hence, despite him not eating this meal again
and not liking his Nan very much, somehow the distinctive taste of
this meal is something he has not forgotten. He is reflecting upon
this taste through a modern day lens that considers convenience
food as lacking. He is simultaneously detailing his taste, knowledge,
and participation (Warde et al. 2007) of a previous UK foodscape, as
well as acknowledging a present foodscape that associates cultural

omnivorousness with high cultural capital (Naccarato and LeBesco 2012). Indeed, it is because he has high cultural capital that he is able to acknowledge a liking for convenience food; this does not undermine his class position.

Ophelia (a 53-year-old married author with two children) also litters her narrative with cultural references from the 1960s and 1970s but adds 'that there was a big divide between what the adults ate and what we ate, as children' and continues:

Later in the early 70s the frozen food revolution hit and Marmite sandwiches were overtaken by cheesy balls and fish bites in batter that sort of exploded fatly in your mouth. I hated them. Frey Benton Steak Pies also made a short visit to our house but were universally loathed. I don't remember eating any salad (apart from ice berg lettuce) and potatoes, which we grew ourselves and frozen peas were about the only vegetable we regularly ate. We had an orchard full of plum trees and apple trees though and helped ourselves to these. The plums were delicious, warmed by the sun with great globs of sticky amber resin where their flesh had burst as they hit the ground. Wasps were a big problem but we always gorged ourselves anyway. I still have a hole in my knee where I ran from a wasp that wouldn't leave my apple alone and slipped on the gravel drive. Everything suddenly became 'easy care and pre packed'; Butterscotch Angel Delight was my absolute favourite.

Again, as in Fred's narrative Ophelia is positioning herself as someone with knowledge of changes in the UK foodscape. Hence, her family are introduced to foods considered cutting edge at the time and had the cultural capital to enable them to engage with these changes. However these commercial foodways are mostly disliked and considered lacking, in terms of care/time spent in their preparation. Ophelia also makes use of cultural markers of high cultural capital and class position; an orchard and gravel drive for example, whilst her references to a lack of salad are more in keeping with contemporary public discourses around children's diets and 'five-a-day' (DOH 2010, DOH 2011). These concerns are indicative of Ophelia's position as a mother and the need to distance the self from association with convenience or 'other' working class family foodways (Parsons 2014a, 2014b).

Family meals

A significant aspect of everyday family foodways for inculcating cultural norms and values is the 'proper' family meal. Anthropologists Douglas and Nicod (1974) commented upon the structure and hierarchy of British meals in the 1970s. They identified 3 types of meal: (1) the main meal of the day, which they considered a social event with rules and a rituals, a focus on time and place, a centrepiece (meat or fish) with a staple (potatoes), a dressing (gravy) and a pudding; (2) breakfast, on the other hand, they documented as a minor or secondary meal; and (3) snacks which they described as unstructured food events without rules. Of course, all three of these food events are influenced by cultural expectations and wider discourses regarding what is considered appropriate or legitimate.

In terms of the family meal one of the ongoing public discourses concerning family foodways centres on a perceived decline of the 'proper' family meal and therefore the decline of the 'proper' family, as identified by Murcott (1995, 1997). The importance of commensality and sharing a family/proper meal in maintaining cultural identity has been well documented (Douglas and Nicod 1974, Fischler 1980, 1988, 2011, Charles and Kerr 1988, Lupton 1996, Murcott 1998, Bahr Buge and Almas 2006, Warde et al. 2007b, Kauffman 2010). Research by Murcott (1982) in South Wales and Charles and Kerr (1988) for example reveal the persistence of the main meal or proper meal as significant in reaffirming family norms and values. In Lupton's (2000) Australian study, 'the baked dinner involved sitting down with the family and taking time to serve and share food, with the emphasis on the traditional British style meat and vegetables as the mainstay of the main meal' (Lupton 2000: 99). Thus, the rituals and rules of this main meal event, these family foodways are considered significant for maintaining social stability. In an era of obesity and continued anxiety regarding the decline of 'proper' families, 'meals help create bonds and serve as an index of the quality of family life' (Kauffman 2010: 138).

This long-standing association between 'proper family dinners, proper families [and] proper children' (James et al. 2009a: 39, Johansson et al. 2013) fed into the 'changing families, changing food' project (2005–2008), the most recent study on family foodways in the UK (Jackson 2009 and James et al. 2009b). The rationale centred on a perceived increase in diverse family forms and the potential impact of these changes on 'feeding the family' (DeVault 1991). It represents the most comprehensive research undertaken in the field of family food studies since the ESRC funded 'Nations Diet' in 1992 (Murcott 1998). Jackson (2009: 10) concludes that the political rhetoric about the decline of the family meal runs ahead of the evidence and that the discourse regarding the decline of the family meal serves a normative agenda, as 'making and eating of a proper family meal remains an important symbol of family life'.

This is certainly evident throughout respondents' narratives as they are keen to keep the 'family narrative going' (Giddens 1991: 54) especially in terms of a fondness for 'roast dinner', which is also a type of 'noshtalgia' (Becket et al. 2002). Hence Laura (a 35-year-old teaching assistant, married with two children) writes 'I think we probably ate like most families in the eighties, roast every Sunday, leftovers on a Monday' and Imogen (a 36-year-old part-time housekeeper, married with four children) notes:

> *I would have to say that my best taste and smell of home has always been and probably always will be a good roast! Very old fashioned but nothing gets the taste buds going like that for me.*

Similarly, Ian (a 64-year-old MD, married with three children) writes:

> *[A taste of home ...] It is Sunday lunch particularly beef, toad in the hole, spaghetti Bolognese. When I was young say 5–8 Mum would take us to Any town to have chicken as a treat. It was expensive then. If I was lucky dad would let me have the end of the joint of beef if it was a little burnt – I loved it. On Sunday evenings there was a ritual as there was for lunch. My dad and uncle would put on clean shirts with armbands and cuff links. This may well have been the only bath of the week! Food was part of this Sunday celebration. I can remember looking forward to the toast and dripping.*

Again, like other respondents' Ian is contemplating the rituals of his childhood family foodways through a modern day lens, here with references to the expense of meat like chicken. There is also an intimacy and identification with his father and uncle, though their concern to dress up for dinner might be considered feminising so Ian introduces the notion that it may well have been the only bath of the week, inferring that as working men they did not have time for such niceties. Of course this also relates to other changes in cultural norms around hygiene. His narrative also highlights the 'treat' of eating out and comfort from the repetition of the Sunday rituals of lunch and dinner that comply with the cultural norms of what Fischler (2011) refers to as 'the fraternal agape of a communal meal [...] a token of Christian fellowship, as held by early Christians in commemoration of the last supper' (2011: 532).

These types of family meal events with their rules and rituals persist as highly symbolic cultural representations, infused with class norms and values as Ian's account implies. It is notable that the 'traditional' Sunday dinner according to Gillis (1997: 94), 'even as it came into being in the mid nineteenth century, [...] was already being spoken of as 'traditional' (1997: 94). He argues that 'we tend to exaggerate the frequency with which families ate together in the past and to underestimate the commitment to the family dinner in the present' (1997: 88). Also, how 'the poor ate out of the same pot around the hearth, but they did not dine as such'. The poor also 'ate whatever and whenever they could, but even the middle classes [...] had no notion of the meal as we have come to know it' (Gillis 1997: 89), indeed, he continues:

> *It wasn't until the middle of the nineteenth century, [that] eating had become a carefully arranged sequence of breakfast, lunch and dinner, in an ascending order of significance.*
>
> (Gillis 1997: 90)

However, despite or because of the cultural association between the traditional Sunday dinner and middle class expectations, an attachment to this type of meal persists and is significant for the display of appropriate middle class family values. In Ian's narrative there are hints of working class family foodways; in Ophelia's account on the other hand, she positions her family quite differently:

> *My parents entertained a lot and my mother loved planning her dinner parties. I remember her long shopping lists of ingredients and the more complicated the better. She was an adventurous cook, born in Another*

Country the first person to serve the exotic and strange 'avocado' and Camembert to friends in our small village in County. She was a brave cook, a bit of a cause celebre amongst her circle of friends and not afraid to try new recipes. To her, cooking was an art – she would spend hours peeling grapes for some pudding if Elizabeth David said so. She was often very late with the food but her guests were always in raptures when it finally arrived. Like many children I sat on the stairs in my pyjamas smelling the delicious aromas of dinner mixed with heady perfumes of the 60s, Arpege, Lanvin and Chanel.

Hence, Ophelia is positioning her childhood on the edges of a glamorous, expensive and rarefied setting. This scene from the 1960s was perhaps not as common as Ophelia implies for 'many children'; however, there is high cultural capital associated with gastronomy in contemporary culinary fields (Naccarato and LeBesco 2012) and Ophelia is aligning memories of her mother with this. However, it is worth noting that although this implies an inculcation of tastes with high cultural capital, Ophelia complains of not being allowed to eat the food her mother prepares nor to help with any cooking or baking. Again these are concerns associated with contemporary middle class family foodways that value inculcation of appropriate cooking skills from a young age. This is examined more fully in Chapter 3 on maternal foodways, but Ophelia is clearly judging her mothers' foodways in light of contemporary concerns about appropriate mothering, the glorification of feminine domesticity (Negra 2009), a fetishisation of the maternal (Littler 2013) and popular discourses on 'yummy mummies' (Allen and Osgood 2009, Littler 2013). When considering gender it is notable that Ophelia refers to her mother as brave and adventurous, which are adjectives not usually associated with women's domestic roles in the 1960s, but more commonly associated with epicurean foodways in a contemporary foodscape (Heldke 2003). Indeed, as Skeggs (2004b: 24) notes, 'cultural capital is always associated with high cultural practices and classifications, though upper middle class femininity would work'. Thus, the intersectionalities of gender and class intersect and position Ophelia's mother with access to elite cultural practices. Ophelia continues:

Sunday lunch was the one-day of the week when we all ate the same food together. Always a roast of some kind. My mother, inevitably no

*longer hungry, hot faced and slightly bad tempered by the time it came
to the table, my father rasping the huge knife and the sharpener together
theatrically to ensure we were all paying attention to his manly role in
this feast. My younger brother, on chicken days, always had given just
the parson's nose as a family joke that had worn tearfully thin. My
stomach churning with the anticipation of the general knowledge quiz
inevitably to follow with my elder brother's arm waving in the air as he
proceeded to answer every question, leaving me feeling thick, tiny and
irrelevant on my red velvet-covered dining room chair. These Sunday
meals were an ordeal, often both my younger brother and myself leaving the table tearfully to sit on the stairs after being teased or taunted
too much by an overbearing older sibling and over-sherried parents. Just
writing about it gives me indigestion.*

It is evident that whilst Ophelia is now describing a domestic,
everyday commensal occasion, it is hierarchical and has a flavour
of 'institutional' commensality, perhaps 'the' family ritual of the
Sunday lunch becomes an 'exceptional' commensality (Grignon
2001: 23–36) or highly stressed event because of Ophelia's childhood dependency and status in this scene, as well as the pressure on
both parents to display 'appropriate' family foodways. Of course, for
Ophelia this is significantly the 'one-day of the week' when she has
the opportunity of eating the food her mother has made, yet this
simple pleasure is spoiled by the formality of the event and adherence to the cultural codes, norms and values prevalent at that time.
Later she writes about her family foodways today and notes:

*A taste of home is everyone around the table, all the generations in one
place from the oldest to the youngest, sharing food, wine, family stories,
love and laughter ...*

Indeed, within a contemporary foodscape Ophelia places less
emphasis on the type of food they are eating – the traditional roast
dinner is missing – and instead there is an emphasis on the role of
'food' in bringing people together, drinking wine (not sherry) and
laughter rather than the stress of a general knowledge quiz. Ophelia's
account demonstrates a shift in everyday foodways from the hierarchical family mealtimes of her childhood to a more informal, relaxed
dining experience and equality around the table. It is notable of

course that the food is still consumed around the table and not in front of the TV, as reminiscent of the symbolic violence afforded by Jamie Oliver to the 'mum and the kid eating chips and cheese out of Styrofoam containers, and behind them is a massive f****** TV' (Deans 2013). Hence 'domestic commensality' (Grignon 2001: 23) continues to be a significant aspect of appropriate middle class family foodways. It is a cultural expectation and a means of 'othering' alternative family foodways (Parsons 2014a, 2014b).

However, when considering family foodways within the domestic sphere, Coveney (2014: 33) argues that there is a distinctive shift within the commensal hierarchy in the home. He comments on research carried out in Australia in the 1990s where he claims they did not find 'patriarchy on the menu'; instead children had a 'privileged voice on household food matters'. Dixon and Banwell (2004) in their report on this study identify how children metaphorically became the head of the family table. Indeed, children are considered equal members within a family as a consequence of individualism and the rise of human rights legislation. Further, these changes in attitudes towards children provide a lens through which respondents discuss their past. Thus Larry (a 48-year-old married managing director with two children and a foodie) writes:

I never really like tomato-based stuff when I was a kid, though Campbell's or Heinz tomato soup was always the exception. Vivid memories as about a 5 year old of Dad getting back from the office and daubing Heinz tomato ketchup all over my dinner ... he was trying to be efficient in distributing the condiment to all and sundry at the table while the bottle was in his hand ... I hate tomato ketchup in any form – even as the base to another sauce such as a barbeque or sweet and sour. I can detect its presence at about 50 feet and still cannot stomach it ... Rarely eat in McDonald's these days because the American assumption that everyone likes ketchup and their burgers therefore must come with it as a standard annoys me. Such choices I like to make for myself.

In Larry's account he complains, as his food preferences have not been honoured by his father, which later turns into a criticism of a multinational company similarly ignoring his individual rights to choose how/what to eat. It is notable here too that it was his father (and not his mother, whom we assume cooked the dinner) who spoiled his food by daubing it in ketchup. In Larry's example as in Ophelia's there is a continued emphasis on traditional gender roles within the family; in Ophelia's her father is wielding a knife (his 'manly role in this feast'), whilst in Larry's vignette, his father has returned to the home from the office. Thus, it is the head of the household that adds the (unwanted) flourish to the meal; the person responsible for preparing and cooking it is notably absent. There is a distinction being made between the instrumental action of the father, coming in from outside, and the potential time and care taken in the preparation of the meal in the home. The association between father, work, masculinity and a global multinational corporation reifies the doxic order; the feminine contribution to food work is naturalised, trivialised, invisible and easily spoiled.

School dinners

In contrast to 'proper' family meals, school dinners for some are considered improper or lacking. Indeed, school dinners differ from family meals that value 'attending to [the] particular tastes and desires' (DeVault 1991: 241) of individual family members, as school dinners are contemplated within a contemporary gaze that values individualism. There is a concern with a perceived 'lack' of care associated with institutional and commercial food production (Pollan 2013), again contemporary issues. For example, Ed writes:

> By contrast, later on, the school dinners of England seemed to echo the drab, colourless, unexciting surroundings in which we now lived, with stringy meat of unsure provenance, floating in watery gravy. Faggots, these unappetizing balls of meat held together with a nauseating membrane, vegetables boiled to within an inch of extinction … My school friends seemed to take all this in their stride, and it was only later that I realised the ordeal the few who ate at [our] table must have endured as Mum served up 'foreign muck' like spaghetti Bolognese, chicken and rice with paprika etc.

Here, Ed's reference to 'school dinners' draws on common conceptualisations of institutional and corporate food as 'lacking' in terms of taste and care. This contrast is stark when considering the richness and complexity of the representation of his childhood in the Caribbean. He not only distances himself from food of 'unsure provenance', but is critical of his peers who he implies also lack taste and/or a cultured palate. Ed's reference to not knowing where the meat has come from is common amongst those anxious or critical of 'other' foodways (Fiddes 1991). It also reflects interests from a contemporary foodscape that values sustainability and democracy within the food system (Johnston and Baumann 2010). He is making clear the distinctions between institutional and family foodways, as well as British and 'foreign muck', in both antinomies the former is associated with food for the masses and therefore lacking in taste or sub-standard. It is noticeable too that he associates his father with the adventurous food of the Caribbean and his mother with the 'foreign muck' prepared in the home. This reifies a gendered doxic order that associates women with feeding the family (DeVault 1991) and men cooking for pleasure. There are also symbols of cultural value here, Ed and his school friends are served meals around a table and although he refers to these as 'foreign muck', within a contemporary foodscape these have cultural value and contribute to his inculcation as a cultural omnivore.

Drew (a 42-year-old senior manager, married with one child, living and working abroad and a self confessed foodie) also refers to school dinners when positioning himself as a cultural omnivore, he notes:

Early bad food memories are around being force fed vegetables and school dinners. Both of which put me off certain foods for a long time ... School dinners, my memory is that each one included beetroot, every meal beetroot, spam, mash and beetroot, boiled fish and beetroot and the only value this vinegary pink thing added was colour – to everything, hands, potatoes in fact anything that touched it. Yuurch ... It took me 19 years to grow to like it/ even try it again – then one day at Borough Market I had a eureka moment, feta, beetroot, mint and lemon pasta – I now grow it, bake it – eat it raw and the Borough recipe is a strong family favourite.

Here Drew equates his school dinner experiences with contamination or contagion (Fiddes 1991), as the beetroot spreads beyond the food on his plate. Again this is food that 'lacks' care and is associated with low cultural capital. In stark contrast to the beetroot he uses in his contemporary family foodways, a 'family favourite', 'he grows, bakes and eats raw'. Hence Drew is clearly considering his past in light of his status as a committed foodie, engaged in a range of elite culinary practices (Naccarato and LeBesco 2012). Drew also associates being force-fed vegetables with school dinners – both practices when considered within a contemporary gaze challenge individualism and the contemporary role of family foodways for inculcating individual self worth. Magenta (a 39-year-old single academic, and vegan) also comments upon school dinners:

I have vivid memories of the school desserts, which I quite literally found very hard to stomach. The worst were bread and butter pudding and spotted dick, which were stodgy slabs of yuck with currents and layers of grease in them. They tasted disgusting and stuck to the roof of my mouth and back of my throat if I tried to eat them and used to make me heave and gag. But the dinner ladies (or dinner-bags as they were known) used to make me sit there with it in front of me for most of lunchtime trying to force it down.

Hence, Magenta's individualism is challenged and the women supposedly charged with her care are objectified and othered. Similarly, Ollie (a 44-year-old married teacher with two children, and a vegetarian) writes:

My earliest memories of eating are probably school dinners. I definitely remember being freaked out by the skin on sausages and struck by the synthetic bright pink and yellow of icing on cakes and custard type stuff. I vividly remember the Primary school canteen and it being warm and sweaty in there ... I remember seeing that film where some scientists are shrunk down to microscopic size and journey through a human body (Fantastic Voyage – I think) and this so amazed me that I was convinced that scientists were trying to put a 'sub' inside me to do some sort of tests. As a result I used to look out for specs in my food, especially mash for some reason, and if there were any suspicious flecks I would put them to one side ... Oh God – I haven't thought of this for years and you'll probably think I need a psychiatrist now!

This memory from Ollie clearly marks his school dinner experience as alien, unfamiliar and uncomfortable (sweaty). It is a foreign and unnatural (synthetic) environment and this is reflected in the food he is served and his anxiety regarding its provenance. He counters this alienating 'institutional commensality' (Grignon 2001: 23–36) by picking over his food as a means of asserting his individualism and as a challenge to authority. This vignette is illustrative of a shift in the contemporary culinary foodscape towards more authentic, natural and locally grown/sourced cuisine (Johnston and Baumann 2010, Naccarato and LeBesco 2012, DeSolier 2013). Ollie's alienating school dinner experience is also vaguely reminiscent of the Jamie's *School Dinners* TV series in which Jamie 'exposed' the 'low nutritional content of school meals ... [and] embark[ed] on a campaign to improve kitchen practices within schools' (Hollows and Jones 2010: 309). Otaline (a 32-year-old PhD student, living with her partner and new baby), on the other hand has a different 'school dinners' experience, she writes:

I was a school dinners kid and I hated that when I grew old enough to know what that meant. I was the only one in my group. When I was younger it was fine, but later in my teens when my mum's partner left and we were really poor we'd get like 50p to go to school so it was our only meal of the day and I was always starving.

Thus, she continues:

School dinners I loved. My step great aunt, Mavis was a dinner lady at my school. She was such a lovely, lovely woman, so frail and tiny, even then. With a tiny gentle voice. She'd always give me seconds and I'd always go for seconds. I'm really quite greedy with food and it started young. I loved, loved, loved the school's roast potatoes with macaroni cheese. When I got older and everything became standardised they used to have portion control – God, I'm laughing – I can't believe I did this, let alone remember it – and I used to ask for a cake or something – whatever was behind the dinner lady so I could lean over and nick a few extra potatoes. I was always starving.

It is noteworthy that the provision of free school meals contributes to Otaline feeling different from her peers and an alienating sense of self. However, this is 'the only meal of the day' and this shifts the focus slightly. This institutional experience is given a more human face, as Otaline's 'step great aunt' is her ally in acquiring 'seconds'.

Hence, the usual dislike of school meals for their lack of 'care' and consideration of individualism is replaced by a need to nourish the self because of a lack of food in the home. Ruth (a 47-year-old MD, married with two children), however, draws upon more widely held cultural norms regarding food served in institutional settings and the position of children attending school in previous decades. She writes:

At pre-primary school the food was disgusting ... I really hated rice pudding in particular and used to try and hide it or throw it in the toilet ... I was about 5 or 6 when one day a friend called Terry and I just couldn't eat it ... We were kept behind in the kitchen after lunch and the headmistress stood over us. Terry tried to eat a spoonful and he was sick into his bowl ... The headmistress then spooned the sick into his mouth ... I will never ever forget it. I was completely shocked ... She saw my face and quickly whisked away the bowls and then we were outside in the playground. The smell of rice pudding makes me retch now.

Ruth has a corporeal reaction to an incident in which her individual food preferences are ignored and her human rights impinged. However, it is the instrumental reaction of the headmistress charged with their care that adds to the distress and 'shock'. The 'lack' of care experienced in institutional settings demonstrates how food care is a cultural expectation within contemporary family foodways.

Food choice

There is a lack of fit between public policy initiatives that emphasise individual choice and the lived reality in which there is often no choice. In a culinary field 'choice' constitutes part of a doxic battle for legitimacy, as it is an embodied, affective practice that sediments over time, rather than a rational and deliberate act. Further, 'choice' is embedded in hegemonic discourses that are politically motivated and morally loaded, especially when choices are made from a limited set of options that are constrained by economics, and/ or cultural norms and values. Indeed, commentators and researchers investigating structural inequalities in the UK have commented that health related and psychosocial behaviours are never truly voluntary (Singh-Manoux and Marmot 2005) and this includes family foodways. An emphasis on responsible individualism and freedom to choose 'appropriate' family foodways belies the reality for those unable to choose the circumstances of their birth. Hence, as Skeggs (2005: 974) notes:

> *Others do not have access to 'choice', all they can display is 'lack'; lack of access to the techniques for telling themselves and lack of access to the right culture; they cannot perform the good self because they do not have the cultural resources to do so.*

Further, not all respondents are fortunate enough to experience elite culinary practices and/or cultural omnivorousness within their childhood family foodways. For example, Otaline writes:

> *I remember being a little girl and often feeling, intensely, the restrictions around food. My mother screaming at us: 'Don't drink the milk – I've just bought it'; 'don't eat the food – I've just bought it'. Free access to food was off limits and I hated that, resented it so much and I really think this established my own fascination with the food I couldn't have. And the food we could have – Jesus Christ – it was bad.*

She explains 'when you're poor there's a lot you can't have' and notes:

> *When I grew older and started going to other friend's homes for tea I really began to realise how different I was from them. In my teens my best friend's mum once made us venison! They all sat down together every night and I loved my time there. I was always inviting myself round. It was a home and it felt safe and cosy and warm and I loved sitting perched on the end of that table with them being a part of it all. Hmm, I still miss them now.*

Indeed, Otaline's narrative demonstrates the power of appropriate middle class family foodways in reinforcing cultural boundaries between those who have access to resources and those who do not. The economic, symbolic, social and cultural capital associated with 'appropriate' family foodways excludes on many levels. It is also about 'lack' and this is not just in terms of economics; in Otaline's account it is a lack of opportunity to learn the cultural codes associated with middle class family foodways. In the domestic commensality she witnesses at her friend's house Otaline highlights how they sat at a table to share a home-cooked meal of 'venison', which has high cultural capital, due to its long association with elite practices of hunting and fishing. Yet, it is sitting around a table and eating home cooked food that demonstrates 'love' for Otaline, not practicing these culinary norms is indicative of a 'lack' of care. Eating food together around a table is a marker of cultural capital, which is also highlighted by Vera (a 59-year-old, divorced, shop assistant, with two grown up children) as she notes:

> *Growing up, we always ate together at the table except Saturday and Sunday teatimes when we usually had sandwiches rather than something cooked and could eat in the sitting room watching TV, but it was still eating together.*

However, Vera neutralises the transgression from the cultural norm of eating around the table by stressing that they are still sharing this activity as a family. Their family identity is not spoiled; eating the same food at the same time together is part of reifying the family. In Faith's (a 30-year-old teaching assistant from Zimbabwe, married with two children) narrative, she writes:

> *Before I turned 7 my siblings and I used to eat together in a large bowl. The food was never enough so we ate really quickly ... When I turned 8 my father was promoted at work and then we had separate plates. I remember how excited we were about the separate plates, which was a sure sign that we had gone up the social ladder. The portions were still very small. I spent all my childhood and my teenage years very hungry. Food was something very precious and we never had anything/leftovers to throw away.*

Indeed, the consequences of Faith's early experiences are felt today:

> *I try not to throw away any food. As a result I sometimes cook small portions for meals, which means my two boys end up not satisfied at meal times.... I also always carry a banana or cereal bar wherever I go even to people's houses when they have invited me to dinner, just in case. I am scared of being hungry ... I don't like 'shared platters' or shared dishes when I go out with friends because I get anxious that I'm*

not going to get anything. Because we were taught never to complain about the quality and quantity of food I would never say anything if I thought I wasn't getting a fair share of food.

Otaline continues her narrative by outlining some of her struggles and strategies to 'learn' the cultural codes lacking from her early experiences:

Moving around a bit, I finally came to live with Luca and Alyssa. He was Swiss French and she was Italian. Again they had the table and God could they cook. Both came from wealthy families. My memories of this time are conflicted. I learned to cook in this house – we ate together often so I really wanted to learn – to be a part of it. My dish was a tuna with Mediterranean roasted veg. I also did great salads – I was very proud of it :)! Once, however, the oven dish slipped out of my hand onto the floor as they were seated waiting for me!! I scooped it all back up and served it! They ate it all and loved it!! But this was also a very hard time for me because they were cultured. Cultured in a way that I didn't even know how to articulate back then. I just felt bad ...

Here Otaline begins her culinary escape, notably with Mediterranean influences from those outside of her family and indicative of a contemporary interest in Mediterranean foodways amongst advocates of a healthy lifestyle (Pollan 2013). The strongest sense throughout her narrative though is her feeling of shame at a 'lack' of cultural knowledge and access to the 'circuits of symbolic [cultural] production' (Skeggs 2005: 975). The power of legitimate middle class family foodways excludes, marks and stigmatises those not familiar with the cultural rules, rituals, norms and values of culinary capital (Naccarato and LeBesco 2012). She continues:

Luca once had friends coming to dinner and I offered to get the wine. We had a specialist winery round the corner from our place and I spend about a fiver or maybe more on a bottle of red but when I got home I could sense his dismay – I'd got it wrong – the wine was cheap I should have spent a tenner I guess. I was so upset. He never said explicitly that I'd messed up and I'm sure he thought I was just being tight but I really just didn't know how to buy the fucking bottle. So I sat at the table with his friends – they were all speaking in French and I just sat there feeling like I really didn't deserve to be there, but without fully understanding why. It was awful. And there were many, many moments like this.

Again, Otaline identifies the class-based associations with 'appropriate' foodways, which can be particularly difficult if they have not been inculcated from a young age and over time. Magenta similarly notes:

I was quite often embarrassed at the very limited knowledge of food I had, so would often eat things just to avoid the shame of admitting that I didn't know what aubergine, for example, was like.

Today Otaline has access to the social, cultural and symbolic resources missing from her childhood family foodways and is able to perform a 'good' self. Therefore she writes 'all that class stuff that I've read loads on and written about', means that '[I have a] self-understanding of that time now, but back then I felt like a peasant'. She adds:

The cutlery thing has followed me. Caught me out, exposed me on more than once occasion. I still feel very anxious eating in groups – especially colleagues, and I avoid it if I can. I still don't know how to hold it all properly – or what order it all goes on that table and I can't bear the shame, the pause to see what everyone else is doing, – and worst of all – not being able to enjoy the food!

Of course, a 'lack' of cultural capital is noticeable in social situations or when mixing with 'other' social groups, especially those with high cultural capital themselves. Generally, Otaline like others clearly documents the development of a type of 'food consciousness' cultivated over time and linked to the acquisition of high cultural capital. Her subsequent education, though, further exposes her sense of alienation from the cultural rules that are not inculcated in her family. Hence, a lack of familiarity with these cultural codes and symbols has the capacity to expose her and this makes her vulnerable. Her narrative is reminiscent of Goffman's (1963) work on stigma, as Otaline is forced to negotiate a discreditable (not visible) status in intimate settings and information management (who to tell). However, in public or more formal arenas she has to mediate a discrediting (visible) condition and impression management. In both scenarios there is an element of shame and fear. This demonstrates the power of everyday foodways in drawing boundaries across culinary and cultural fields. A significant consequence for Otaline is that she is determined that her son will not lack access to the cultural capital missing from her childhood family foodways. She notes 'I do not want him to even know the tastes of my childhood. There are no "grandmother's recipes" to pass on'. Indeed, Otaline is committed to feeding her family 'healthy' home-cooked meals prepared from scratch (Parsons 2014a, 2014b). These contemporary healthy family foodways are examined more fully in Chapter 3 on maternal foodways.

Finally, healthy family foodways reify 'the' family as a site for inculcating appropriate healthy family values. Hence a 'pre-occupation with achieving a "healthy diet" reflects a middle class disposition for being "health conscious" and for taking on board "authentic" health and dietary messages, that are sanctioned by (government) experts' (Wills et al. 2009: 65). The violent repudiation of mass produced convenience foodways (or food of the masses) then becomes part of a hegemonic habitus that highlights privileged idealised feminine and classed dispositions (Parsons 2014a, 2014b). A consensus amongst accounts illustrates how an aspirational model of 'feeding the family' (DeVault 1991) constructs boundaries and distances between sets of practices. An engagement in healthy family foodways requires work, time and a commitment to a particular set of cultural values. These contribute to the symbolic vilification and cultural hostility regarding alternative foodways and the reification and valorisation of 'healthy' family foodways. Put simply, middle class 'healthy family foodways' are presented as the norm and others pathologised (Parsons 2014a, 2014b).

3
Maternal Foodways

There are two interrelated issues for maternal foodways, the valorisation of healthy 'home-cooked food prepared from scratch' (Pollan 2013) and the significance of home-baking. In respondents' accounts both are markers of high cultural capital and bound up with notions of appropriate middle class maternal foodways and intensive mothering (Hays 1996). Further, as highlighted in Chapter 2 on family foodways, respondents are keen to distance themselves from commercial/convenience foodways, ready meals (chilled, dried, canned, frozen) and take-away food. This dismissal of convenience foodways as inferior runs counter to research carried out by Carrigan et al. (2006) who identify a hierarchy of potential cheats when it came to the use of convenience products by women when feeding their families. Yet, commercial foodways are considered to 'lack' on many levels, mostly due to a perceived 'lack' of care due to a symbolic vilification of 'other' maternal foodways, such as the mum who feeds her children convenience foods, like 'cheese and chips out of a Styrofoam container' (Deans 2013).

This is despite a compound annual growth rate in the UK ready meals market of 3.1% in 2011, with the performance of the market forecast to follow a similar pattern of 3.2% for the five-year period 2011–2016 (MarketLine 2013). Indeed, the ready meal market as a whole is valued at £2.6bn (Winterman 2013). Moreover, alongside a steady rise in sales of ready meals is an increase in retail sales of home-baking products between 2009 and 2013 from £1.41bn to £1.79bn. Notwithstanding these contradictions, home cooking and baking is indicative of a commitment to intensive mothering (Hays

1996) and having time (economic resources) to prepare home-cooked food from scratch. Certainly women with dependent children at the time of the study were committed to 'creating [healthy] meals from raw ingredients' (Little et al. 2009: 204) and this reinforces the doxic order that this is woman's work, and a means of doing appropriate middle class mothering. Indeed the medicalisation and individualisation of everyday foodways is pertinent as there is an 'implicit assumption that healthiness is a product of home cooking' (Hollows et al. 2010: 310) and women's domestic labour. This obscures:

> The food industry's role in constructing people's food desires and behaviours and blames the individual ... [and] since food is a woman's responsibility, the corollary of individualisation of food-related health problems is that women are to blame.
>
> (Allen and Sachs 2007: 11)

Indeed, part of the problem with convenience/commercialised food products is that they are associated with less healthy diets, obesity and related chronic diseases such as cardiovascular disease, diabetes and cancer (Jabs and Devine 2006, Celnik et al. 2012). Hence, the rise in consumption of these types of meals is associated with unhealthy diets and therefore unhealthy families, it links junk food with a 'junk childhood' (James 2010: un-paginated). In Jackson's (2009: 10) work 'junk food' is associated with working class mothers, whereas the 'making and preparing of a proper (home-cooked) family meal from scratch', whilst accommodating 'the individual food preferences and tastes of different family members', is part of a middle class habitus and a means of displaying a 'healthy' family life (Parsons 2014a, 2014b). This raises obvious issues in terms of how individuals negotiate or counter the stigma/contamination associated with commercial foodways (ready meals, take-away food). Strategies include considering them as treats (a rarity), or in response to a work/life balance that means cooking from scratch is difficult (on occasion), or as 'authentic street food' and significant in the accumulation of culinary capital (Nacarrato and LeBesco 2012). However, *ALL* women with dependent children at the time of the study prepared healthy home-cooked meals from scratch (Pollan 2013). This accentuates the power of this cultural ideal for the display and performance of appropriate mothering and legitimate maternal foodways.

Throughout this chapter I demonstrate how maternal foodways continue to be influenced by gender and class. Hence, there is a consistency over time regarding who is responsible for 'feeding the family' (DeVault 1991) and subtle shifts in the display of appropriate middle class maternal foodways as markers of high cultural capital. It is notable that recent research on gender tends to focus on family foodways as leisure or lifestyle activities for men. Hence, men engage in foodie or gourmet practices or 'choose' to become involved in the domestic sphere (Johnston and Baumann 2010, Meah and Jackson 2013, Szabo 2013). Neither of these lifestyle/leisure options is considered possible for mothers/women engaged in maternal foodways or the invisible work of feeding the family (DeVault 1991). Indeed, in terms of the individualisation thesis, 'motherhood' severely restricts everyday movement and future possibilities for women (Beck and Beck-Gernsheim 2002: 70). Hence, individualisation can be conceptualised as masculine (Lewis 2007).

Intensive mothering and 'yummy mummies'

Hays (1996), Douglas and Michaels (2004) and O'Reilly (2004) argue that intensive mothering is an ideology based on white privilege and that this therefore 'others' alternative mothering practices such as mothering on welfare. Hays' (1996) definition of intensive mothering is referred to in Chapter 1. She adds that:

> *Good childrearing requires the day-to-day labour of nurturing the child, listening to the child, attempting to decipher the child's needs and desires, struggling to meet the child's wishes, and placing the child's well-being ahead of their own convenience.*

> (Hays 1996: 115)

Further, Allen and Osgood (2009: 7) discuss distinctions between the 'yummy-mummy' and the 'chav mum'. They note that McRobbie (2008) identifies this 'yummy-mummy' as a distinct consumer 'tribe', consisting of women 'who have established a successful career before embarking on a family'. It is an aspirational identity, occupied by white, middle class professional women. Ringrose and Walkerdine (2008: 232) argue that the 'yummy-mummy' falsely 'universalises middle class femininity and pathologises working class women', especially younger women who have been unable to 'choose' between career and family. In Tyler's (2008: 30) analysis the 'chav-mum represents a thoroughly dirty and disgusting ontology that operates as a constitutive limit for clean, white, middle class, feminine respectability'. She contends that the vilification of alternative mothering practices outside of intensive mothering ideologies links:

> *New sets of norms about femininity, in which the ideal life trajectory of middle class women conforms to the current government objectives of economic growth through higher education and increased female workforce participation.*
>
> (2008: 30)

Hence, in the context of neo-liberal discourses, the 'yummy-mummy' 'embodies self-responsibility and self-sufficiency'; the chav-mum on the other hand 'is constituted as the unplanned result of improper and immoral behaviour that results in welfare dependency' (Allen and Osgood 2009: 8). Respondents did not refer to conceptualisations of the 'yummy mummy' or 'chav mum' in their narratives, however they would certainly have been aware of wider discourses regarding intensive mothering ideologies, the glorification of feminine domesticity (Negra 2009) and the fetishisation of the maternal (Littler 2013).

Indeed, it is argued that 'intensive mothering' (Hays 1996), 'requires symbolic and material resources' due to the desire of middle class parents 'to maximise [their] children's opportunities for success' (Lareau 2003 cited in Francis 2012: 374). This includes appropriate maternal foodways, (Elias 1978, Mennell 1985) and etiquette for example inculcated within the family as an 'all consuming project' (Francis 2012: 374). If this does not occur it can be viewed as a failing of the family (mother) in the duty of care and responsibility. Francis (2012) argues that 'intensive parenting' ideology is entwined with neo-liberalism, one that 'emphasises individual responsibility and self-management alongside a focus on managing risk' (Shirani et al. 2012: 26). There is an assumption therefore that parents (particularly mothers) can manage and plan their children's lives through 'concerted cultivation' (Vincent and Ball 2007). This ensures that their children are turned into responsible citizens. Hence, in an era of concerted cultivation with regards to childcare (Lareau 2003) or intensive mothering (Hays 1996), maternal foodways are even more significant in the display or performance of legitimate middle class mothering. Similarly in an age of obesity, with the medicalisation of eating along with other aspects of everyday life, and when neo-liberal government discourses charge families with the responsibility of enforcing dietary guidelines, mothers especially are implicated as the guardians of family health (James et al. 2009a) and eating (McIntosh and Zey 1989). Thus, in terms of contemporary constructions of new femininities, women today have to negotiate the twin poles of traditional femininity whilst embracing neo-liberal values of the autonomous self (Budgeon 2014).

Indeed, despite the demands placed on women by the dual burden or 'second shift' (Hochschild and Machung 2003) 'women are still responsible for the care of the house [and], the home [and family] regardless of the presence of a spouse or participation in paid work' (Robinson and Hunter 2008: 479). In DeVault's (1991: 22) study 'half of the women worked outside the home for pay'. In my study, not only are boundaries between home and work increasingly blurred, but the 'feminist political dilemma of housewife versus career woman has been replaced by narratives of renaissance women' (Allen and Osgood 2009: 7). These centre on the notion that women balance their careers alongside motherhood, that they 'simultaneously work in paid employment' whilst working 'to produce a successful child' (Hey and Bradford 2006: 61). In my study, the majority (80%) of female respondents are working. The extent to which these are full-time or part-time occupations or carried out outside of the home, is not investigated. There are nine women (out of 49) who self-identify as 'housewives', which included Celia (a 79-year-old 'retired farmers wife', married with four grown up children). Yet, for mothers with dependant children at the time of the study, even (or especially) those working full-time demonstrated a commitment to feeding the family healthy home-cooked meals from scratch. Further, it is well documented that the 'pre-occupation with achieving a "good diet" reflects a middle class disposition for being "health conscious" and for taking on board "authentic" health and dietary messages, that are sanctioned by (government) experts' (Wills et al. 2009: 65). This is something that cannot be delegated or negotiated. It is integral to the identity of a good mother and the positioning of the self in relation to one's own childhood experiences.

Thus, respondents (men and women) complied with a gendered division of labour within the domestic sphere particularly when allocating the work of 'feeding the family' (DeVault 1991) and this emphasised continuities, rather than disjunctures in social relations. Despite accommodating individual family members' preferences and maintaining an occupational identity, providing 'healthy' home-cooked meals from scratch is a means of displaying high cultural capital and appropriate maternal foodways (Parsons 2014a, 2014b). These represent much more than domestic practices, they are embedded in notions of what it means to be a 'good' mother. Specifically, this incorporates intensive mothering practices (Hays 1996) associated with maternal foodways, both the everyday 'proper' food work, such as home cooking from scratch (Pollan 2013), as well as baking and sharing this with children as representative of a middle class habitus and high cultural capital.

Maternal foodways 'past'

Although not all respondents were parents themselves, many including non-parents linked the good mother, both past and present with notions of good maternal foodways. The extent to which everyday foodways would be so embedded within a normative script of appropriate parenting was not anticipated, nor its significance in positioning the self as a good mother. In most cases feeding the family healthy home-cooked meals from scratch was used to 'display' (Finch 2007) appropriate family values and as a source of high cultural capital (Bourdieu 1984). This applies to those reflecting on maternal foodways from the past as well as those from the present. Again, as in the previous chapter, respondents reflected upon the maternal foodways of their childhoods, through a contemporary lens that focused on how they developed their own subjective positions. Thus Simon notes:

My mother was a competent but unadventurous cook, whose style was shaped by rationing, she loved to go to the hawker stalls for dim sum and takeaways that came home wrapped in banana leaf.

It is notable that Simon presents his mother's competency as a cook in the context of living abroad. This is a central aspect of his own food story and transition to becoming a professional cook. He is acknowledging that his mother cared about his food/welfare, but was unadventurous in contrast to his own style of cooking. Similarly, Paula, (a 55-year-old food/web writer, married with two children) makes the connection between her mother's foodways and her own contemporary interests:

> *Mam did a very good Sunday roast with a very small piece of beef (always cooked 'through', as she would call it) with Yorkshires, roast potatoes and mashed potatoes, greens, carrots and always, mushy peas. I now wonder at how she managed to get it all onto the plates. Has to be my most vivid memory from childhood. A very early memory is of Mam trimming the rind off bacon before cooking it and giving me rind to chew on. She was a lover of nature and showed me which wild things were pleasant to eat. Chewing on new rose stems or new long grass, eating wood sorrel and primrose flowers, picking brambles. Also where to find crab apples and sloes, and that great field mushrooms would usually be found in a field where there had been a horse! Foraging is a habit to this day. Something for nothing being irresistible – and wild flavours being much better for not being tampered with and tamed.*

Thus Paula locates her current food interests within the context of her mother's skills. Similarly, Connor (a 27-year-old, single musician) frames his interest in cookery within the context of his mother and grandmother's skills, he writes:

> *My Mothers Yorkshire Puddings (of which were always perfect) to go with the Sunday roast; how she would mash in turnip (swede to the southerners) into the mashed potato because I would turn my nose up at it; the spaghetti bolognaise recipe that was full of carrots, mushrooms and peppers to bulk it out cheaply (I still make it that way-the 'real' Italian one is good but I still prefer my Ma's) and also, not forgetting her fudge recipe that comes from the far North-East from my Grandmothers hand written scrap/cook book which is a combination of the traditional English fudge and the Scottish tablet. In fact all of these come from her mother and no doubt from her mother before her.*

Hence, as noted previously respondents begin their food narratives within a past family setting, in which mothers are judged on their cooking skills. Alison, for example, notes: 'food was very important to my mum – [she was] a real homemaker which meant feeding her family – lots!' This reinforces the doxic order, whereby feeding the family reifies maternal identity and naturalises a division of labour within the domestic sphere along gender lines. Connor valorises his mother's and grandmother's taste, participation and knowledge within a culinary field that usually associates high cultural capital with Italian cookery. Thus, he positions himself as a gourmet, who appreciates cultural omnivorousness with the taste and discernment to appreciate the difference. Dalia (a 50-year-old painter living with her partner) is similarly engaged in epicurean foodways in later life and therefore views her mother's cooking through this lens. She notes:

> *Our Mums have a big advantage in that their cooking is all we know as kids and is often, therefore, the 'best' cooking. I now realise how unimaginative and probably bad my mother's cooking was. With six kids to feed it was probably not an easy task and I forgive her for treating food as fuel ... well, almost. The big upside to her cooking was that it was homemade and probably healthy (in part) and not just reheated processed ready meals.*

In Dalia's account she is also judging her mother's cooking skills in terms of a contemporary middle class concern for appropriate maternal foodways that stress the importance of healthy home-cooked meals prepared from scratch (Parsons 2014a, 2014b). This would not have been a concern in the 1960s or 1970s, nor the connection between home-cooked and healthiness or the 'implicit assumption that healthiness is a product of home cooking' (Hollows et al. 2010: 310). This has the effect therefore of romanticising maternal foodways and adds to the continued valorisation and reification of healthy home-cooked meals cooked from scratch as the only appropriate way to feed children. Fred on the other hand writes about his mother's cooking:

> *What I do remember is that around the age of 10–11, I became distinctly aware that the food my mum was preparing was really boring. It wasn't her fault. At the time my dad ate no garlic, nothing spicy, nothing heavily flavoured, no rice, pasta or much else other than meat and two veg. His favourite meal of all time was a roast dinner. I found all this bland and uninspiring. I put it down to the meat. So I became a vegetarian. Not a complete one as my dad said I needed meat and*

wasn't there any I liked – I didn't mind chicken and so I ate chicken about 4 days a week for about 6 months. I was so over chicken by then I dumped that too. I was a veggie for about 17 years and it was during that time I guess I fell in love with food. My mum told me she wasn't going to cook separate food for me (she would have done – it was a ploy to get me in the kitchen). Because I was just cooking for me I could experiment more. Also at the time the range of pre-made veggie food was limited so I had to be more creative. I developed a passion for cooking. I discovered Italian food, Indian, Thai. There wasn't much I didn't like. My mum started eating what I cooked and I used to cook for my parents too (as well as my friends).

Thus, like Connor, Fred positions himself as an expert in cookery and a gourmet, but unlike Connor, this is in spite of his mother's 'boring' cooking. It is notable that in not blaming his mother Fred reinforces that notion that being a 'good' cook is a natural attribute associated with being a 'good' mother. In this case it was just unfortunate that his mother's good (natural) cooking skills were curtailed by his father's tastes. Cooking 'proper' healthy family meals is therefore a skilled practice (Short 2006: 89), a significant aspect of meaningful family-integration (Mosio et al. 2004: 265) and an essential element of doing appropriate mothering. On the other hand, Faye (a 46-year-old, secretary, married with one child) writes:

My mum was a fabulous, creative cook; she loved reading cookery books and took great pride in her cooking. We didn't have a lot of money when we were young, but my mum was a very creative cook and every meal was completely delicious and homemade.

Thus, Faye considers her childhood through a contemporary foodscape that places a high cultural value on home cooking from scratch (Pollan 2013) and a glorification of feminine domesticity (Negra 2009). Otaline on the other hand claims:

My mother was a really terrible cook. She could do mince – 100 different varieties of mince – and I can remember that she would never drain the fat so when the mince cooled you could feel the fat stuck to the roof of your mouth. God, I can still taste that now; it makes me sick to think about it. Safe to say I don't eat mince now – and if I did, I'd drain the

*bloody fat! She once burnt our sausages black and when we complained
she told us they were Chinese!!*

Thus, Otaline valorises home cooking from scratch as an indicator
of high cultural capital that is also indicative of maternal care and
exhibits a kind of matrophobia (Rich 1986). It is notable that in both
accounts a 'lack' of money has an impact on food provision, however
whilst Otaline equates this to 'lack' in terms of cultural capital and
'appropriate' maternal care. Faye argues that her mother was able
to counter the association between 'lack' of money and a 'lack' of
care by being a 'creative' cook. Thus, being creative and interested
in reading cookery books has high cultural capital and puts a floor
on a potentially disadvantaged position (Skeggs 1997). In Otaline's
account on the other hand her mother is not creative in the kitchen,
nor in the excuses she provides for burning the sausages. Further,
Otaline comments on the association between convenience food and
'lack' of taste. She writes:

*Then there was the microwave meal. Thick bubbling, congealed beans,
over-cooked and the plastic tray crisped and melting into the beans and
whatever else was in those godforsaken things – three little triangle com-
partments of sheer poverty. I cannot believe she fed me that shit. But
then, when we were children my mother worked nightshift in a factory –
a thread mill. She'd come home at 7.30 and put out our breakfast before
we woke at 8. I remember asking her to please stop putting the milk into
the cereal before we got up as it was a soggy, gooey mess by the time we
did but she was just so desperate to sleep, to get to bed that she'd do it
just to have one less thing to do ...*

Thus, maternal foodways are firmly embedded in notions of cultural capital and status, with the provision of good 'healthy' home-
cooked food equated with a good 'healthy' maternal identity. It is
about time and the lack of it. A lack of time is due to having to work
outside of the home and the lack of time to prepare or care about
preparing healthy meals from scratch. Convenience food is therefore
clearly associated with low socio-economic status, a particular working class habitus and lack of care. It is an unauthorised culinary practice associated with a subordinate group, these are not the legitimate
foodways practiced amongst the elite. Otaline continues:

I hated the shit quality of everything we ate. It just tasted shit. Long before we had the discourses on healthy eating we have now I knew this stuff was crap. And it made me really angry – even as a kid. I didn't know what the hell else was out there mind – but I knew that somehow this deal was raw.

The food Otaline's mother provides is therefore alien, unnatural and unrecognisable as nourishing on any level. It fails to provide any cultural capital because it is lacking in taste and does not incorporate any of the 'healthy' cultural references enjoyed by those with access to resources. Indeed, as DeVault (1991) argues, 'feeding the family' is care work that takes time. Otaline's mother did not have time to care because of a lack of material resources. However, a lack of time and 'poor' mothering was not only associated with mothers who were working. Ulrika (a 46-year-old property developer, living with her partner) writes:

I do have good memories associated with the feel good factor of being made soldiers to dip in a boiled egg. I think that this was my grand-mother who was fab. I probably spent the rest of my childhood days hoping that I might persuade my mother to do something of that ilk ... She was a busy bird and I came along to consummate her 2nd marriage (I have 2 older half brothers).

Ulrika identifies her mother as 'lacking' time for her, to feed or prepare the food that she liked. Instead it is Ulrika's grandmother who nourishes her through food. This is further reinforced when she writes about missing being fed baby food from jars:

I also remember the jars of baby food, which at the time I really loved. I remember missing them so much that I did actually persuade my mother to buy me one when I was 5ish, and discovered that it tasted horrible. So although I had clearly realised that they did not satisfy my taste buds I felt this sense of loss, as I knew I had to resign my self to life without Jars. This might be explained, as I was not breast fed at all. Apparently my mother managed less than a week before she gave up (mastitis). Not only was I fed formula milk but I am told solids as well from about two weeks old (Probably Jars!!) so that sense of loss when I no longer saw jars was perhaps explainable and a bit like been weaned!

The irony here is that by persuading her mother to buy her a jar of baby food, Ulrika is further alerted to the fact that her mother no longer feeds her. This therefore has the effect of making her feel bereft all over again at the loss of the closeness and comfort she craved and identified with the jars of food. In DeVault's (1991: 228) work she claims that whilst 'not all women feed the family, they live in the shadow of the social demands for the normalcy of care'. DeVault (1991: 237–9) expresses concern with being prescriptive about the caring aspects of feeding the family as it reinforces the association of women with nurturance and emotion. She asks, 'what are the consequences of calling this activity work and not that one? Who benefits from such a distinction?' She distinguishes between 'caring for' and 'tending', 'a kind of maintenance work and caring about an emotional, personal dimension of an activity' (1991: 237–9). Thus, maternal foodways are judged significant markers of legitimate mothering. A lack of care in the kitchen is therefore indicative of 'lack' on many levels and especially in terms of a lack of interest or care for the mother child relationship.

Contemporary maternal foodways

When, considering contemporary maternal foodways, respondents such as Faye, despite working herself and in common with many women juggling the second shift (Hochschild and Machung 2003) positioned herself as responsible for feeding her family. Indeed, Faye's comments are strikingly similar to those in DeVault's (1991) research from over 20 years ago; one of De-Vault's (1991: 56) participants says:

As soon as I get up on the morning or before I go to bed I'm thinking of what we're going to eat tomorrow.

Two decades later Faye comments:

Oh my goodness! I wake up each morning and the first thing I think about is what are we going to have for supper! It's such a drag, as I can never think of anything new or inspirational, despite the fact that we have lots of lovely cookery books!

Hence, these comments serve to reinforce further the status of 'feeding the family' (DeVault 1991) as central to maternal identity. Faye in contrast to her own mother has the additional pressure in an era of *Renaissance* woman (Allen and Osgood 2009) of having to cook new and inspirational food. Indeed, if preparing and purchasing food for herself or her family she notes:

I would make a packed lunch of something I really enjoyed eating, that's healthy, balanced and nutritious, with a little treat tucked in! I just buy things that are healthy and nutritious and things that might be interesting to appear in [my daughter's] daily lunch box!

Therefore by 'just buying things that are healthy' Faye contributes to the notion that feeding the family healthily is easy and natural care work. She positions herself in the mother role and as the 'guardian of health' (Beagan et al. 2008: 662, James et al. 2009b). This demonstrates the extent to which the caringscape and healthscape can be intertwined (McKie et al. 2002: 603), as well as, how health discourses seep into family foodways, whereby a 'good mother' ensures the health of her children through cooking/providing healthy food or by being engaged in emotion (food) work. Faye reiterates this by writing: 'if I have time [my cooking skills] ... are very good, if I don't they are rumbled together! But everything I cook is cooked with love!' Hence, this emotion work is not considered work at all, but an expression of love. This is what Erickson (2005: 338) following Hochschild (1983) considers the 'illusion of effortlessness' and 'part of doing the work (of mothering) well'. It contributes to the pervasive trivialisation of the work of managing meals (DeVault 1991) and reifies food work as part of a naturally occurring female disposition. Jocelyn writes about the transition from cooking to please herself to having to cook for her children:

I used to spend many hours cooking for friends before I had children; nowadays complicated looking recipes put me off, too busy I guess. I'm really 'in' to the 5 a day fruit and veg idea and am much more conscious nowadays of the fat-content of food. I read labels in supermarkets, especially when buying for the children, and tend to avoid stuff with too many additives.

She contrasts feeding children with preparing meals for her husband:

When I cook meals for Philip and I, I tend to open up the fridge and create something and hardly ever follow a recipe for a main course ... Though I say it myself I come up with lovely dinners this way ...

Jocelyn is making a distinction between food work done to provide healthy meals for the children and the more creative aspects of food work she carries out for her husband and herself. Jocelyn is thoroughly engaged in the skilled practice of feeding the family (DeVault 1991); she has to accommodate government dietary guidelines and advice on appropriate healthy feeding, rather than being creative. The complex character of caring work, the effort and skill it requires, the time and resourcefulness of those involved in feeding the family is highlighted. Ophelia notes that:

After 15 years of daily cooking for my family I have become much more confidant and proficient in food and what it really means. Today I balance the weekly meals between vegetarian, pasta, fish and meat and we have a lot of salad. I have been trying to cook less meat, maybe twice or sometimes including a roast at weekends, three times a week. Teens need carbs so I cook them most evenings but I don't eat carbs myself in the evening now unless it's a pasta dish we are all sharing.

Ophelia highlights here how she had time to learn appropriate middle class maternal foodways that emphasise healthy home-cooked meals prepared from scratch and eaten together. She has the skills and is able to work within a culinary field that places a high value on taste, participation and knowledge of the rules of the game (Peterson and Kern 1996, Warde et al. 2007). She engages in a middle class habitus, that values balance and control, responsible individualism and self-care. Further, home cooking healthy meals from scratch is aspirational and a way of accumulating cultural capital (Parsons 2014a, 2014b) and as Hannah (a 43-year-old secretary, married with two grown up children) claims:

Once I started to work at buying good wholesome healthy foods and making every meal from scratch, I started to dislike the taste of chips and pizza's.

Therefore, in terms of inculcating middle class tastes and cultural capital within the family, Hannah's education in healthy 'wholesome' cooking for her family has lead to change in her own tastes. However, the need to display appropriate mothering through feeding the family healthy home-cooked meals prepared from scratch, was especially pertinent for women working and living on their own with children, in order to put a floor on a disadvantaged social position (Skeggs 1997). Hence Valerie (a 46-year-old website designer, living on her own with her daughter) notes:

I am also responsible for feeding my daughter ... I make a great effort to make sure she is getting a balanced diet. To this end I nearly always cook meals from scratch. I use meal planners to get organised. I also have to budget quite tightly and meal planning helps with this. I aim to ensure we eat fish a couple of times a week, chicken a couple of times of week, red meat maybe once or twice and vegetarian once or twice a week. We always sit down to eat together at the table, even if it is just the two of us. It gives us a chance to talk and focus on each other.

It is notable that Valerie insists that they sit down to eat at a table. This is a particular aspect of a middle class habitus and one that distinguishes Valerie's family foodways from others, despite their low income and family status. Hence, 'proper' mothering is about cooking 'proper' meals from scratch, even or perhaps especially if on a limited budget or having the sole responsibility for childcare. Chloe (a 46-year-old occupational health advisor, co-habiting and living with two of her three children) claims:

I like to cook from scratch and meals can take time so I have to plan that around work ... I use cookbooks for ideas for quick suppers ... thinking about it I do spend quite a lot of time thinking about what I'm going to cook. I shop with meals in mind for each night of the week ... this will depend on what's available in the shops and what looks good, and then what time I get home ...

In DeVault's (1991: 230) study she argues that whether women embrace or resist the responsibility for feeding the family, they are subject to the cultural expectations and discourses of caring that shape action. She contends that the work full characteristic of

feeding is unrecognised by those who do it and it is problematised only when the work is not done, or perhaps when there are difficulties in doing it. Hence, mothers use home cooking from scratch as a means of demonstrating a commitment to appropriate middle class tastes. They are 'good' mothers because they understand the value of food, symbolically and metaphorically as well as in terms of its nutrients and heath benefits. The assignment of a high priority to the health promoting aspects of maternal foodways is a particularly middle class concern (Wills et al. 2009).

Men and maternal foodways (past and present)

In terms of the intersectionalities of gender and class within maternal foodways, respondents tended to draw upon traditional hegemonic masculinities. For example, Faye comments:

> *One of my very favourite things to eat was roast lamb (this was my mums craving when she was pregnant with me!) and my mum made it at least twice a week for lunch when I was at playgroup – my dad hated the smell of lamb so we had to eat it when he was at work!*

Faye's mother is therefore only willing to accommodate her daughter's food preferences when her father is at work. This reifies a traditional gender order, with the male head of the house taking precedence. Here the power relationships embedded in the gendered domestic division of labour, the breadwinner role and the homemaker are revealed through the cooking of a meal; as Beagan et al. (2008: 665–6) note, emotion work in the domestic sphere includes activities that enhance others' emotional well-being and provides emotional support. However, food work strategies such as these are framed as individual decisions rather than being seen as collective normative constraints or a result of wider gender divisions/inequalities. Faye describes her early childhood memories from the perspective of a cultural climate that values neo-liberal individualism, whilst simultaneously acknowledging the gender expectations and possible constraints of a previous era. She continues:

> *My dad and I loved opening a packet of crisps and adding pepper and vinegar to them and shaking the bag up to spread the vinegar before eating the soggy crisps inside!*

It is notable that references to her father are about sharing a snack, or leisure time, reinforcing the gendered division of labour in the home. Similarly Beth (a 57-year-old housewife, married with two children) claims:

> *My earliest memory of food must have been when I was five or under as I remember my father showing me how to make a pie out of all the food on my plate. You mash it all up together with a fork, but you can leave the peas whole if you like to make the pie look prettier. He made it into a pie shape then I could pretend it was a cake and cut it into slices and eat it. It was fun.*

The light-hearted and intimate experience of this encounter is given greater significance by Beth:

> *When I told my mum this, years later she was surprised because she said he was a stickler for good table manners, so maybe he showed me when she wasn't around. He did like to play. He died when I was five so I can place my memories in a timeline easily.*

Here, playing with food, changing it on the plate and making it fun undermines the serious business of 'feeding the family' (DeVault 1991) that mothers do. Beth's mother assumes that this must have occurred outside of the formal eating arrangements around the table. Or when the person who had spent time and effort preparing the meal was not around. Again, this example assumes an invisibility and effortless in preparing food for the family. The cultural scripts of femininity relating to appropriate middle class mothering assume a taken for granted naturalness and an effortless around preparing food for the family. These are all part of the continued glorification of feminine domesticity (Negra 2009) and the fetishisation of the maternal (Littler 2013). Thus, feeding work is a central aspect of maternal foodways; when mothers with dependent children discuss their partners these are framed in terms of hegemonic masculinities. Otaline, for example, writes about her partner's role in the kitchen:

> *Justin now does all the cooking. It started when I was pregnant and he felt rather useless, I think. He wanted to show me care, show me love and so he fed me and, of course, little Ethan who was growing inside.*

*Justin is a fabulous cook: reckless, meaty. Back then he would attend to
my dietary needs and make me eat buckets of Spinach for Ethan (lol).
He fed me mackerel so much I haven't been able to eat it since – or
salmon. And he loved doing it.*

There are contradictions here between food as work and food as
pleasure. It is notable that Justin's approach to cookery is 'meaty
and reckless', or qualities associated with hegemonic masculinities
that emphasise risk and adventure (Connell 2005). Otaline is also
clearly identifying the role of time in the preparation of food and the
association between cooking from scratch as an expression of love/
care, as opposed to the convenience food she endured in her childhood. She goes on to explain that her partner has become a gourmet.
Although since they have had their first child, the routine of having
to cook for her from Justin's perspective has become:

*Much more of a chore but still he is there cooking each night. It
was Chinese-spiced pork belly tonight with rice and Spinach. Damn
delicious – though I hate the fat. Anthony Bourdain is his hero. He
came to Brighton just before Ethan was born and Justin queued to have
his book dedicated to Ethan, I loved that. He fantasises about teaching
him the pleasures of food.*

Here, there is an emphasis made on the notion of 'food work'
(feeding her) as a chore alongside the notion of foodways as leisure
and pleasure. There are markers of high cultural capital as well, with
reference to specialist chefs associated with epicurean foodways.
Justin is participating in this and looking to pass on this cultural
habitus to Ethan. However, when it comes to feeding the family and
her new child:

*Today Ethan had his first bit of toast. I was anxious but Justin and I
were both delighted – gleeful – watching him sucking marmite on toast!
He loved it. I cook all his food. On occasion I will buy an organic pouch
but I want to cook for him because I love him. I am deeply concerned
about what he eats. I do not want him to even know the tastes of my
childhood. There are no 'grandmother's recipes' to pass on. He eats
three meals a day now and mostly I cook it fresh because I never seem*

to have the time to cook and freeze – though I know life would be easier if I made the time.

Hence, Otaline positions herself engaged in contemporary maternal foodways, with an understanding of legitimate cultural capital. Unlike 'the tablet recipe' in Connor's narrative, for Otaline there are no grandmother's recipes to pass on and she engages in a kind of matrophobia (Rich 1986), reminiscent of Lawler's (2008) argument on how upwardly mobile women dis-identify with their working class mothers. Thus, Otaline refers to her mother's maternal foodways, the 'lack' of interest in taste, participation in and knowledge of middle class culinary practices as well as 'lack' of time and money, in contrast to the time-consuming practices of preparing healthy home-cooked meals from scratch for her son. She does confess to buying 'an organic pouch on occasion', but the potential stigma associated with this is alleviated by cultural references to 'organic' which is expensive and uncontaminated; it is also in a pouch, not a tin or jar. Indeed, despite her lack of time, she insists on home-cooked meals from scratch and is deeply concerned that he has three meals a day (and not the one main meal a day she had as a child). Otaline continues:

I can eat whatever I like now … But it does play a big part in our lives still – the joy of it that is. Financially it's not an easy time but food will be the last thing we skimp on – it's fundamental to a good life for me – money or not.

Again, Otaline is reinforcing the association between good mothering and appropriate middle class foodways. Also, that despite a lack of money they are committed to legitimate forms of middle class foodways and inculcating these within their family. It is notable therefore that whilst Justin cooks for her, Otaline cooks all of Ethan's food, which reifies the dominant cultural script that defines a good mother through her appropriate middle class maternal foodways. A middle class approach to feeding the family is therefore a significant aspect of high cultural capital, and the appropriate means of doing good mothering. This reifies the doxic order that women engage in food work for children and men in food play for pleasure or for their partners.

It is notable that other female respondents wrote about their partners' aptitudes as cooks and how this influenced the domestic division of labour in the home over time. Laura, for example:

I moved in with my boyfriend (now my husband) when I left home. He's a few years older than me and had already been married, he'd also been to catering college for three years and although he hadn't finished the course and wasn't working with food he did have a good idea of how to cook. Over the next year or so he taught me some basics and we learnt together how to prepare meals ...

Laura learned to cook from her husband and shared food work with him at this stage in their lives. This follows Kemmer (2000) who interviewed a small number of couples who were just beginning to co-habit. She found that there was a much greater sharing of food work before couples had children, although the symbolic value of eating a meal together remained unchanged. However, once Laura had their first child:

We had our first daughter when I was 20 and this really ramped up my interest in cooking. I avidly read every baby magazine I could get my hands on and took a lot of notice of any advice given in them. I was determined that my child wouldn't eat food from a jar and that I would feed her the best, freshest food I could. This involved hours of cooking, pureeing and freezing ice cube trays full of various fruits and vegetables that were suitable ... From there my interest and pleasure in cooking continued, although I wasn't (and still am not) wildly experimental, I took great pleasure in preparing meals for my family ...

Here, Laura is positioning herself in terms of appropriate middle class maternal foodways. Taste, knowledge and participation of these carries high cultural capital and is the legitimate means of doing good mothering well. The transition to motherhood therefore ensures that Laura now has all food work responsibilities in the family. There is no democracy in the kitchen (Meah and Jackson 2013); indeed hers is a restrained, considered, feminised cooking practice, an emphasised femininity in the kitchen. She is not 'wildly experimental', which is more likely to be a trait associated with male cookery for pleasure and hegemonic masculinities (Connell 2005).

Kemmer's (2000) findings are pertinent when considering Nadia's (a 40-year-old artist, living with her partner and child) account of her partner, Dan who:

Was a pretty basic cook when he moved in and he has taken such an interest in it he is now much more polished than I am. He has fancy recipe books (that he uses!)

Again, men cooking for pleasure reinforces 'natural' distinctions between everyday food work carried out by women and the more exciting or expert food play men enjoy in the domestic sphere. Here, in contrast to Laura's experience but similarly to Otaline, Nadia's partner has become more of a gourmet engaged in epicurean foodways. Notably he has time outside of the domestic responsibility for feeding the family to 'use' fancy recipe books:

I am very lucky as Dan often cooks now ... I sometimes buy organic mince or free range chicken so he has variation. I do enjoy the taste but would be happy, and used to be, without it. I previously bought treats like ice cream as he loves it but ended up eating too much so bought him an ice cream maker and he prepares healthier versions.

In this extract from Nadia's narrative, like other respondents whose partners 'often cook', she positions herself as 'lucky' in this regard. However, she compromises her vegetarianism (as men need meat, Adams 1990) and her concerns about her weight/eating too much sweet (unhealthy) food. Nadia is therefore still responsible for the less visible aspects of everyday foodways, such as shopping, planning meals and as the guardian of health for the family Beagan et al. 2008, James et al. 2009b).

Zoe (a 44-year-old, recruiter, married with two children) also draws on her relationship with her husband when outlining how she became proficient in cooking and distances herself from convenience food or ready meals:

But when I met Rex in 1997 aged 30, it all changed. He is an excellent cook and used to own a restaurant so I was educated pretty quickly and now am a good confident cook and cook far more simply but with better ingredients and flavours. I cook most days particularly since having

children, but he will still cook 40–50% of the time … Now we eat good
interesting food every day at home and a takeaway once in a blue moon
(2–3 times a year). Ready meals are unheard of here and we eat out
sometimes (once a month). But food is a big social thing for us and we
have friends and family over a lot to eat.

Again, like Laura, Zoe has been educated by her husband (the
expert) and now cooks 'far more simply' (not restaurant style) most
days for the family. This reifies the notion that 'male' cookery is far
more complex than everyday maternal cooking, but as Zoe is also
responsible for the family's health the ingredients are better. Zoe also
highlights how inculcating a cultural habitus that values commensality (eating together around a table) are significant markers of high
cultural capital and important in the display of legitimate culinary
capital (Naccarato and LeBesco 2012). It is notable that in Laura,
Zoe and Otaline's narratives, their men are good cooks. However,
this has not led to a 'democratization of the domestic sphere' (Meah
and Jackson 2013). Instead the transition to parenthood ensures an
'increased production or display of gender' (Baxter et al. 2008: 262)
and a reinforcement of intensive mothering (Hays 1996), or 'an all
consuming project' (Francis 2012: 374), in which a 'good' mother
continues to put the needs of her children above her own.

Home-baking and (in)convenient foodways

When referring to 'baking', respondents may have been influenced
by the BBC TV series *The Great British Bake-Off (GBBO)*, first aired in
the UK in 2010. Indeed by October 2011, it was argued that:

On the high street, the effect is visible. Marks & Spencer have reported
sales increases of up to 20 per cent in baking ingredients, with spikes in
specialist sugars and cake decorating equipment flying off the shelves.
At John Lewis, customers buying cake tins and muffin trays have
increased by 15 per cent, while vintage-style tins and stands have more
than doubled

(Jarvis 2011 un-paginated)

It is notable that the commercial outlets reporting these increased
sales can be coded 'middle class' – these are not discount stores. Of
course the impact of *GBBO* is impossible to discern, yet the notion

of baking or even making a cake for someone has strong emotional as well as high cultural capital. Further, cake symbolises food as a 'gift relationship' (Mauss 1990), it is not just the cake but also the act of preparing and baking it specifically for someone else which is significant. To give a cake in modern westernised and Christian cultures is usually associated with love, caring, special occasions, birthdays, christenings, weddings as well as religious ceremonies such as Christmas and Easter. Hence Warin et al. (2008: 104) note that the:

> *Serving of food reflects Mauss's (1990) classic definition of the gift in that food creates and sustains caring relationships between people and displays an ethos of care ... [As food is prepared it] reaffirms her concept of self and sense of identity as mother and wife.*

The gift relationship implicit in baking a cake is also bound up with appropriate middle class maternal foodways. Thus Laura writes:

> *As soon as my daughter was old enough we cooked things like cakes together, she would stand on a chair and later a plastic step to reach the worktop.*

It is also a means of demonstrating care/love as Ophelia notes:

> *I love to cook for people and I especially love to bake, make chutneys, marmalades and jams and to give the surplus away as gifts; to me making food and giving it to people I care about is 'giving love' in some way.*

The theme of giving love through food is interwoven throughout her narrative and when reflecting upon her life before children she writes:

> *I baked bread quite a lot and I was good at that so I loved doing it to surprise people.*

Again, later:

> *Ah yes, cooking and baking and sharing. I do love that; it makes me feel warm inside. I love everything about it from planning the menu to making it and serving it or bottling it and giving it away. I much prefer to feed other people than to feed myself.*

Although Ophelia is referring to 'people' and not her family per se, there is a connection made between baking/cooking for others as an expression of love/care. Notably she finds it difficult to nourish or nurture herself in the same way. Similarly Connor notes:

I love cooking for/eating with people. The more the merrier. The content usually is decided by the others food preferences (veggies, mushroom haters etc. vegans can sling their hook though). And also the bank balance, if I am feeling flush then I would happily prepare a banquet of many dishes. But also I get a bit of a kick out of making a 'free meal' where I don't buy anything extra and still get to feed a house full of hungry students.

Hence, there is something deeply nurturing about feeding others (Lupton 1998). Bryony (a 33-year-old PhD student, living with her partner) writes:

I much prefer baking to cooking though. I like the whole process of measuring and mixing and that there's something sweet at the end of the process. Also, my baking seems to come out better. My favourite things to bake are apple crisp, apple pie, and oatmeal chocolate chip cookies. I haven't made the last two for over a year now. Mostly because I'm afraid I'll eat them! But I've been thinking recently that I should make it for someone else, which removes the temptation to eat a whole batch while letting me create something that I love.

Further, high cultural capital is associated with baking what are ostensibly snacks, whereas buying commercial snacks and snacking is not. For example, Fischler (1980) in his discussion on commensality draws a distinction between two basic categories of feeding 'commensalism and vagabond feeding'; during vagabond feeding 'individuals range freely [...] in loose formation each taking small items of food for himself (sic)'. Further, that the impact of 'urbanization, industrialization and their social correlates has tended to break up or erode the sets of rules, norms and meanings associated with food' (Fischler 1980: 947). This is significant for Fischler (1980) as it relates to his concept of 'gastro-anomy', a kind of normlessness related to food and feeding. Similarly, Kaufmann (2010) argues that the notion of the 'proper family meal' is eroded by a secularisation of everyday meals, with an emphasis on pleasure, a decline or relaxation of some of the more formal rules and rituals around eating', as well as a rise in more highly individualised dietary practices. The more relaxed types of eating are what Kauffman (2010: 62) refers to as 'meals without a compass'. Indeed, the demise of commensality or the structured food event in favour of what Bahr Bugge and Almas (2006) refer to as 'one hand food' or fast food dishes that can be eaten anytime, anywhere, leads to a 'pattern of ragged and discontinuous but frequent snacks' or what food marketers have come to call 'grazing' (Caplan 1997).

However, when snacks are prepared with care this counters the symbolic violence associated with 'other' foodways that lack care and consideration. Baking a cake for example is a family event, one in which the family is made and remade over time. Indeed, respondents negotiated the stigmatising effects and 'lack' of care associated with 'vagabond' feeding or 'one hand food' by recourse to home-cooked snacks prepared from scratch. Indeed, respondents tend to anchor their meals and snacks; they were not unstructured or free-floating meal events, but significant family rituals. For example, Annie (a 50-year-old, separated life coach with five children), when asked to describe a taste of home writes:

Well I guess it would be from my childhood so would say flapjacks and drop scones ... always a favourite my mum would make. Finding it hard to pinpoint anything that is more up to date ... I guess it would be brownies. Something that is a frequent favourite enjoyed by all in the family and demolished as quickly as it's made!!!

Here, Annie is drawing links between snacks and home, as well as past and present maternal foodways. That these home-made snacks were 'a favourite my mum would make', reifies the connection between home-baking and appropriate maternal foodways: baking is mothering. So Annie is clearly having her preferences catered for and of course it is 'mum' providing the care. Indeed, it is the act of sharing freshly prepared home-cooked food, rather than the distinction between meals and snacks that reformulates this crucial cultural distinction. Hence, taking time to make home-made chocolate brownies weakens the symbolic violence associated with 'snacking', 'grazing' or 'vagabond feeding' (Poulain 2002).

There is an idealisation of maternal foodways and mothers nurturing through baking woven throughout respondent's narratives, whether they were parents themselves or not. Thus Bryony writes:

My mom also used to make her own bread (still does) and dinner rolls (she also made her own granola, ketchup, mustard, and cashew nut 'cheese' among other things) … The dinner rolls were a key element of Sabbath lunch. A Saturday meal with out them would bring an apology from my mother who, although in full time employment as a teacher, saw it as her duty to provide her family with homemade food as a rule. Those rolls accompanied meals also made from scratch in the old-fashioned two veg and meat composition, except there was no real meat. I grew up vegetarian, eating soya based meat substitutes.

It is notable that Bryony's 'mom' apologises for not baking bread on Saturdays, reifying and valorising the doxic order that 'good' mothers bake and cook home-made food for the family. Jade (a 37-year-old, single architect) on the other hand writes:

My mother was usually too busy to bake and make a home; life was quick and geared towards work, sports, and homework. Now she bakes and likes to take time for it, because she has the time. I had a babysitter who baked for me and friends had mothers who stayed at home and made pancakes when they came home from school. I always envied that! But my mother had a career and so do I, so less time for homemaking. My father liked going out for shopping and cooking with me as well, but baking and doing the traditional mother-thing, no.

Hence, Jade is making clear distinctions between 'home-baking' and making a home, also that this was what 'other' non-working mothers did. Her mother had a working identity the same as Jade, so there is simply no time to bake. Also, that despite her father's interest in food, he did not engage in the highly feminised activity of baking with his daughter. Hence the connection between shared baking activities and 'home making' are synonymous and naturalised, it is what mothering is and what a good (non-working) mother does. Ophelia on the other hand notes that:

As a young child I was allowed to watch but I never made a cake or anything with my Mum, although I could lick the bowl when she had finished. She was a perfectionist and didn't like to share this particular love of hers with anyone else. She hated mess. I remember tasting things like a sauce for kidneys and scraping out the bowl which had contained creamy puddings she had cooked for other people and finding them delicious, but I never got to eat them as part of a meal.

This is part of Ophelia's story, always feeling hungry and missing the maternal love associated with baking and sharing food. In Nadia's account she notes:

Mum did bake which was a blessing after her pretty average meals ... biscuits and cakes, crumbles and upside-down puddings, rice pudding (my favourite). Unfortunately many memories tinged with sadness, as there were often arguments at dinnertime, not a particularly peaceful household.

Further, in Nadia's narrative her mother provided comfort (lacking in the home-cooked meals she prepared for them) through baking. Nadia continues:

My love for homemade cakes, biscuits and deserts is definitely linked to my mum's baking. Times of comfort in an often-discordant home (grumpy father!)

Nadia, also discusses the distinction between food work (the drudgery of preparing home-cooked meals every day) to the pleasure of baking and sharing this activity and writes:

Transition ... I moved out of home at 21. I would have started cooking for myself then. It is not a clear memory. I did not cook much in the family home, just helping with baking, licking the bowl! Now I think about it, it seems strange that I did not cook before then. I suppose my mother cooked because she had to, so perhaps it wasn't an environment to inspire me to try.

Thus, Nadia is highlighting a rigid division of labour in her childhood home, in which the only comfort for her and her mother centred on baking. Again, this reifies the connections between nurturing, or maternal foodways and baking.

To summarise, in an era of heightened neo-liberal individualism there is little evidence of a 'negotiated family model' (Beck and Beck-Gernsheim 2002). The 'symbolic violence' (Bourdieu and Wacquant 2002: 167) afforded to mothers who transgress the boundaries of appropriate mothering by feeding their children convenience foods meant that mothers in my study only fed their children healthy home-cooked food prepared from scratch (Parsons 2014a, 2014b). It would be inconceivable to admit to 'other' inappropriate mothering practices. Generally, there are rigid cultural scripts regarding appropriate middle class maternal foodways, with a middle class maternal identity and intensive mothering practices (Hays 1996) associated with elite/legitimate cultural capital. Hence, despite working full-time or part-time and the blurring of boundaries between home and work (Hochschild 1997), women are committed to feeding the family healthy home-cooked meals (and snacks) prepared from scratch. Dualist and absolutist approaches to foodways means that unhealthy, convenience foodways are demonised within family discourses. These foodways are derided and considered indicative of a lack of care. They are associated with 'other' (working class) mothering practices, with a lack of care, indicative of a lack of education, economic and cultural capital. Thus, 'good' mothers engage in appropriate middle class maternal foodways whether they are working or not.

4

Health Foodways

Generally, in the current foodscape, taste, participation and knowledge of 'good' food are considered indicators of high cultural capital. Further, Naccarato and LeBesco (2012) argue that 'sustainability, health and dietary restraint' are key markers of status within contemporary culinary fields. Indeed, the links between food, health and morality are not new. Brillat-Savarin [1825], for example, wrote that 'gastronomy should bring together pleasure and good health and the enjoyment of food is no longer a sin' (Drouard 2007: 266). However, despite public and media discourses purporting the importance of health foodways, a minority of respondents, (mainly gourmets), did not refer to health at all, although they did discuss 'good food'. This raises questions in terms of what constitutes 'good' food and what 'good' food is good for. It is certainly good for drawing distinctions and boundaries between legitimate high status foodways. Indeed, gender and class intersect in the performance of health foodways, because health has high cultural capital and neo-liberal aspirations towards self-care or 'health-consciousness are [an] ideal vehicle for the performance of femininity' (Moore 2010: 112).

Food, health and morality

It is notable, following Foucault (1973, 1977, 1979, 1988), that health foodways can be considered part of a disciplinary regime that contributes to the personalisation and rationalisation of the surveillance of the self (Bordo 2003, Howson 2004, Petersen 2007). In terms of an internalised moral gaze, Warde (1997: 174) notes that all four antinomies of taste used by advertisers in food marketing – 'novelty and tradition', 'health and indulgence', 'economy and extravagance' and 'convenience and care' – are potential sources of guilt and anxiety. Thus, inappropriate or unhealthy foodways compromise an individual's sense of self and 'in the field of social relations is a sign of moral turpitude or impropriety' (Warde 1997: 173). Thus, 'eating healthily is a way of constructing a moral self, of being a good person' (Balfe 2007: 141) and this forms part of a repertoire of disciplinary techniques, self-surveillance medicine (Armstrong 1995) and a Foucauldian internalisation of a medical gaze (Howson 2004, Petersen 2007). There is a 'duty to be well' through highly individualised practices of self-discipline (Turner 1997) with the body of the population managed via expert forms of knowledge in relation to diet and exercise (Armstrong 1995). This is not to assume that 'health' is a fixed or stable category; as Nettleton notes (2006: 170) 'health is not a unitary phenomenon and is a highly elastic cultural notion'. Similarly, Rousseau (2012: 14) argues that 'healthy is one of the most semantically unstable words in the English language'. However, some respondents engage in a kind of healthism, with health identified as feeling and 'being' good (Bendelow 2009: 136).

Indeed, in a highly individualised, neo-liberal era, health is capital (Bendelow 2009) and the performance of health foodways a key aspect of responsible-individualism and self-care. These health foodways position the self within a moralising medical discourse (Foucault 1988, 1991) that reifies a Cartesian dualism and absolutism regarding good/bad foodways (Levi-Strauss 1969). Thus, these rigid dichotomous approaches have implications not only in terms of health/self management but also for individual and social identities. Further, the increased medicalisation of everyday life (Crawford 1980) and 'food-related health problems' (Allen and Sachs 2007: 11) increases the pressure on individuals to engage in the micro-management of the self and everyday foodways. Hence, some respondents adopt health foodways in order to treat underlying health issues, such as Irritable Bowel Syndrome (IBS), *Myalgic Encephalomyelitis* (ME) or Chronic Fatigue Syndrome, Eczema, Drug Resistant Epilepsy (DRE), Candida and an ovarian cyst. Or in an effort to counter unexplained symptoms such as feeling 'sluggish', 'sleepy' or 'rotten', or to feel 'comfortable'.

When looking to treat conditions through health foodways, these narratives are reminiscent of Frank's (1995) four types of illness narrative, the 'chaos' narrative that includes emotional anxiety caused by the loss of health status, the 'restitution' narrative or coping with this loss, the 'quest' narrative or search for a cure/resolution, and finally the 'testimony' narrative that includes reflections on what has been gained or lost by the experience (Kennedy and Kennedy 2010: 49). Similarly, respondents' narratives are redolent of Bury's (1982) conceptualisation of biographical disruption, as respondents outline how they negotiate the impact of their health foodways on the life course and everyday life. Both Bury's (1982) and Frank's (1995) typologies also have religious and moral overtones; if medicine fails, then it is the individual's tenacity in overcoming obstacles, not giving in to the 'battle' with the condition or the authority of the medical practitioner, that has moral or heroic status. Finally, these narratives, in keeping with 'illness narratives' more generally, demonstrate how respondents negotiate and/or manage a spoiled (illness/health) identity, either their own or others in social situations, with echoes of Goffman's (1963) work on stigma.

In this chapter, therefore, the focus is specifically on health foodways or ways of doing health through foodways. This incorporates notions of food as treats and/or treatment, whereby treats can be a source of pleasure but can also lead to suffering and anguish. This can be a corporeal reaction or an emotional one, because of overeating and feeling out of control, or just eating 'bad' foods (however comforting). It is worth noting that what might be considered good or bad, like health and illness are not fixed concepts and our understanding of them is influenced by wider social and cultural norms and values. For example, distaste for convenience foods amongst middle class respondents, as documented in chapters 2 and 3. However, there is a level of agreement across narratives on what constitutes a treat as well as consistency amongst respondents about the types of food to be avoided in order to be well. There is a consensus that eating 'healthily' is important in maintaining 'health' and feeling 'good'. The 'bad' or 'unhealthy' food categories are alcohol, dairy, meat, sugar and wheat products. These categories incorporate specific items such as beer, wine, cheese, chocolate and bread. There are degrees of avoidance or acceptance of these and it is in the context of treating other ailments that they take on particular significance, which leads to subjective monitoring/surveillance of the self and/or others. Thus, it is through these 'moral narratives' (Nettleton et al. 2010: 296) that the individual gains or regains control over foodways and therefore health.

However, foods coded as 'bad' within hegemonic health discourses can actually be 'good' in the treatment of certain conditions. This is the case with the ketogenic diet, which relies on a high intake of fat and protein in order to send the body into ketosis. When the body is in this state, it is more likely to be free from seizures. This has implications for those involved in implementing a dietary regime outside of what might be considered 'normal' and/or 'healthy'. I explain more about this later on in this chapter. Suffice to note at this point that because of the rigidity of the boundaries between good/bad foodways and the extent to which these are embedded within moral discourses, any dietary regime however beneficial for health causes problems if it utilises food items from the 'bad' category. It means a negotiation of Warde's (1997: 174) 'indulgence' versus 'health' antinomy, as noted earlier. This contributes to feelings of anxiety and guilt and these antinomies have powerful moral overtones that can compromise a persons' identity (Warde 1997: 193).

Throughout this chapter I consider health foodways as a form of medicine and dietary regimes as part of a repertoire of Complementary and Alternative Medicine (CAM) (Bendelow 2009, Kennedy and Kennedy 2010). It is notable that respondents did not refer to CAM directly, but nutritional approaches and herbal remedies are considered to be CAM (Bendelow 2009: 21). Hence, not only are respondents grappling with strict dietary regimes in the interests of controlling symptoms, they are managing the implications of practising non-orthodox treatments. Bendelow (2009) and Kennedy and Kennedy (2010) consider the practice of CAM a potential source of stigma within Goffman's (1963) framework on the management of a spoiled identity. This means that those engaged in CAM engage in both information and impression management in social situations, especially if they adhere strictly to unusual dietary regimes. It is notable that CAM is a typically female activity (Petersen 2007: 119) and usually associated with higher educational attainment and socio-economic status (Bendelow 2009: 111).

Gender and health foodways

Health foodways, or ways of doing food that incorporate strict dietary regimes in order to benefit one's health status are gendered (Connell

1995, Beagan and Saunders 2005, Gough and Conor 2006, Gough 2006, Gough 2007, Robertson 2007). Indeed, health foodways are coded as feminine. Further, if and when men 'do' health they tend to position their engagement in terms of hegemonic masculinities (Connell 2005, Gough and Conor 2005, Gough 2006, Gough 2007). Thus, Fred notes:

My ex (who I was with for 7 years) was really into her healthy eating and didn't do carbs so it was very easy to avoid them and in fact the chances to eat them were few and far between … She was very interested in healthy eating. I was interested to see if it made any difference. I don't feel it did although apparently I don't look as old as a lot of my friends but don't know if that is diet or genes.

Hence, Fred is only interested in healthy eating to please his (now ex-) girlfriend. Thus, he distances himself from the potentially contaminating association with feminised health foodways and discourses of responsible individualism. Indeed, a concern with the health benefits of food, particularly dieting to lose weight is considered a feminine preoccupation (Lupton 1996, Bordo 2003, Gough 2007).

Fred also claims:

I think I have a good idea what healthy eating looks like (and I think its quite different to a lot of people I believe who seem to think there are healthy convenience meals and that low fat options are 'healthy' irrespective of the rubbish they load them up with to give flavour etc.). Whether I always choose the healthy option is debatable …

Here Fred is directly criticising a diet industry that sells 'healthy convenience food' and 'low fat options' possibly because the target market for these products tends to be women. Fred also displays condescension and cultural hostility towards an imaginary subordinate group, who are ignorant of how they are duped by commercial foodways. However, Fred is also a gourmet (see Chapter 6) and 'good' food prepared from scratch has higher status than the mass-produced commercial products he is referring to here. It is notable too that despite knowing what 'healthy' eating looks like, he may choose not to eat healthily because that too has associations with femininity. Indeed, refusing to comply with dietary guidelines and wider public health discourses can be construed as risky, 'living on the edge' or 'edgework' and is a strategy for performing dominant masculinities (Collinson 1996, Robertson 2007: 48–9).

Indeed, the turn towards 'healthy' non-commercialised foodways is common within respondent narratives and not just amongst mothers preparing healthy home-cooked meals from scratch as noted in Chapter 3. Also, despite the associations between femininity and dieting, respondents differentiated between 'the thin ideal' (Germov and Williams 2004: 355) and changing one's diet for health reasons. Nadia for example, explains the difference between a 'diet' to lose weight and eating or not eating for health reasons:

> [I have been on] a proper diet once, from a book when I was 22ish. I followed it strictly, exercised and lost heaps. It was basically a fat free diet. It taught me about low fat foods. I have also been on many wheat free, low sugar, detox type diets. These were to deal with problems like candida. I have a weakness for sugary things so have to take it in hand now and then!

Hence, Nadia argues that a 'proper diet' was useful in terms of developing her knowledge of low fat foods, but has since followed 'other' dietary regimes to cure specific health problems such as candida. It is notable that health consciousness is a means of performing femininity (Moore 2010) and that Nadia has a weakness for sweetness, which is similarly coded as feminine (Mintz 1985, Lupton 1996). In Mark's (a 45-year-old consultant, married with three children) account, he notes:

> I still am [conscious of what I eat on a day-to-day basis], in that I only eat salads and maybe scrambled eggs for lunch. This is based on being healthy rather than trying to lose weight ... I feel guilty now if I eat a pie or pasty for lunch but never usually worry about having a 'healthy' dinner.

Of course, the rationale for Mark's distinction can be understood in terms of hegemonic masculinities and the association of dieting with emphasised femininities (Connell 2005, Gough 2007). However, like Fred, his health consciousness has limits and he does not worry about having a healthy dinner. Again this is about distancing the self from the feminine attributes associated with health, and engaging in slightly risky behaviour or edge work as a performance of dominant masculinities (Collinson 1996, Robertson 2007: 48–9).

Dietary regimes and technologies of the self

In Foucault's (1973) work the *Birth of the Clinic* he highlights how medicine became a form of social control; what Turner (1987: 219) refers to as 'the regulation and management of populations and bodies, in the interests of a discourse, which identifies and controls what is normal'. There is therefore a social and individual concern with the normative, the good and the proper in both public and private life. Similarly, the development of disciplinary regimes from Foucault's (1977) work in *Discipline and Punish* and the elements of 'rationalisation embedded in the personalisation of surveillance' (Warde 1997: 173) is significant. The continued internalisation of the disciplinary gaze is exposed through the intricacies and intimacies of respondents' highly regulated, individualised eating plans. Thus, in an era of self-surveillance medicine (Armstrong 1995) tracking food and exercise and other health foodways are increasingly the means of performing a good self. Indeed:

To be a good citizen one should play one's part in managing one's risk, promoting one's health or preventing illness, regulating one's diet, and so on.

(Petersen 2007: 10)

Of course, 'beliefs about what constitutes health and illness are at once individual and social' (Herzlich 1973: 1). They are subject to historical and cultural change. One of the most significant changes since Parsons' (1951) research and articulation of the medical model and the sick role, has been the rise in chronic conditions of late modernity, such as:

Diseases associated with the life course ... chronic illnesses, which require management (such as diabetes) ... and complex disorders of late modernity such as anorexia, depression, eating and anxiety disorders and including the proliferation of acronym disorders such as IBS, CFS and ADHD ... [as well as] multifactorial degenerative diseases such as cancer.

(Bendelow 2009: 26)

In the contemporary milieu these conditions challenge the functionality of the sick role and the medical model, which was developed in an era when the purpose of medicine was curative or to get people back to work (Parsons 1951). Further, because some of the chronic conditions of late modernity are often difficult to medically define and/or treat this raises problems for those with chronic conditions or who do not fit the medical model. Is it still important for conditions to be medically sanctioned by trained medical practitioners? What are the consequences of blurring the boundaries between what might be considered a chronic condition and issues associated with the life course? Is someone with a chronic condition always ill, or is it a matter of only being ill when the management of that condition falters?

Generally in matters of health and illness, orthodox medical discourse encourages individual responsibility, as Nettleton (2006: 42) claims:

> *Conceptualisations of health and illness in contemporary Western societies ... reflect the values of capitalism and individualism ... imbued with notions of self-discipline, self-control and will power.*

Thus, there are links between the individual and the political body, with individuals charged with finding solutions to health problems, whereby gaining control of one's everyday foodways is part of a 'normal' life trajectory and a growth in personal autonomy (Petersen 2007, Turner 2008). However, foodways not sanctioned by orthodox medical experts can be considered 'alternative healing systems [and] still regarded with suspicion and hostility' (Bendelow 2009: 22). Despite the potential benefits of alternative foodways as useful coping mechanisms when managing chronic conditions and/ or negotiating a (spoiled) illness identity (Goffman 1963), there is a double burden for those regulating conditions through health foodways. Thus, the stigma associated with a change in status from healthy to 'sick' can be further compromised if managing the condition via health foodways or CAM. This is part of what Turner (1987: 225) identifies as:

> *The Foucault paradox [in that] the provision of citizenship tends to require the expansion of regulation, control and surveillance from the state [which leads to a] contradiction between individual rights and*

social surveillance. The medicalisation of society involves a detailed and minute bureaucratic regulation of bodies in the interests of an abstract conception of health as a component of citizenship.

Hence, the medicalisation of every day life (Crawford 1980), or the process whereby medicine has made inroads into the domain of 'ordinary life' previously controlled or regulated 'through moral, religious or legal jurisdiction' (Bendelow 2009: 11), ensures that the conceptualisation of health foodways are an appropriate means of 'doing health' (Moore 2010). Paradoxically, if the individual is practising a form of CAM, either treating conditions not sanctioned by orthodox medicine, or practising unhealthy/unusual foodways the individual is breaking the rules of the sick role and therefore potentially liable to punishment (Parsons 1951). Or if following a dietary regime outside of what might be considered appropriate within the normalising discourses of health, individuals are forced to engage in the management of a spoiled identity (Goffman 1963).

This is particularly pertinent for those monitoring their food intake because of dietary intolerances or other health-related issues. Dalia, for example, makes clear distinctions between changing one's eating habits to treat a condition and going on a diet to lose weight:

I have only been on one diet in my life! Not that I didn't need to on several occasions. This one diet was brought on by avoiding light surgery in favour of changing my diet to cure a small ovarian cyst. It seems to have worked ... but what it has also done is made me eat more healthily.

The distinction here is clear; going on a diet to lose weight is connected to aesthetics rather than health and therefore not quite as serious as following healthy foodways because of health benefits or medical cure. Here the association between the feminised practices of dietary restraint to lose weight and the 'curing' of a sanctioned medical condition is significant.

Others documented highly regimented health foodways and ate almost the same things on most days; Hannah is a good example, and notes:

I love food, I have to have regular meals and mid meal snacks, I always have a good breakfast, what ever I am doing I have to start the day with breakfast otherwise I feel grumpy and tired. As I have got older I have become more aware of what I eat and drink, I try to eat healthily, when given a choice I always buy food which contain granary or whole grain, nuts and seeds.

Here, Hannah illustrates knowledge of her body and its require-ments. She discusses her potential mood, 'grumpy' and feeling 'tired' if she doesn't eat a 'good' breakfast. Generally, respondents engaging in health foodways are keen to explain how, when and why they developed this approach. These are narratives about emotions and feelings; they are embodied, corporeal rebellions to an increasingly alienating foodscape. They are responding in part to what Fischler (1988: 948, 2011) refers to as 'gastro-anomy' in which:

Modern individuals are left without clear-cut socio-cultural clues as to what their [food] choice should be, as to when, how and how much they should eat. Food selection and intake are now increasingly a mat-ter of individual, not social decisions. And they are no longer under ecological or seasonal constraints. But individuals lack reliable criteria to make these decisions and therefore they experience a growing sense of anxiety.

Whether this growing sense of anxiety manifests itself in a cor-poreal sense on or within individual bodies is difficult to measure. Certainly, respondents explain how they developed their health foodways in response to anxiety about when, how and what to eat, but this is an affective practice, a response to embodied experiences (Wetherell 2012). It is a learnt health consciousness inculcated over time. Fischler (1980: 949–50) argues that:

Food fads, fad diets, food sectarianisms, new trends in culinary aesthet-ics may be indicative of an aspiration to re-establish dietary regulations and norms in the face of growing normlessness ...

He critiques the shift towards heightened individualism with regards to foodways and how this serves to undermine the com-mensal aspects of sharing food. This is not lost on respondents and some, such as Imogen, note that despite following fairly strict health foodways, 'If I go out I'll eat whatever I'm presented with as it's maybe a bit rude not to'. Fischler's (1980: 949) use of the term 'food fad' implies something temporal, fleeting and unimportant. Respondents' health foodways are far from brief or short-lived crazes. Indeed, these 'quest' narratives (Frank 1995) highlight how they are eventually able to control difficult to treat symptoms and biographical disruption (Bury 1982) by changing their dietary habits.

Food for health

Of course, generally speaking a commitment to healthy eating can be understood as a means of performing responsible individualism and a middle class habitus. In terms of affective practices (Wetherell 2012), eating the wrong things or bad food has consequences for the individual in both a social, moral and corporeal sense. So, whilst the focus for respondents is on good/bad foodways in the context of health discourses and the medicalisation of the practices of everyday life (Crawford 1980), sometimes it is not necessarily that the food itself is 'bad' but that certain foods cause 'bad' physical and/or emotional reactions. The association of items such as bread or chocolate or sugar (sweets) for example with pleasure, childhood innocence and/or comfort is common. Yet, excess consumption of these is sinful, reinforcing the connection between food and morality (Coveney 2006), as Nadia writes:

My general rule is if healthy at home then that is a good base to then have treats when out and about. If there is nothing too evil in the fridge then there is less chance of me eating badly. If I have chocolate at home I have little self-control, I would snack on it before an apple so it's best to not buy it.

Her use of the word 'evil' is notable; this is a strong word to use when describing food, especially something that maybe an innocent or potentially comforting treat like chocolate. This underlines the moral contamination from association with improper foodways. Notably these foodways are coded feminine (chocolate), with issues of discipline and control similarly associated with femininity (Malson 1998, Riley et al. 2007, Malson and Burns 2009).

In Imogen's 'quest illness narrative' (Frank 1995), she writes:

I also started to listen to my body more, recognising what made me feel uncomfortable or upset my stomach and this led to my beginning to cut out white bread and over the following five years or so most wheat products. I explored food combining and gluten free diets and have tried cutting out dairy but have kind of settled on a mostly wheat free diet that is otherwise very varied ...

It is notable that Imogen 'listens' to her body, which whilst reminiscent of Cartesian dualism and mechanistic medical models of health, 'moves the locus of causality back towards the self' (Lowenberg and Davis 1994: 587). Hence, although she identifies a more 'holistic' or CAM approach towards her health foodways, this is still framed within a medical discourse that assumes the body is a machine that can be controlled by appropriate regimes (Turner 1982, 2008, Petersen 2007). She continues:

I started cutting out wheat when I was about 25 because I found that every time I ate bread my stomach and right cheek would swell! My face became hot and itchy and would take days to go down. After seeing 2 different doctors they said I had an allergy to wheat so I stopped eating it and probably 80 per cent of the time went gluten free. This cured my stomach problems which I still have if I cant resist a pizza or garlic bread once in a while but not the face swelling which after seeing a specialist turned out to be a narrow parotid gland which could be operated on but has a chance of facial paralysis so I've left it! The reason I think I associated it with wheat for so long was because I was snacking on bits of toast when I got really hungry but it was the hunger and production of saliva that was triggering it not the bread! Now I manage it by eating something like nuts or cheese to stop me getting too hungry so it doesn't swell.

Thus, in Imogen's 'quest' and 'restitution' illness narrative (Frank 1995), she discovers and then learns to deal with symptoms associated with her narrow parotid gland. Notably, though, this is not due to changes in her diet, which instead 'cure' an altogether different ailment. Then, she writes:

I tried going dairy free for a while to see if it made any difference to the skin on my arms and legs, which was getting pimply. It did help and I still have soya milk on cereal and in drinks but I eat other dairy stuff. I've got so used to the soya that I don't like the taste of cow's milk now.

Here, Imogen notes how her 'tastes' have changed in line with alterations to her foodways over time, which is now part of a middle class cultural habitus; she is fully immersed in closely monitoring her embodied responses to food and has internalised the medical gaze (Petersen and Bunton 1997). This is also an important element in the performance of emphasised femininities (Connell 2005). She finishes with a testimony on what she has learned:

> *I think probably it's taken me this long to work out what I can eat in good amounts without having a detrimental effect on my health as I basically love food! I love eating good quality nice things but always hated the heavy full tired feeling I had after eating too much stodgy food as a kid.*

Imogen notes that as a child her diet left her feeling 'very full quite often', but for Imogen, like others, this is not a desirable state, it is uncomfortable, it is not how a 'healthy' body should feel; thus, feeling full is not healthy. Today she likes to eat 'good quality' things and is therefore displaying a kind of neophilia (Lupton 1996) and distancing herself from the inappropriate foodways of her childhood. She continues:

> *I think there is a lot more information available to kids now regarding a healthy lifestyle. I don't remember ever being told about healthy diets at school or at home for that matter.*

Hence, Imogen's knowledge and expertise with regards to her health foodways were not inculcated at school; she has had to learn these for herself, as part of becoming a responsible neo-liberal citizen and engaging in health foodways associated with high cultural capital. Willow (a 55-year-old senior lecturer, living on her own with a grown-up child) on the other hand, documents a number of dietary changes over the life course and in response to health issues:

> *In my twenties I cut down on sugar and meat, sometimes giving both up completely, and started to eat a lot more whole-grain based food. In my thirties I would cut out milk products occasionally for a few weeks when I had problems with asthma. In my forties I had a period of eating more meat (mainly organic) in an attempt to eat less dairy produce to help my*

asthma, and also because my daughter enjoyed meat. When my teen-age daughter became a vegan I gave up meat again and didn't miss it. When I got IBS I experimented with diet changes and cutting out wheat and milk products seemed to work well and make me feel good, so I've tried to stick with this since, with occasional lapses, either to be polite to people I'm with, or just because I'm very tempted by something.

Willow's account is similar to Imogen's in that she finds she lapses her health foodways in order to be social (Warde 1997).

Healthy food

There is also a consistency in accounts around 'feeling full' or 'heavy' or 'tired' which is associated with eating too much or consuming 'bad' foods. These are embodied notions that equate feelings with healthiness and unhealthiness. Zoe writes:

We had a cleaning lady who used to cook for my father and leave food in the fridge … sausage rolls and vol-au-vents. Hideous lumps of pastry that needed a litre of tomato ketchup to make them palatable. He [father] used to eat sandwich spread sandwiches … My mum's cheese scones were and still are great. Going out for a meal was a huge event … as a child, we always ate at home. The thought of all that pastry is making me feel quite sick though!

Zoe also notes:

… Mum left home when I was a teenager (12/13?) so I learnt most of my cooking skills and planning skills at school.

This may account for the strong reaction to the food left by some-one other than her mother and emphasises the links between food-ways and nurturing/care (Lupton 1996). Zoe continues that now:

I like salads, lots of crunchy textures and good flavours. And light food – and its generally down to the way it makes me feel. My body goes into sleep mode if it has to digest anything too solid and I like having energy.

Hence, 'good' food is light food and this means that Zoe feels light and this is important. Here, 'lightness' is associated with health and healthiness (although also possibly lower body weight) and morality (Coveney 2006). In all of the health foodways there is an emphasis on feelings; these are embodied and emotional responses to food, the environment and the social context in which this food has been consumed or prepared.

Overall, respondents expressed an engagement with contemporary health discourses and knowledge of the correct foodways deemed beneficial for one's health. Thus, knowledge, taste and participation in health foodways could be considered an aspect of elite cultural capital (Naccarato and LeBesco 2012). Indeed, health foodways are integral to being a responsible moral citizen and 'Coveney (2006) reminds us, that the discipline of nutrition informs the construction of notions such as responsibility and health' (cited in Nettleton et al. 2010: 746). Hence, Hannah's narrative is littered with references to healthy and importantly this healthiness is strictly controlled:

The above food diary is a fairly typical day – always a healthy start ... From here on the day always starts out to be controlled and healthy, but at work someone always has a reason to bring in cakes/sweets, I cannot resist and indulge with the rest. Always a healthy lunch, same crackers, marmite and cheddar, apple and or yogurt. Supper, again, always home-cooked, healthy main course with fresh fruit optional.

Hannah's health foodways are disciplined, highly regular and always home-cooked (Pollan 2013), which all have high cultural capital. Yet she is still able to conform in social situations and, like Imogen, she indulges in (unhealthy) 'cakes/sweets' and joins in with 'the rest'. Hannah will suspend her health foodways in order to fit in with social norms and values around the commensal aspects of sharing rituals in the workplace (Fischler 1980). Nadia writes that she has a:

Strong dislike for unhealthy, overly processed food e.g.: junk with additives. I generally prefer vegetarian options so I am uncomfortable with takeaway animal foods such as chicken or burgers. I prefer vegetables and wholefoods. This developed from health issues when in my 20's and learning more as a result about wheat free, low sugar, less fat etc. I choose organic when I can afford it ...

Again, this is indicative of how respondents distanced themselves from contamination from convenience foodways. This is part of a commitment to a disciplinary model of the self (Petersen 2007) and associated with high cultural capital (Naccarato and LeBesco 2012). Nadia's dietary concerns began because of issues to do with her health and she describes unhealthy food as:

… Anything too 'plastic': food that has become too removed from its original natural source. I stay away from meats that I feel have not been humanely produced, I only eat free range and/or organic meats and in small quantities. I eat soy as an alternative to meats and dairy, and prefer organic dairy produce when possible. I check labels and avoid too many numbers, or even too many ingredients. I am wary of too much sugar so avoid lollies and soft drinks.

In Nadia's narrative, unhealthy food is so alien as to be not even 'food' but plastic and indicative of an alienating contemporary foodscape (Fischler 1980, 2011). There is also a concern raised regarding animal welfare, which can be aligned to more sustainable approaches to foodways but is not a wholesale engagement with democratic or sustainable foodways; this is common amongst respondents and differs to other studies such as Johnston and Baumann (2010). Later Nadia attributes a 'complicated' relationship to food to the problems of negotiating 'a Western culture of plenty' in contrast to the spirituality and ascetic feelings she associates with her experience of other cultures:

I have experienced returning home from a ten-day silent retreat where I've enjoyed wonderful mindfulness choosing what to eat and slowly chewing each mouthful to finding myself at a dinner party mindlessly gorging myself.

Nadia's account is reminiscent of the problems of negotiating the boundaries between the 'orgy' and 'the feast' and the pleasures of the flesh (Coveney 2006, Turner 2008). Nadia has become health-conscious and developed health foodways because of problems with candida, which she blames on an over consumption of sugar (hyper-femininity). Her health foodways are also a response to Fischler's (1980, 2011) notion of gastro-anomy, whereby her dislike of overly processed 'plastic' junk food and health foodways are a means of countering the impact of an alienating and highly industrialised foodscape. Again, this is associated with the accumulation of cultural capital, as processed 'junk' food is considered low status food.

Food as CAM

Although 'good' food is conceptualised as significant for a healthy diet/lifestyle (way of life) the use of food as a treatment for certain conditions is not wholly sanctioned by orthodox medicine. Nettleton et al. (2010: 297) note that the 'avoidance of food because of food intolerances is associated with alternative and unconventional lifestyles, fashion and trends which in turn implicate the person who suffers'. The question is how do those involved in using food as a treatment negotiate these contradictions? This has significant implications for those forced to adjust their dietary habits because of health or illness. In an era of responsible individualism there is a moral imperative to be well and to be unwell can be stigmatising (Goffman 1963).

In health foodways, respondents considered certain foodstuffs as treatments for particular conditions, such as a high fat (ketogenic) diet as a treatment for DRE. However, 'treats' for some had to be excluded from the diet in order to avoid becoming ill (wheat and dairy for example). For others the avoidance of what might be considered 'treats' alleviated pain and discomfort. In all cases, respondents are forced to participate in a kind of hyper-surveillance of foodways in the interests of controlling health and/or illness, either theirs or others (children, partners, families). Again, in terms of taking responsibility for health (Petersen 2007) this has high cultural capital. Similarly, an emphasis on CAM/holistic approaches places the 'responsibility for health and illness in the hands of the individual' (Baarts et al. 2009: 727).

However, the route to health foodways as treatment tended to arise as a result of the inability of orthodox medicine to diagnose and/or treat symptoms. Although in some cases a medical opinion was not sought and the respondent had just heard that this was a possible means of treating the condition, notably those already engaged in holistic approaches to everyday health and well-being. This seemed to be particularly pertinent in cases of eczema. For example, Kevin (a 47-year-old consultant, living with his partner and two children) comments:

[When planning meals] I have to think of their favourites and veggie options and our youngest is off dairy products due to eczema ... We never feel sure [if it works] – we have also done soya free and tomato

free – overall I think his eczema is improving but honestly couldn't say if it's the dairy – occasionally bad spells have seemed linked with a lapse in diet but also that hasn't always happened – not very definitive sorry.

Similarly, when positioning the self in the role of a 'proper' mother, with responsibility for the health of the family (Wills et al. 2009), Chloe notes:

[I have] never been on a diet but have moderated type of ingredients in family cooking for health reasons ... i.e. family health ... eczema ... daughter can't eat too much dairy.

On the other hand, for Nick dietary change in the interests of health if not sanctioned by orthodox medicine is problematic. When asked why he was avoiding bread, for example, he replies:

The white bread thing is probably a bit faddish but I have read/ heard/ seen the odd thing which says us humans were never designed to eat flour of the highly refined type we pass off as bread anyway. I like the idea of nuts, meat, fish berries, root veg etc. like cavemen and not much else. The Romans had bread but it was pretty much spelt I believe. Tudors also had a good diet ... or at least those eating inside Hampton Court with a healthy veg soup on the go all the time ... a pottage ... cooking away in a giant cauldron ...

He presents his rationale within a historical context and distances himself from the feminised and faddish practices (Fischler 1980) associated with health foodways. On the other hand Bryony writes about bread:

And then there's the bread. Ah the bread. I'm trying not to eat it at all at the moment. I've had some gastric problems over the last three of years and an extra sluggish metabolism. I'm convinced I've developed some food intolerances, but am not sure to what. Not eating bread seems to have helped so I'm going with that for the moment. Though not religiously, I just spent a couple of weeks travelling and ate bread the whole time. I don't think I have any outright allergies, but rather that stress has lead to my immune system being strained and my digestive system finding it hard to work over some foods.

Thus, Bryony has an emotional attachment to bread, whilst Nick continues:

We get spelt from the cult weirdo's in the market and one slice is all you need for breakfast ... slow release etc.... Whereas you can eat slice after slice of manufactured white bread and still feel hungry/ empty/ bloated etc.

This highlights how certain dietary practices if not fully sanctioned by nutritional science are difficult to legitimate. Nick's engagement with the practice of purchasing spelt bread is positioned elsewhere, on the boundaries of the intimate self. Nick is able to distance himself from its production, whilst simultaneously making it 'other'. Thus, Nick trivialises the benefits of the bread as a 'fad' (Fischler 1980) and again as a means of distancing himself from the possible stigma of association (Goffman 1963). Further, a concern with health foodways and fads are potentially feminising. Nick's comments position him in opposition to the consumption of highly processed or mass-produced 'manufactured' white bread, which has low cultural capital due to its association with unrefined or working class tastes or food for the masses. In a contemporary foodscape he is also registering his distaste and intolerance of the excessive industrialisation of food (Mennell 1985). Indeed, Mennell (1985) notes that it was prestigious in medieval times to eat white bread amongst elite groups, who associated unrefined bread with the unrefined classes.

Generally, respondents who changed their diets for health reasons either to manage symptoms for themselves or their children, were aware that nutritional approaches to treatment were potentially illegitimate and outside of orthodox medical practice. For some, orthodox medicine was actually at the root of the problem in the first place. For example in Kelly's (a 30-year-old PhD student, living with her partner) 'quest narrative' (Frank 1995), the cause of her IBS:

Was certainly somehow connected to the four or five instances of tummy flu and food poisoning that I had had, but forgotten. Also, the tons of antibiotics I have ingested thanks to their liberal prescription by Bulgarian doctors in the 1980s. Also the change of food due to my immigration to the UK. And even stress (only then did I realise that I was anxious in the mornings – but later I also found out that the IBS

actually feeds a physical feeling of anxiety, so the relation between stress
and IBS is more complicated). And I also started realising that I may
have had a hidden food-absorption problem for years without even sus-
pecting. This could be one of the reasons for my strikingly bad health
and constant low-level inflammations I've had since I can remember
myself, i.e. really bad teeth ... very early arthritis ... persistent tonsil-
litis ... peripheral neuropathy and carpal tunnel syndrome of the arms
at 18 ... osteopenic bones at the age of 25 ... reproductive problems ...
problems with sleep and concentration ... etc. etc. etc. I also came across
stuff that blamed candida for many of these food related problems ...

Thus, in Kelly's narrative, food is the main protagonist in the story;
following a 'military metaphor' (Lupton 2003: 65), Kelly engages in
a 'battle' with food as she asserts, 'however, my "food story" would
be incomplete, if I didn't mention the battle with that pesky thing
called IBS that I've been fighting ever since I came to the UK'. It is
notable that she refers to her condition in a familiar, light-hearted
way, this 'pesky' condition, as if it is a mere nuisance and yet uses
a military metaphor. This is an emotional narrative and following
Frank (1995: 7), the condition is not so much a 'disruption', but is
seen as 'part of life's map or journey'. Indeed, Kelly's narrative utilises
heroic, tragic, ironic and comic sub narratives in dealing with the
biographical disruption of her IBS (Bury 2001: 263). She continues:

Currently I am not the master [sic] of my own decisions. Or at least it
is not my tongue any more or my waistline, but I'm trying to 'listen' to
what my body actually 'wants' to eat, for its own good. This is a new
concept and a new skill I wish I had acquired earlier. Perhaps if I had,
I would not have 20 fillings in my teeth or thin bones, or feel tired and
unable to focus all the time. So, yeah. The IBS, after scaring me to death
and depressing me (mentally and, as it turns out, also physically!), has
finally turned out to be my best food teacher ... It is also kind of ironic
that after two decades of fighting against my mother's food regime I'm
now forced to build a rather similar food regime for myself! Very annoy-
ing. But I've gone past annoyance.

Hence, Kelly highlights the impact of changes in her diet on her
sense of self, notably a feminine identity that associates food with
her 'tongue' and 'waistline'. Instead, she is 'trying to listen to what
her body actually wants to eat, for its own good'. Again, this is

reminiscent of Cartesian dualism and an alignment with the medical model, despite engaging in holistic medicine or CAM. This represents an interesting dichotomy therefore, as a focus on individual responsibility for health and illness supports a de-medicalisation thesis; however, the application of a health-illness paradigm to nearly every domain of life represents increased medicalisation (Lowenberg and Davis 1994: 584).

Kelly adds that she is no longer 'master' (sic) of her own decisions but having to radically reconsider her diet as a means of preventing suffering. This has knock-on effects in all aspects of her life as a postgraduate student and implications for her identity. She concludes that:

Food is no longer the innocent pleasure it was when I was younger, I've grown to be a bit afraid of it, since it can cause me weeks of suffering if I'm not careful.

She writes that her IBS has become her 'best food teacher'. Her narrative like others in this theme is illustrative of some of the issues faced by individuals managing their diet for health reasons and highlights the significance of cultural rules and rituals in the management of a spoiled (illness) identity (Goffman 1963).

Kelly though, has only recently developed these health foodways and identifies contradictions in managing a student identity that would usually entail a more carefree and convivial attitude towards food. She claims:

The two things I've not managed to eliminate from my food (for longer than my heroic forced 2-month diet in April and May this year) are coffee and cakes! :-)

Although, she has strategies for alleviating any side effects if she is caught out by 'bad' food choices, in social commensal eating situations:

I tend to not be too careful about what I eat in restaurants ... but then I carry around enzymes and charcoal and stuff just in case. My best find are good Italian restaurants in which I can eat a load of olives before the main meal, that is delicious and seems to make me feel good after, too.

Typically for those engaged in health foodways as a means of controlling conditions or symptoms, many respondents suffered from more than one ailment. This was not a matter of having the 'high cholesterol mantra humming in the background' as Ian notes, but for someone like Edith, (a 54-year-old Arts Co-Ordinator, single and living with one of her three children), for example:

> *I have many food fads as I suffer from IBS, Acid Reflux, Hypothyroidism and some allergies, all of these things can dictate what, how and when I eat ... I am very conscious of what I eat, but I do not always listen to my body and rarely pay attention to what I am supposed to eat, I go in fits and starts of being super healthy, and I mean really healthy to junk food ... reasons for this could be time, money, laziness, lack of family unity at meal times, all very informal these days.*

Edith's narrative contains a confession to not 'always' listening to her body, it signals an ambivalence and resistance to the power of dominant healthy eating discourses. She presents reasons for not complying, yet by referring to 'really healthy' dietary practices as food fads (Fischler 1980), she manages to reinforce the notion of them as temporal and fleeting and not that serious anyway. Willow on the other hand writes:

> *My friend had bad eczema and I had asthma so we read a lot about allergies and intolerances and vitamins (Adele Davies) and had a period of eating a lot of liver and wheat germ and drinking a lot of goats' milk.*

Thus, not all eating for health is necessarily what might be considered healthy eating. Queenie (a 62-year-old married, and retired hairdresser) though explains how she developed her healthy foodways in response to physical conditions triggered by grief at the loss of both of her parents and the stress of dealing with their deaths. This 'lack of appetite' is considered by Lupton (1996: 33) to be 'an emotional response' to life events (the link between death or loss and dietary change is another thread picked up in Chapter 5).

However, Queenie writes that she was already practising CAM, by making reference to a *Retail Outlet* in her local town that specialises in 'natural products and remedies'. She notes:

Obviously I should have gone to the doctors, but didn't, by the time I did eventually go I'd stopped eating wheat for quite some time and a celiac test could not be done. In the meantime a visiting Iridologist in Specialist Shop told me to avoid all wheat products, which I did. It was like a miracle I felt so much better immediately.

She continues:

The memory of the unpleasant symptoms from eating wheat means that I don't ever lapse, it just isn't worth it; at the very worst I'd get a stomachache. My/our friends kindly do wheat free meals for me; I do sometimes take a particular ingredient or food item if I am staying somewhere. It's not that difficult, most supermarkets do a 'free from' range now and even [Italian restaurant chain] have gluten free pasta on the menu!

Here, by referring to a mainstream Italian restaurant chain, she positions her dietary habits within popular cultural norms. Therefore, her dietary requirements are acceptable outside of a specialist CAM arena. She acknowledges that her strict dietary regime is potentially problematic in social situations, but claims that most of her friends are very accommodating of her diet. This counters Warde's (1997: 173) contention that 'because people eat in social situations even the most self-disciplined will relax their abstemious personal regimes'. And challenges his assertion that 'people are not generally known for their eccentric eating habits' (Warde 1997: 182). Queenie also explains how her intolerances may have developed:

In recent years I've become very interested in the mind/body connections and it has occurred to me through thinking about your questions how, why and when I became intolerant to wheat, that there may be a possible connection to the extreme stress I was feeling at the time. In the space of about three years my father became ill and died and 18 months later my mum died. Being an only child and very close to my parents I found all that happened during that time very difficult (I know I'm not alone in that) but did my very best to help them in every way. Somehow I went in to some kind of 'overdrive', which I'm sure most people do at these times, but on reflection it must have taken its toll on my body, I became very thin and was completely exhausted.

What is notable here is the notion of being 'very thin', 'completely exhausted' and therefore ill or requiring treatment. Queenie links a loss of appetite with the death of her parents, which is typical for those engaging in 'holistic health that stresses, grief and friendship in terms of a direct causal relationship with health and illness [and a] medicalisation of lifestyle' (Lowenberg and Davis 1994: 592). However, what is interesting is the notion that a thin body is indicative of illness, as this runs counter to the cultural ideal of the thin body as desirable. There is an evident contradiction here between being thin as a result of illness, loss or bereavement (i.e., perhaps due to factors beyond individual control) and being thin as a result of purposely following a weight loss regime in order to conform to the elite aesthetic of the thin ideal. Again, this is examined in Chapter 5. However, it is notable that conditions that might be alleviated through adherence to strict dietary regimes can be 'disorders related to stress and lifestyle [which] do not lend themselves to simple solutions or what we might call 'heroic medicine' (Turner 1987: 224). In other words, some of the illnesses of late modernity appear to be untreatable with conventional medicine. However, this does not mean that these conditions or ailments are less prone to the need for medical sanction and distinctions continue to be made so that:

> *Medical professionals have become the moral guardians of contemporary society, because they have a legitimate domination [monopoly] of the categorization of normality and deviance'.*

> (Turner 1987: 217)

If health is considered the norm then anything that deviates from this is automatically stigmatised; it is how individuals learn, manage or adapt to this that becomes significant. This is especially pertinent when practising a dietary regime that similarly deviates from what might be considered a normal health diet.

Food as treatment

In Faye's account, there is a hint that her daughter's drug resistant epilepsy began shortly after her MMR vaccinations. She claims:

> *Poppy first presented with seizures at the age of four and a half months, just after her immunizations.*

Hence, Faye, like Kelly explains how they began to use 'food' as a treatment due to a failure of orthodox medicine. Faye writes about the difficult and lengthy route through an alienating orthodox medical landscape for her daughter's drug resistant epilepsy. To begin with their daughter's neurologist told them that it was:

"A revolting diet that doesn't have a very good success rate" and "you have to eat packets and packets of butter and jars and jars of mayonnaise". I told her that I didn't care what you had to eat; we wanted to try the diet for Poppy, because it was our only hope. It took over a year to persuade her to let us try the diet, and in the end she gave in.

Faye continues:

We came home with a menu plan from the hospital for mackerel floating around in olive oil, whipped cream with artificial sweetener with a few grams of kiwi fruit stirred into it. Yes, we had a very creative dietician – not! Poppy ate all her food without hesitation and I cried buckets because of what I was forced to feed her.

Eventually, Faye and her husband devise:

New meals for Poppy; containing, amongst other things, healthy oils (safflower, sunflower, olive and grape seed), salmon, asparagus, avocado, swede and goats cream.

So, for Faye, whilst the introduction of the ketogenic diet alleviated all of her daughter's symptoms, it challenged the notion of what it was to be a good mother in an era that values health foodways and associates high cultural capital with home-cooked healthy food prepared from scratch (see Chapter 3). In her narrative, Faye cannot bring herself to describe the food as 'bad' or 'unhealthy' and in the end it becomes a diet of 'healthy oils'. This is despite the positive and life changing impact the diet had on her daughter's drug resistant epilepsy. As Faye declares:

We noticed a positive difference in her seizures and overall well being almost immediately. It was as if a veil had been lifted ... We continued weaning [her off the] medication and as the days and weeks went by her seizures lessened in frequency and severity. We had won the lottery!

No! It was better than winning the lottery! The diet quickly became part of our daily lives and it was a real blessing because we got to meet the daughter we had longed for – the little girl hiding behind a huge array of medication and their side effects.

Similarly, the idea that Faye might compromise her daughter's diet in the interests of social interaction due to the 'quasi-moral conflicts between the imperatives of asceticism and conviviality tomorrow and today, control and abandon' (Warde 1997: 182) appears highly unlikely. To begin with the preparation of food is rigorous and immensely time-consuming:

Each meal took us 2 hours to calculate, but we soon devised a selection of healthy, appetizing menus. It took over an hour a night to weigh up and label Poppy's meals for the following day.

Yet, as already highlighted the impact of the diet on her condition is immediate. Faye explains her daughter's reaction to the diet:

Poppy was a complete angel about it all and never once tried to eat anything that wasn't Keto friendly. She would have friends around for tea and she would attend birthday parties, the whole time eating only her own ketogenic food we had prepared for her. I find it very difficult now, knowing that she never once had a slice of her own birthday cake. I don't know why I should find this so upsetting looking at the full scale of things, but I do. I suppose it's because it's such a simple pleasure, and one most parents take for granted.

Hence, even though Faye is occupied in the immensely time-consuming act of mothering through the provision of such a highly specialised diet for her daughter and despite the rewards that this brings, she has the added pressure of managing her daughter's 'spoiled' illness identity (Goffman 1963). This is particularly pertinent on social occasions such as birthdays. Her daughter is excluded from the act of sharing the birthday cake that her mother made especially for her and this adds to the tragedy of the situation for Faye. It denies Faye the ultimate opportunity of being a good mother as displayed through the baking and sharing of a birthday cake. This emphasises the current cultural capital associated with the glorification of feminised domesticity (Negra 2009).

However, when considering rigid dietary management practices Balfe (2007: 138) notes that:

> *Disciplinary practices are often not completely disciplined ... people might fail in their ability to articulate the practices of one discourse because they are equally committed to the practices and ideals of another.*

It is difficult to imagine how Faye would not be completely disciplined regarding Poppy's dietary regimes, given the implications of lapsing. This is about 'social' eating and the pressures to belong and fit in and in many ways this is what Faye found difficult about her daughter's diet, that it marks her out as different and unable to participate in 'normal' social activities, as unusual food regimes can be stigmatising (Goffman 1963). So, whilst a disciplined approach to eating alleviates conditions for Faye's daughter, it does have repercussions for social interaction and the management of a spoiled or stigmatised identity, even beyond the notion of the condition marking the individual out as different. In social situations the previously hidden dietary regime is made public and forces the individual to engage in the management of a 'spoiled' identity (Goffman 1963).

Hence, if everyday foodways are positioned within moral discourses it can be difficult for individuals to negotiate alternative foodways when food rules are so rigid. So that even when supposedly 'bad' foods, such as the high levels of fat needed in the ketogenic diet, have far-reaching and remarkable health benefits the identity of those entrusted with carrying out the dietary regimes can be challenged by the act of feeding 'bad' foods, particularly when feeding healthy food to children has such high symbolic and cultural value. Indeed, as indicated previously feeding the family healthy home-cooked food is part of a middle class habitus. It is a way of displaying cultural capital; to be forced to transcend the boundaries in this field is risky. Of course, Faye is not engaging in these dietary practices lightly, or through lack of knowledge, but instead is performing intensive mothering (Hays 1996) practices. Her dedication to her daughter's dietary requirements and the emotional work involved in her care is admirable. That she should need to justify her actions is testimony to the rigidity of the symbolic and cultural division between what is considered good and bad food. This reifies the power of legitimate foodways practised by a dominant group. Generally, most respondents in the study demonstrate a tacit awareness of health as capital (Bendelow 2009). This has symbolic value; health foodways are a moral act and a responsibility (Coveney 2006, Petersen 2007). Those committed to health foodways convey an understanding of, and a commitment to disciplinary regimes of self-surveillance (Armstrong 1995) through the monitoring of their own (and/or others') health foodways and by listening to the body's responses. However, whilst health foodways, as an aspect of responsible individualism fit with the social norms and values of a medicalised society and a middle class habitus, the use of food as a CAM does not. Hence, those adhering to food as CAM need to justify their decisions to do so and are forced to manage a stigmatised or spoiled identity, particularly in social situations (Goffman 1963). It is notable again, that health foodways are classed and gendered. CAM is a particularly middle class, feminised concern. Similarly, technologies of the self, including the monitoring and micro-management of diet or health foodways are ideal vehicle[s] for the 'performance of femininity' (Moore 2010: 112).

5

Embodied Foodways

The desire for a thin body has long been associated with elite cultural capital (Naccarato and LeBesco 2012). It is connected to issues of self-restraint in dietary and sexual practices, as women's bodies are considered in need of control (Inckle 2007). In Judeo-Christian ideology the duality central to Western morality focuses on the control of the body through fasting and chastity (Counihan 1999, 101–3). Hence, the links between food and sexuality have a long history of dualist and absolutist rhetoric that positions women as 'other' whose appetite for food and sex needs to be controlled.

This chapter focuses on the control of (sweet/fat) food/bodies and the problems associated with being out of control in an era of obesity, when self-restraint and self-governance are desirable (Foucault 1988, 1991) and have high cultural capital (Naccarato and LeBesco 2012). In examining respondents' embodied foodways, they learnt to read their own and other bodies as a means of doing gender over time (West and Zimmerman 1987). This draws on anthropological research on 'fat talk' (Ambjörnsson 2005) and 'lipoliteracy' or literally the reading of fat on bodies (Graham 2005), when women especially became body conscious as a means of conforming to the cultural scripts of appropriate hetero-normative femininity (Inckle 2007, Moore 2010).

These embodied foodways encompass complicated relationships with food and the body, including eating disorders or dis-ordered eating. It is evident that none of the female respondents self-reported as obese or used any 'O' words (Wann 2009: xii). Indeed, struggles with body weight are about negotiating the boundaries of what might be considered a 'normal' body weight as well as trying to achieve a thin body shape as the cultural ideal (Germov and Williams 2004). They are also about distancing the self from associations with fat bodies due to a fear of fatness (Murray 2008, LeBesco 2009). Instead the performance of femininity centres on adjudicating a 'heroic' middle ground of acceptable embodiment. Again, this centres on the intersectionalities of gender and class, as men and women conform to rigid cultural scripts of appropriate embodied foodways.

Sweet femininity

This theme was anticipated at the start of the study; I wanted to consider the extent to which individual food histories were related to issues of weight management if at all. I argued in my proposal that this was because of my reading of feminist literature such as Orbach's (1982) *Fat is a Feminist Issue* that explores women's complex relationship with food. This finds expression in terms of dissatisfaction with the body, a desire to please and an ongoing unwavering commitment to dietary and weight management practices (Lupton 1996, Bordo 2003). Thus, despite a 'love' of certain foods (mostly 'sweet things') these foods are avoided. Further because respondents' narratives are embedded in wider socio-historical contexts the avoidance of 'sweetness' can be interpreted as a denial of femininity (Mintz 1985, Lupton 1996).

Indeed, the types of food denied for weight loss are often those most strongly associated with femininity; as Lupton (1996: 105) notes, 'chocolate and sugar are traditionally coded as feminine foods'. Likewise, Barthel (1989: 431) claims those who self-identify as 'chocoholics' are predominantly women and that 'the chocoholic identity is a regressive identity celebrating weakness and surrender to temptation'. However, within embodied foodways, these 'bad' foods are not avoided or denied for health reasons but because of a commitment to a thin ideal (Germov and Williams 2004). Indeed, Counihan (1999: 4) argues that women and men both hold standards of female thinness for women that reproduce female oppression. Hence, the themes in this chapter relate specifically to embodiment and elite cultural scripts of hetero-normative femininity in a contemporary obesogenic environment. These centre on lacking control as expressions of femininity, as Ophelia notes:

> *One summer holiday she [stepmother] told me not to drink Coke even though everyone else was, because I was fat. I sat sipping water mortified whilst everyone else drank gallons of Coca Cola. Back home, now aged 15 I started to drink coffee in my bedroom with sugar in it to comfort myself and eat chocolate whenever I could … If I ate anything she thought might be 'bad' for me she would tut and give me that 'are you stupid' raised eyebrow glare, which just made me feel guilty and so I ate 'naughty' foods when I wasn't with her … I would never ever eat anything like chocolate in front of her so my sweet addition was forced to go underground!*

Thus, there is a moral imperative to control one's food intake, which for Ophelia, means control of 'naughty' foods such as chocolate or sweet drinks. However, like many embodied foodways, this early experience is she believes the source of 'a pattern of self sabotage', which she 'struggles with today' and how connections between sweetness, fatness, desire and control are established. Further, embodied foodways are articulated in terms of 'loss', such as weight loss and a loss of control over the rational masculine self, expressed as a moral failure or as giving in to uncivilised, (feminine) urges for certain foods. In Moran's (2011: 117) autobiography, *How to be a Woman*, she argues that 'over eating has come to be regarded as the lowest ranking of all the addictions'. However, Moran (2011: 116) makes it clear that she is referring to 'those for whom the whole idea of food is not one of pleasure, but one of compulsion'. In Ellen's (a 61-year-old dance teacher) narrative, thinking of chocolate as an addiction does not necessarily fully explain her 'emotional' need for it. Although she explains:

> *I consider that I have an addiction to chocolate, so that I don't (or indeed can't) keep any in the house, without eating it. I have managed to give up smoking, and drinking, for the most part, but chocolate seems to be the hardest thing … I have smoked on and off throughout my life. I have given up successfully at least three times. The last time was around ten years ago. I know I can 'give up' things. But at the moment, as much as I would like to, I cannot give up the sweet food in my life …*

Even Hannah who is committed to health foodways claims:

*My downfall is chocolate; I love chocolate – not a lot but small nibbles
... I feel quite annoyed if I don't eat some sort of plain chocolate in a day.*

Thus, women write about longing for foods that they deny themselves in an effort to lose weight, whether this is chocolate, crisps or
bread. Ophelia comments:

*I have also always had a love / hate relationship with bread. I love it but
it definitely isn't good for me and for a while between having children
I gave it up entirely and found that I could keep my weight pretty static
and eat whatever I liked, but in the end, I found it too hard and it crept
back in to my diet, just like I find giving up sugar hard. Both of these
foodstuffs puff me up but I love them, it is a battle ... I try not to eat
sweet things and for me it is better if I give them up completely because
once I start I just can't stop and the chocolate bar is gone! I know it's
ridiculous but there you are ... My weight has always fluctuated usually
because of my love of sweet things ...*

Thus, Ophelia's narrative details a common vocabulary (Mills 1959)
amongst women engaged in embodied foodways, in which pleasure
needs to be contained and controlled. There is a longing for foods
that cannot be eaten in the pursuit of thinness coupled with a longing to be thin or thinner (not fat). This is a battle and one of the contradictions at the heart of contemporary femininity, aptly summed
up by Kate Moss, a model and minor celebrity: 'nothing tastes as
good as skinny feels' (Wardrop 2009: un-paginated). The implication
being, you can either eat or be thin. Of course, as Ophelia notes, even
when she was thin she 'never believed [that she] was thin enough'.
Eventually she has learnt that she does not 'have a thin body shape
and would never have been able to achieve the impossible that [she]
longed for'. It is perhaps only for gourmets engaged in epicurean
foodways that pleasures are unbounded (Chapter 6).

A thin/fat binary

Women practising embodied foodways identify strongly with the
thin ideal and/or distance themselves from being fat or fatness
(Murray 2008). Beardsworth and Keil (1997: 178) argue that the:

Preoccupation with thinness is so powerful that 'fat oppression, the fear and hatred of fat people remains one of the few acceptable prejudices still held by otherwise progressive persons'.

(Meadow and Weiss 1992: 133)

Further, the thin ideal (Germov and Williams 2004) differs from other body conceptions such as slimness (Lupton 1996, Beardsworth and Keil 1997) or slenderness (Chernin 1981). However, embodied foodways focus on a corporeal self governance or surveillance in which weight and dietary management techniques became part of an internalising patriarchal gaze and ongoing body project (Lupton 1996, Bordo 2003, Murray 2008). The thin body ideal in Western societies is an elite, masculine body, hard and in control; it eliminates any feminine curves or references to hips and breasts. It is, according to Saguy (2013), considered an element of elite cultural capital; rich women are associated with thinness (interestingly though not necessarily thin men):

Achieving and maintaining thinness is an important way in which the contemporary elite in rich nations, and especially elite women, signal their status ... pursuit of (female) thinness is an integral part of elite and middle class habitus.

(Saguy 2013: 13)

Added to this are the current concerns related to the medicalisation of the fat body and the contested correlation between obesity and ill health (Rothbum and Solovay 2009). So not only is the thin body shape desirable as a cultural marker of success (Naccarato and LeBesco 2012), but is also an indicator of health and beauty/femininity, regardless of what means are used to secure or maintain it. In other words, embodied foodways are not health foodways, as the problem of 'obesity' and the focus on 'weight' 'obscures the health benefits of diet and exercise', and crucially, 'weight loss can be achieved at the expense of health' (Aphramor 2010: 30).

Respondents committed to embodied foodways detail the origins of their relationships with food and body weight. They have strong emotional attachments to certain foods and avoiding these is akin to the pain of unrequited love, as Bryony expresses so eloquently: 'I love bread but it doesn't love me'. Yet the social milieu in which respondents are writing is one in which 'fat' bodies are reviled and 'thin' bodies considered an indicator of high cultural capital, health and beauty/femininity (Naccarato and LeBesco 2012, Lupton 2013, Saguy 2013). However, although documenting a pursuit of weight loss, successes and failures, female respondents did not self-identify as fat, nor did they make use of the BMI as a key measure of appropriate body weight, their own or anyone else's. Only Ralph mentioned the BMI and in the context of 'my BMI is ok'. Further, men did not express angst or anxiety about weight or controlling appetites.

Indeed, Inckle (2007: 92) claims that 'gender is played out upon the body, which is already marked as "other", female, through the norms of femininity'. The anxiety and trauma expressed in some of the women's narratives, of having to control one's femininity is not unlike having to manage a 'spoiled identity' (Goffman 1963, Saguy 2013) in a society that values maleness. Woman is the 'deviant category, the other from a male model of a normal subject' (Frost 2001: 31). This resonates with Frost's (2001: 31) other 'prescriptions for womanhood'; that man *has* a body, whereas 'woman *is* her body', she must 'be slim and beautiful' and that 'feminine sexuality is passive and defined by men'. Fatness is about femininity, it is held in adipose tissue that marks gender and:

> *Fat functions as a floating signifier, attaching to individuals based on a power relationship, not a physical measurement. People all along the weight spectrum may experience fat oppression.*
>
> (Wann 2009: xv)

Like many respondents I learnt to talk about fat amongst my friends as an adolescent and engaged in 'fat talk', which is not only about fat bodies, but is a way of 'establishing friendships with some girls and ostracizing others' (Ambjörnsson 2005: 114). Indeed, 'the expression of dissatisfaction with one's body becomes an important way of performing one's identity as a girl' (Ambjörnsson 2005: 117). Hence, 'this dissatisfaction becomes a normal female state, so that talk about fat becomes talk about being a girl' (Ambjörnsson 2005: 119). Further, Ambjörnsson concludes that:

> *Fat talk is a way of staking a claim, of making yourself visible and legitimate, of showing people that you have independence, individuality and style. But at the same time fat talk ironically signals the opposite: it*

indicates conformity ... it is an 'absent presence'. It is present as talk only
to the extent that it doesn't actually materialise on people's bodies ...
(Ambjörnsson 2005: 120)

I also learned to read fat bodies, my own and others. This 'lipo-literacy' (Graham 2005: 175) refers to the act of learning about fat by reading about it as well as reading fat on bodies, for what 'we believe it tells us about a person in terms of their moral character and their health' (Kulik and Meneley 2005: 7). Hence, 'the fat body is pathologised independently of what the body actually does with food or movement' and leads to an oversimplification of the notion 'of fatness as compulsive over-eating and average size as healthy' (LeBesco 2009: 148). Similarly, the conflation of health and beauty with thinness is contentious, because of the assumption that a thin body is a healthy body and a fat body is not (Aphramor 2010). This masks a diverse range of potentially unhealthy eating, purging and exercise practices that are not considered problematic so long as the individual's weight is within a normal weight range. Again, 'the average sized body is taken to be healthy regardless of whatever det-rimental practices' the individual may engage in (LeBesco 2009: 148).

The pre-occupation with the moral value of food and the over reli-ance on weight as the chief indicator of health (Jutel 2005) reinforces the stigma attributed to bodies that do not conform and pathologises fatness, as Malson (1998: 105) contends:

The fat body is constructed as ugly, unattractive, disgusting and shame-
ful. It signifies gluttony and uncontrolled sexual activity. The 'fat self' is
unhappy and lacking in self-control and self-confidence.

Again, the focus is on a lack of control, which is associated with femaleness and the working class (Skeggs 1997). Indeed, the 'homogenisation of healthism and pathologisation of fatness' are tied to notions of appropriate womanhood; this is expressed through multiple cults and symbolic representations of thinness (Eckerman 2009: 10). This ensures that:

Even those people who do not view themselves as particularly fat find
themselves implicated in this constant struggle over food consumption,
leading in some cases to anxiety, guilt, shame and self-disgust as they

attempt to conform to normative standards of health, beauty and self control

(Jallinoja et al. 2010: 125)

Indeed, respondents practising embodied foodways are uncritical of the notion of body weight as an indicator of health. Hence, the need to present themselves as healthy responsible citizens, even when exploring the potential problems that this entailed in negotiating food likes and dislikes. Unlike Lupton's interviewees in the 1990s, respondents in my study did not demonstrate a 'disdain for the asceticism required of them by weight control edicts' (Lupton 2013: 99). Some catalogued highly emotional struggles with controlling body weight, but did not consider this an imposition or a problem, more a fact of life and how they had to live. It was part of 'doing gender' (West and Zimmerman 1987). A concern with dietary restraint is associated with elite cultural capital (Naccarato and LeBesco 2012) and by narrating this struggle respondents are claiming these class aspirations for themselves.

Respondents' embodiment

The majority of women tended to distance themselves from any notion of being considered fat and this word tended to be avoided, as were 'O' words, such as overweight and obese (Wann 2009: xii). This counters Lupton's (2013: 71) assertion that 'people who identify as fat or overweight often represent their efforts as a battle with overwhelming urges to indulge in food'. The women in my study did not identify themselves as 'fat', yet still expressed a longing for certain foods and/or body size. This was normalised, part of a hetero-normative cultural script of femininity. Respondents want to eat food they love; bread, chocolate, crisps, though these tend to be 'negotiated pleasures' and rationalised within a 'will to live a healthy life' (Jallinoja et al. 2010: 125) and/or part of a 'weight loss script of femininity' (Malson 2007: 29).

Indeed, as discussed in Chapter 4 health and body weight are both a means of doing gender and performing femininity. However, women engaged in embodied foodways placed a lot more emphasis on their bodies and their weight as significant aspirations, rather than referring to health issues. They write about relationships with food in the context of what they eat in order to manage body weight.

Food intake is something in need of control and being out of control is considered a problem, as Ophelia writes:

I started to eat things that I normally wouldn't, e.g. almond croissants, pizzas, puddings, crisps. I suddenly didn't care about what foods I put into my body and over the next six months I continued to eat badly especially in the evening and my weight has crept up to perhaps the highest it has been for a long time. I just couldn't stop eating the wrong things and I was dealing with a new feeling of 'what's the point' now I am 53 and just one big blob of cellulite. I had to get a grip and I hated the feeling of being so out of control. It hasn't been a good year for me and my body and food and this is partly due to my age and the way the body changes after the menopause.

Being out of control is significant, as Malson et al. (2006) attest, self-monitoring and self-control; health and well-being are constituted as matters of individual responsibility. Hence, a high value is given to practicing appropriate self-care and maintaining control is a means of securing cultural capital. Also, as Howson (2004: 114) claims:

Feminists identify the control of food intake as part of the pursuit of slenderness, a form of tyranny that distorts the female body and creates a sense of alienation from their bodies.

This is perhaps evident in the extent to which respondents reflected upon their past selves. In looking back they viewed their bodies with a less critical lens and without the emotional intensity of those earlier times, as Ophelia declares:

I never felt thin and I wanted to – of course when I look back now at pictures of myself, I was really slim … Looking back at pictures of me at this age I can see that I am holding a huge amount emotionally in my body rather than being fat and this gave the impression that I was a bit podgy …

Thus, Ophelia is longing for a thin ideal, yet does not position herself as 'fat'. Similarly in Ellen's narrative:

I noticed that I was pear-shaped when I was 21, which came as a bit of a surprise – I'd always been thin, with a good (big) appetite. My sister was heavier than me so when we shared a year at college together, I was then about 25, she suggested we did a low calorie diet together. I obviously believed that I was too heavy then, and so went on this very successful diet. I felt sexy and attractive when I was that much slimmer – I was around 7 stone (as I remember). I never liked my shape, and it is only in hindsight that I look at pictures of myself from any previous time and see that I did not see myself clearly. (I think that that is still the same now). I associated being slim/thin with being attractive ...

Further, Ellen documents a development of body consciousness over time and Bryony similarly writes:

From pictures I can see that I had put on weight between 13 and 14 but I was by no means fat.

Hence, both Ellen and Bryony are aligning themselves with a cultural ideal that equates thinness with beauty and being sexually attractive (Germov and Williams 2004, Lupton 2013, Saguy 2013). This reinforces an association between fatness, low cultural capital and a lack of femininity. These narratives are about body size and weight, losing it and gaining it. As Ida (a 54-year-old midwife, married with two grown up children) claims, she 'lost/gained/lost/gained, currently losing again' and began her narrative with the following statement:

I've just embarked (again) on a journey to lose 4 stone EEEEK!!! I want to get married and I want a much smaller dress size to do it in

Ida is thus identifying a history of weight cycling that forms part of a hetero-normative cultural script of femininity. She wants to lose weight because she is getting married; again this is complicit with the cultural ideal that a woman needs to be 'attractive for her husband by being slim and fashionably dressed' (Charles and Kerr 1988: 33). Ellen also writes about her history of weight cycling. She embarks on a low calorie diet with her sister and 'lost well over a stone in weight – I was thin again. I could feel my hipbones sticking up when I lay down. I felt fabulous'. Her weight loss though did not last and:

I had put on weight and was putting on more – this bothered me. Food was a source of consolation and celebration – so giving myself treats (sweet things) became more regular. When my mother died, I felt able to take on another diet (this is only the second time in my life that I seriously dieted) ... I lost weight, felt good, my digestive system speeded up considerably (where it had been quite sluggish) .... I lost weight, steadily and successfully. I felt more attractive, of course ...

Notably Ellen relates her weight loss at this time with the death of her mother, but again equates slimness with being sexually attractive and feminine. In Bryony's narrative, she explains how 'her mom' 'sent [her] to water aerobics class' because her mother thought she 'was getting a bit too chunky' (not fat). Notably, as in Ophelia's account, Bryony's mother is charged with monitoring Bryony's body, as part of a hetero-normative script of appropriate mothering/femininity. Bryony, also documents a struggle with 'weight', weight gain, controlling weight, maintaining a healthy weight, losing weight, fluctuating weight and weight creeping back. She writes:

The next time I gained a substantial amount of weight was during University. The first year I was ok, but the weight crept on over the next three year until the last year I was a bit hefty to say the least. That weight dropped off after graduation thanks to a bad break up. Since then my weight has fluctuated greatly, but hasn't reached anything I would call obese until this Christmas. Throughout my 20s I would periodically diet if I thought I was putting on too much weight. I tried the South Beach diet once. I couldn't handle the first two weeks of it, so didn't do it ever again, but I continue to use some the recipes from the later stages of the diet and the whole grain emphasis. I've also done shake replacements. I used to use Carnation Breakfast shakes, but as they're dairy based I haven't used them recently.

It is clear that Bryony attributes weight loss after University to a 'bad break up', underlining the interconnections between emotional turmoil, loss and weight loss (Squire 2002, Burns 2009).

In Melissa's (a 46-year-old viola player, married with two children) narrative she begins:

Food was never really an issue for me until I went to boarding school at 14. Suddenly a girl was not considered pretty unless she had a 'great body'. I'd never contemplated this notion ever before and remember

*being surprised by it and noticing my own for the first time ... We were
always dieting in my boarding school and weighing ourselves every day.
I went through a phase of eating only breakfast and lunch and lost a lot
of weight, thus gaining a 'great body!' I particularly remember the joy
of weighing in at 8 stone one day when I was 16 or 17 and 5 feet 5½.
When we were hungry in the evenings we used to go into the tuck room
and smell the food, oohing and ahhing in pleasure!*

Thus, Melissa is participating in the cultural norms and values prevalent amongst her peer group at the time. These foodways are social
activities, a means of performing hetero-normative scripts of femininity. Indeed, Melissa and her friends were clearly focused on a weight
loss goal, perhaps at the expense of health (Aphramor 2010: 30). At
the end she writes:

*I've put on a lot of weight but feel my body is testament to my love of
good food (I weigh about 11 stone now) and have come to terms with
my bigger size and quite value it. At least I don't look haggard and
wrinkly! And my husband says I look 'bountiful'*

Melissa's use of 'good' food here is ambiguous, can 'good' food
make you put on weight? Or is she referring to what might be considered 'bad' food. This reinforces the problem of considering everyday
foodways within dualist and absolutist discourses. Earlier Melissa
writes about her commitment to organic, home-made and home-
grown produce. A concern for healthy, organic food has high cultural
capital and is part of a middle class habitus (Naccarato and LeBesco
2012). Epicurean foodways are examined more fully in Chapter 6,
but focus on 'good' food and a concern for authenticity. Notably,
gourmets in my study rarely if ever mentioned their body weight and
presented their food narratives within the context of acquiring good
taste and as a form of high cultural capital. This creates a problem
for women, as elite cultural capital is associated with a thin body
shape, whilst elite cultural capital for gourmets (men) is about fine
dining or 'good' food. Here Melissa is trying to marry a number of
conflicting aspirations. She distances her body size from those that
might be considered fat (or 'big') and thin ('haggard and wrinkly!')
and instead considers herself 'bountiful'. However, earlier on she
notes 'I was 8 stone one day when I was 16 or 17 and 5 feet 5½'.

This means that she would have had a BMI of 18 as an adolescent, which would locate her body weight at that time in the underweight category. Now at 11 stone her BMI is around 25, which is within the healthy body weight range. She may even be taller now than she was at 16 or 17. In other words, although she claims to be a bigger size than she was, her BMI is not in the overweight or obese category. In Ophelia's narrative on the other hand she notes that 'she wasn't overweight'. Instead, she is 'struggling with puppy fat', 'emotional padding' or 'all over puppy fat padding' that gave the impression that she was 'a bit podgy', and is avoiding the 'O' words (Wann 2009: xii). She admits that 'I have never liked my body much' but that this 'isn't about being fat'. Ophelia's concern is about thinness, as elite cultural capital and an aspiration to be thin:

I had a new friend Tania who lived in a nearby village and we became close. She was at boarding school in Any Town and was completely obsessed about being thin. Until I met her I hadn't really thought about it much, nor really considered that being 'thin' was in my control ... I started to want to be thinner although I was too lazy to really do something about it ... I spend a lot of time reassuring her that she is thin and vice versa, this is pretty much all we talk about in our letters [at that time].

Again, like Melissa and Ellen in Ophelia's narrative there is a development of body consciousness at the time of adolescence; thus, as individuals become sexually aware they become more pre-occupied with their bodies (Becker et al. 2002, Becker et al. 2007, Ambjörnsson 2005). This appears naturalised in these accounts, part of becoming a woman. Ophelia continues this part of the narrative by introducing another friend:

I had a beautiful friend called Sophia who lived down the road and all the boys flocked round her. She was thin, much more 'developed' than me (i.e. she had a woman's body whilst I was still struggling with this all over puppy fat padding) and I felt invisible when she was around. My elder brother who I worshipped went out with her and I felt like I lived on another planet.

This reaffirms Ophelia's suspicion that she has not yet developed as a woman. She is alienated from her body, whilst her friend's body is womanly, sexually attractive and therefore otherworldly. Later, Ophelia 'was very very thin' when she got married, 'under 8 stone' because 'she had been extremely ill' and 'had to put on weight to get pregnant'. Ophelia did not detail the specifics of her illness at this time and this is not seen as a desirable or wanted thinness, especially as it interferes with other normative scripts of femininity, namely motherhood. The association between thinness and illness is similar to Queenie's healthy narrative explored in Chapter 4, when she writes about being thin and ill after the loss of her parents (Squire 2002, Burns 2009). However, Ophelia in a similar vein to Melissa writes about her battle with weight, but claims to never having actually been that big:

> *I feel that I have always battled with my weight since teenage years, but in fact I have never been larger than a size 12 at my largest and most of my clothes are still size 10. Having big breasts has made me feel bigger than I am as my frame is really quite petite but up top I look bigger and this has, I think been my biggest problem. I look bigger than I really am underneath and that has been annoying. If I was rich and I wasn't worried about having an unnecessary operation I would book a reduction tomorrow.*

Ophelia identifies herself as accepting of elite cultural values and thinness is a longed for aspiration in a narrative reminiscent of Weir's (2010) memoir *The Real Me is Thin*.

Fat pasts

A couple of respondents referred to how they had been fat in the past. Ulrika, for example:

> *I historically have had to be very careful, as a flat footed bow legged fat child I was forced to lose weight as a part of my treatment I was on an 800 calorie a day diet aged 8. That was tough at that age. I remember running for the first time I fell over as I was going so fast, it was brilliant. I still have awareness in food choice and some (a lot less) self-control, but am not obsessed but with that I am recently at least a stone heavier as a consequence. Oops!*

Here, 'fatness' is medicalised and needs to be treated. It is not part of a performance of femininity. Ulrika is not engaging in 'fat talk' (Ambjörnsson 2005) or reading fat on her own or other bodies (Graham 2005). She was a fat child and therefore put on a strict dietary regime in order to treat this condition. She is aware of eating too much and has some self-control despite this, though she is a stone heavier. However, this is trivialised somewhat with her 'oops!' reference. Henry (a 42-year-old director, married with two step-children) was 'fat' in the past as well. He writes that he was 'fighting' with his weight since his middle 20's, but went on to lose almost five stone and has 'maintained' this 'weight ever since'. And his rationale for losing weight:

As you guessed, obvious answer, because I was a fat bugger. Saw a photo of me and decided that I could no longer be that fat.

It is interesting that Henry and Ulrika give these past selves a 'fat' label. Monaghan (2007) argues that the use of this sort of pejorative term is a pre-emptive strike against others deriding one's body size. On the one hand this positions Henry and Ulrika as bodies resistant to hegemonic healthism and embracing of the pleasures of eating and drinking, and distances both of them from the 'feminine coding' of 'dieting, body consciousness and obsession with one's appearance, which are considered negatively and as stereotypically female' (Lupton 2013: 64). On the other, because these fat bodies were in the past, Henry and Ulrika are complicit in the objectification of themselves and other fat bodies; this is not how they are now. Henry's weight loss is also in his control. Even when he does not comply exactly with his diet plan, as he can not avoid alcohol, he writes: 'my biggest downfall has always been alcohol which is packed with carbs, but if I give up people tell me I might live longer, I think it will just feel that way!' This is presented as not a problem; it is just a matter of conforming to a cultural script of hegemonic masculinities (Connell 2005), such as drinking (in stark contrast to Ellen's narrative). Henry explains that his diet is so successful he has to moderate it and therefore distances himself from potentially contaminating association with feminised forms of dieting and weight cycling:

I went from almost 110kgs (17st 4) to 78kgs (12st), but people were asking me 'how is the treatment going?', cheeky buggers! I felt great, but my wife and very long-standing female friend managed to convince me that 80's to early 90's was perhaps healthier. So I now fluctuate between 85 (13st 5) and 90 (14st) depending on how good I am being. The training remains fairly constant and my avoidance of rice, potatoes, pasta and bread also remains constant. However if we are at friends and they have just baked fresh bread or a rice dish then no prob. I just avoid it when I can ...

Henry's weight loss is pragmatic and devoid of emotion, other than feeling 'great'. He presents himself as unconcerned with his health and it was only the significant women in his life as the arbiters of the family's health who managed to persuade him to moderate his highly successful diet. In terms of comparing this account with those of the women respondents, it is perhaps the framing of his diet as a success and a continued success that differs. A change in weight from 78kgs (12st) up to 90kgs (14st), for example, could be considered a failure or a loss of control, or indicative of weight cycling and none of these issues are problematised. Further, this weight loss is controlled and framed in terms of a rational choice. It is not a feminised pre-occupation nor longing for a thin ideal (Germov and Williams 2004). Similarly, Larry writes:

Last year I broke through the 100kg barrier (not good) peaking at 102kg (16 stone) so I decided to try the 'no whites' diet and dropped, potato, bread and rice for about three months. I also cut out alcohol and joined the gym. I was pretty religious about going ... at least five times per week. I lost more than 11 kilograms over about three months and actually began to feel better. Sadly it all went a bit pear shaped when we came to England for three weeks ... Mum's cooking, English ale, all the usual treats you enjoy when on holiday.

It is notable that Larry's diet is spoiled by his mother's cooking. However, occasional lapses can be considered 'negotiated pleasures'; or strategies used to manage a spoiled identity when mediating 'food pleasures and the will to live a healthy life' (Jallinoja's et al. 2010: 125). In Henry's account his inability to avoid alcohol, fresh bread or a rice dish at a friend's house is considered an 'unhealthy treat', it is 'negotiated, balanced and rationalised'. Larry's negotiated pleasure is contextualised as a holiday treat, it is notably 'English ale' or beer drinking, distancing him from the potentially feminising associations with dieting (Lupton 1996, Bordo 2003). In neither account do they engage in an emotional struggle or battle. These 'negotiated pleasures' resemble what Coveney and Bunton (2003) term 'disciplined pleasure', Sassatelli (2001) refers to as 'tamed hedonism' and others 'pleasure in moderation' (Crawford 2000, Pajari et al. 2006). In other words, they do not fall outside of the chosen dietary regimen and are therefore not considered lapses or a loss of control and a source of guilt and anxiety.

Masculine embodiment

Some men did write about weight loss practices. Walt, for example, writes that all his family 'watch their weight', so it is not that he is interested in the feminised practice of dieting for aesthetic reasons or the thin ideal (Germov and Williams 2004). He therefore checks the calories of food that he buys on a regular basis so that he rarely buys products with over 400kj per 100gs. James writes that '80–90 per cent of the time he loosely follows the point system developed by weight watchers'. He has followed 'weight watchers twice, but would never follow them exactly' and 'lost about 6 or 7 kilos both times, but exercise is better for keeping it off'. Again, there is no notion here of individual failure if weight loss is not sustained. The reference to six or seven kilos is dismissive as if it is an arbitrary figure, when it is around a stone in weight. His claim that he would 'never' follow the diet exactly indicates his resistance to the feminised performativity of such dietary practices (Lupton 1996, Bordo 2003). His diet is bespoke; changing an element of it gives the illusion of control and makes it different from feminised dietary practices.

Men also tend to explain weight management practices in terms of forms of hegemonic masculinities (Connell 2005), such as beer drinking. Hence, Ollie notes:

> *I was always skinny and don't like the idea of getting a belly (although, this probably has more to do with beer than food ...) although I reckon I'm the least fat of my contemporaries ... I eat out much more than I used to. I always thought of it as a waste of drinking time, which for many years was the main reason for going out – but I enjoy it now.*

Notably, Ollie is also skinny, which is not usually associated with dominant forms of masculinity, however this is countered by references to beer and drinking. That said, he has put on weight, but he notes that he is the 'least fat of his contemporaries'. Similarly, Fred writes:

> *I've never been one to watch my weight (I'm 6 foot 8 and only just over 12 stone) so I'm on the skinny side. That said I drink a lot of alcohol so do sometimes watch what I eat if only to balance the calories from the booze.*

Ralph claims:

> *There have been occasions where I've stopped drinking beer for a few weeks to lose weight, but BMI is generally okay ... I never last long as I want to be on a beer diet.*

And Sam (a 50-year-old yachtsman, married with one child) when reflecting on what he ate as a young man says:

> *I guess we must have eaten other stuff as well ... I don't really recall much more, generally speaking it was mostly a diet of beer.*

Thus, Fred cuts out food in order to be able to drink more and Ralph wants to be on a beer diet. These examples exemplify the power of cultural displays of masculinity through beer rather than food (Gough 2006, 2007, Gough and Conor 2006). There are also references to meat eating, as well as drinking, in men's embodied foodways. Tom (a 37-year-old occupational therapist, married with one child), for example, writes:

> *I have always had to force myself to eat as I could quite happily go without if I knew I would survive and maintain a good weight ... I was once told in my late teens that if I wanted to put on weight, I should drink Guinness and eat steak. The Guinness has done me well now for nearly 20 years, but I've never been a big fan of steak ... I have to be [food conscious on a day-to-day basis] as my energy levels suffer easily if I don't eat well. I am constantly grazing on something.*

Hence, Tom like Fred and Ollie was skinny and did not comply with hetero-normative cultural scripts of appropriate masculinities.

In Ian's account he notes that he has never really changed his eating habits in order to lose weight, although he:

> *Messed with protein only deal for a week at a time ... Lost weight rapidly and felt odd – light headed ... Quite conscious because I have the high cholesterol mantra humming in the background ... Bacon sandwich for breakfast and a burger for supper – oops! (Today) granola bar only (its 17.20), still full from last night ...*

Ian distances himself from notions of seriously attempting to lose weight, which has feminised connotations (Lupton 1996, Bordo 2002). Also, despite needing to pay attention to his cholesterol, he does not comply with health foodways either. Nick on the other hand writes:

> *I don't like too much stodge. I hate the feeling of anything making me fat! Try to stay slimmish. Try to avoid too much white flour / white bread. Try to eat spelt bread only. We get spelt from the cult weirdo's in the market and one slice is all you need for breakfast ... slow release etc. Whereas you can eat slice after slice of manufactured white bread and still feel hungry / empty / bloated etc. Rubbish foods are pretty much for me all processed foods. An example I can give is the M&S ready-made mashed potato. It looks fab in the packaging in the shop and continues to look fab in the fridge at home. I wonder how many days ago it was made and what they've put in it to make it keep its looks etc.*

Thus, in Nick's account he is aligning himself with forms of high cultural capital, practising health and dietary restraint (Naccarato and LeBesco 2012). He is also distancing himself from low status foods such as white bread and convenience/commercial foodways, which are associated with lack. Further, he writes:

> *Try to not eat if not hungry. Very impressed with Prince Charles who still fits uniforms that were made for him 35 years ago. I know he misses supper where he can. I still fit my morning suit that I got married in – even though the jacket is a bit tight across the shoulders – and I am determined not to buy another one!! Absolutely love it. It is all part of the sensual experience of life, like music, paintings, and sex.*

Hence, Nick is positioning himself as concerned with the pleasures and aesthetics of food, but again practises restraint when he can. Thus, he is engaged in a form of culinary capital that values dietary and weight control.

Dis/Ordered eating/bodies

One of the original aims of the research was 'to consider the extent to which individual food histories were related to issues of weight management if at all'. The University Ethics Committee responded by insisting I strongly advised potential participants 'not to participate if they had suffered from an eating disorder' and I fully complied with this request. Despite this, notions of dis/ordered eating were always going to be part of the study, because there is not a fixed ahistorical definition of what constitutes an eating disorder, and as Malson (2009: 137) identifies:

> ... eating dis/orders are complex, heterogeneous and shifting collectivities of socio-historically located subjectivities, bodies and body management practices that are constituted within and by rather than outside of the normative discursive contexts of contemporary western cultures.

Indeed, because a controlled thin body shape is considered culturally desirable for women in Western societies, weight management practices and dis/ordered eating tend to be highly feminised preoccupations (Lupton 1996, Bordo 2003). Hence, they can be trivialised and/or pathologised. Certainly, body weight is considered a master signifier of health and according to Malson (2009), Anorexia Nervosa (AN) enacts par excellence the masculinised, individualised, hyper-disciplined and almost revered micro-management of the body. However, the British Psychological Society and Royal College of Physicians guidelines on eating disorders in January 2004 (CG9), claim that the preoccupation with body weight, fear of fatness or pursuit of thinness are considered significant in the aetiology of Anorexia Nervosa, Bulimia and Eating Disorders Not Otherwise Specified (EDNOS). Similarly, the National Institute for Mental Health (2001) in the US defined eating disorders as 'serious disturbances in eating behaviour, such as extreme and unhealthy reductions of food intake or severe over eating, as well as feelings of distress or extreme concerns about body shape or weight' (Giovanelli and Ostertag 2009: 294). Again, these feelings are considered a constituent element of hetero-normative femininity.

It is notable that in proposals to change the Diagnostic Statistical Manual (DSM) IV, for AN the usual measure of 'underweight' as a BMI of less than 18.5 is to be removed and 'markedly low body weight', based on the individual clinician's judgment, used instead. This indicates a shift away from the certainty of the BMI as an accurate indicator of AN. The removal of amenorrhea as a criterion is also under discussion. These changes to the DSM suggest new variations in those presenting with eating disorders and the problems of having fixed psychiatric criteria. This highlights the problems of quantifying something that is subjective, culturally specific and medicalising of feminised practices.

In terms of conceptualising eating disorders Sam writes:

A particular memory that sticks in my head is there because it was, at the time, a bit of a watershed, I had been battling with an eating disorder of sorts where I would get very nervous around eating food in the company of others, this was awkward because I was going to college at the time and had to attend lunch in the canteen, I would often not bother as I could not face it, the symptoms would generally be a feeling of intense nausea while trying to eat. I never bothered to talk to any sort of specialist about this, just worked my way through it eventually ...

Hence, Sam positions himself as having suffered with an eating disorder 'of sorts' which centres on his inability to eat in company. However, although this is an embodied experience, it is not related to anxiety about his body size or weight and we have no sense of this, which is reminiscent of the assertion that a 'man *has* a body' whilst 'a woman *is* her body' (Frost 2001: 31). Later, Sam notes:

My relationship with food started out stormy, I really had very little time for food or eating, it got in the way of everything else that I was doing with my life and slowed me down. This grew into a standoff as I've already described where I could not face eating even though I was hungry, I never actually got physically sick from this disorder but felt very ill often, basically a series of panic attacks would overcome me when ever I had to deal with eating anything more that very casually ...

I use this example from Sam to challenge the medicalisation of eating disorders and the conceptualisation of them as feminine. Sam is male; what makes his account different is the lack of rhetoric about embodiment. He was anxious about eating, but this was not about a longing or desire to be thin. Helen (a 54-yer-old publisher, married with two of three children living at home), on the other hand discusses an anorexic friend; despite having had anorexia herself, which she refers to as an 'attention seeking venture', she writes:

> *One of my friends had anorexia – very serious, dropped to 4 and a half stone at the age of 16. She was off school for quite a while and when she returned she put on a massive amount of weight and ended up being huge. Once she had returned to school I remember her sitting at the dining table and scooping up the rashers of bacon (still in the fat) and stuffing them in her mouth and then picking up the plate and pouring the fat into her mouth ...*

This visceral account from Helen demonstrates a real fear of and repulsion towards fat on many levels. Similarly, Ophelia writes about a couple of girls at her school:

> *Olivia Huntley-Palmer had anorexia though, with her huge head and red hands but nothing was ever said. She came top of the form always, exercised endlessly always playing in every sport and every match going and was always cold and every bone showed. It scared us and we used to whisper about 'anorexia' as if it was something you could catch. On the other hand, Justine Cookson-Snell was enormously fat, smelly and allegedly snored. No one wanted to share a room with her – even at 12/13 we were discriminating against fat people in our little world.*

Again, for Ophelia there is a horror of bodies out of control on all levels and this concern feeds into other stereotypes and labels that associate unpopular characteristics with body size and the reading of bodies for what they disclose about morality and other characteristics (Petersen 2007). There is a fear of contagion and stigma associated with these extremes of female embodiment (Goffman 1963). She also comments that:

> *It would have been hard to put on weight but some girls did starve themselves to be thin – interestingly no one considered them to be heroes.*

Thus, Ophelia makes an equation between heroism and starvation, reminiscent of the Middle Ages when saints and martyrs fasted for a cause (Coveney 2006, Turner 2008). However, in a contemporary milieu women are concerned to negotiate a 'heroic' middle ground of appropriate body weight. There is an added dread of being judged too thin or too fat. She also writes:

When my mother died as I turned 12 I lost a lot of weight very quickly and my dad and various relations were very worried about it. I found them wittering on about it very very annoying, it seemed to be all they talked about but as I saw it, I didn't want to eat much and I didn't see the problem. I had just lost my appetite that was all. It took months for me to regain it. Being thin at that time didn't make me feel any differently about myself, I certainly wasn't doing it on purpose and gradually my weight returned to normal. I also had a delayed puberty because of the shock, even though I already wore a simple bra at 12 nothing else happened until I was about 15 and my periods didn't start until I was 16.

Hence, Ophelia is clearly drawing a distinction between the weight loss/gain of others and her own experiences, which in this instance were not about longing for a thin ideal. Burns (2009: 131) argues that if we consider the meaning and experiences of these practices rather than the body image of the anorexic or the bulimic, it is possible to consider how women are articulating themselves. Thus, they can be understood as 'managing mourning, emptiness and anxiety through embodied practices' (Burns 2009: 131). Thus, in Ophelia's account, the loss of her mother is intertwined with the loss of her appetite and weight loss. This is an embodied reaction to trauma that is interpreted by those around her as a wilful act of self-starvation. Ophelia is keen to explain that she did not 'feel' better being thin at this time and why would she? If women are positioned as being obsessed with their body weight and thinness then their behaviour is interpreted within this frame. Indeed, Squire (2002: 61) argues that her experience of bulimia was an emotional response to the death of her mother:

I found that bulimia was a way of managing anxiety in the absence of other forms unavailable to me. My weight gain in the early stages of my mother's illness, and subsequent weight loss prior to, and following, her death, provided a context which was unlike the tales I had read of teenage girls dieting and starving themselves in an effort to be slim. I began to understand my bulimia in terms of grief ... In the numbness of grief bulimia was also an attempt to feel less empty through an intensely embodied and physically invested space ... one of a number of practices in the absence of an embodied mourning ritual ...

Again, this highlights how embodied foodways can be misinterpreted and/or understandable responses to external trauma. Indeed, Gaby (a 51-year-old architect designer, married with two children) writes about her anorexic and bulimic behaviour between the ages of 11 and 16, which was a series of embodied responses to trauma, a car accident, a hospital stay, her parents splitting up and being an only child dealing with these significant life events. I represent her narrative here as it was sent to me, written in just one long stream of consciousness, with lots of short sentences, all of them not quite finished, but quickly following on to the next, in a rush to get to the last sentence:

At 11 years old when I had a car accident and lost some weight and was told I looked better (I'd always been the heaviest in my class and teased for it) and then when I got out of hospital I decided to lose more weight ... started to eat less and to find out how little food I could survive on ... almost as a scientific test. Also parents split up at this time and I was an only child so maybe needed more attention ... Refused to eat calorific food and ate cottage cheese, lettuce, raw carrots, apples. I avoided anything with calories even if I was hungry. Drank black coffee and water and took laxatives ... lost so much weight that I was taken to a specialist who told me that if this pattern of eating continued, I would never have children ... that comment sparked a change in my eating habits I guess. Also at 16 I met a guy and fell in love and we were going to pubs and I drank beer and ate crisps and embarked on more of a student diet plus my self confidence started to develop, so there just wasn't time to worry so much about what I was eating. Realised that I could eat more and not put on masses of weight. When pregnant, I enjoyed putting on weight but still controlled it ... swam every day with first baby ... to stay toned I guess ... but the swelling side was good! Ate whatever I wanted but ate healthy nutritious food. After that, it was a case of eating with the family and enjoying everything we ate together, which I had prepared ... but still controlled the content. Now eat enthusiastically and quite a large amount, considering my size!

Gaby is keen to get to the end of her embodied narrative, in order to demonstrate that despite AN her life conforms to the usual cultural scripts of hetero-normative femininity, she 'met a guy', 'fell in love' and has children. At the beginning of the narrative she is teased for being the heaviest in her class at school, but hints that she is now small (although she eats enthusiastically and *quite* a large amount). Her account represents a 'fear of fatness' that 'is assumed to underpin the disordered eating practices that lead to exceptional thinness' (LeBesco 2009: 146). Indeed, it is argued that the fear of the imperfect, fat self is stronger than the hope of a perfect thin self, particularly for young women today (Dalley et al. 2013).

Gaby was not the only woman to refer to pregnancy; in Hannah's health foodway, she positions herself as a responsible individual practising self-care but also as a middle class woman she complies with government guidelines on healthy eating and drinking during pregnancy:

> *Being pregnant with Felix at 22yrs stopped me drinking alcohol for 9 months, the take-aways and fast food purchases rapidly reduced and a sensible daily diet began ...*

Further, in her second pregnancy:

> *Being pregnant with Felicity at 24yrs again stopped me drinking alcohol, again a healthier approach to food began, and I stopped eating pate, as I was advised with the 2nd pregnancy.*

Thus, health foodways and embodied foodways interconnect and are significant in the display of appropriate middle class values. Abstaining from alcohol and eating properly when pregnant have high cultural value. Indeed, these findings run counter to those of Charles and Kerr (1986) who conclude that 'virtually all women have a relationship with food that is problematic [and that] except when pregnant, it was virtually impossible to be relaxed about food' (cited in Beardsworth and Keil 1997: 179). Today, in an era of heightened awareness of responsible individualism and an internalised medical gaze (Howson 2004, Petersen 2007) as highlighted in previous chapters, the idea that women ever relax about food, especially when pregnant, appears incongruous. Indeed, Earle (2003) found that pregnancy was not the opportunity to transgress gendered norms and values regarding one's body. Although her study focuses on women's attitudes to bodies and not food, she found that women are not changed by pregnancy. They wish to be seen by others, as they were before (Earle 2003: 251). In Ophelia's account, she also identifies how she had to put on weight in order to get pregnant and then:

> *Pregnancy didn't suit my body terribly and I got a lot of cellulite, which means that I don't feel confident on the beach nor sailing or anywhere where I need to keep cool.*

Thus, post pregnancy embodiment is also problematic for women who continue to be judged on their appearance. Indeed, all of these narratives contribute to and reinforce 'weight based stigma' and discrimination (Saguy 2013: 16). There is an uncritical acceptance of the 'cultural prescriptions of feminine beauty as thinness' (Malson 2009: 139) and therefore the 'fat' body as 'other'. In none of the accounts is there any mention of double standards or inconsistencies between the sexes for example. The notion that big male bodies are associated with power, whilst female ones are not, is not problematised. Bergman (2009: 141), when passing for a 'big dude', suffers no abuse but notes that when she is 'seen' as a fat woman:

> *Packs of boys follow me mooing; women with aggressively coordinated outfits accost me in the grocery store to inform me that I can lose thirty pounds in thirty days and that they would love to help. There are pig calls ...*

She claims that 'my fat, taken together with my height and confidence in my body while I am out in public view say "man" in this culture' (Bergman 2009: 142). Indeed cultural concerns with 'individualistic competitiveness and personal display' (Malson 2009: 139) and persistent Cartesian dualisms (Levi-Strauss 1969) lead to tensions that feed directly into the condition of 'being a woman' in contemporary Western cultures. Hence, to even accept notionally that 'other' alternative body sizes are admissible undermines constructions of 'good femininity' (Day and Keys 2009: 91). Further, qualities such as self-sacrifice, self-denial and restraint are written on a thin body and therefore assumed to be missing from a fat one. Indeed,

Burns notes (2004) that good or ideal femininity is achieved via the restraint and control of food intake. Gard (2009) also suggests that talk about food and dietary restraint is central to modern white 'girl' culture, whilst boys and men concern themselves with discourses that celebrate bigness and deflect public pressure to show dietary restraint (Gard 2009: 41).

I therefore argue that all female bodies regardless of their size are 'marked categories'. Thinness may have high cultural capital, but as such it is no longer an unmarked category. Indeed, references to thin bodies can evoke as much fear and hostility as fat bodies. It seems that when reading the bodies of others the boundaries of acceptable or appropriate body size are subject to moral appropriations and a pathologising of all body types. Respondents in the study are therefore concerned to negotiate a heroic middle ground of appropriate embodiment; they could not be too fat, but they could not be too thin either.

Thus, embodied foodways highlight how the contemporary cultural milieu marginalises and stigmatises individuals on the basis of a constantly shifting notion of appropriate body size. Yet, this is not just about fat or thin embodiment; because these bodies are gendered, it is the female body that is implicated here and a critique of fatness (or thinness) implies a critique of femininity. My female body is mutable; it can change over the course of the reproductive cycle throughout a lunar month. Indeed, the size of my body has ebbed and flowed throughout the whole of my life. However, in a civilised, dualistic and absolutist society that values masculine notions of control, management, willpower and rationality, the 'other' female body is always in need of containment. Some female respondents expressed disgust with their bodies at times, especially if they felt they were out of control. Of course, body dissatisfaction is ultimately about not having an appropriate body and this is linked to cultural norms and values, or the intersectionalities of gender and class. The body with the highest cultural capital is actually male.

6
Epicurean Foodways

In the previous four chapters I outline how women and men negotiate dominant discourses of responsible individualism and the contradictions inherent in hetero-normative cultural scripts of appropriate gendered and classed foodways. Mostly these foodways (family/maternal/health/embodied) are conceptualised as feminised approaches to food work carried out within the domestic sphere. This therefore raises questions when considering how men negotiate their engagement in foodways within the home. One way of avoiding contamination by association with feminised domesticity is by recourse to hegemonic forms of masculinities (Connell 2005) that centre on 'traditional' masculine attributes, such as 'meat-eating, beer drinking and womanizing' (Gough 2007: 237). Indeed, Gough (2007: 237) argues following Connell (2005) that 'all men are complicit in supporting hegemonic ideals through their practices, whether it be weight training, promiscuity or high alcohol consumption'. Further, economic success, knowledge and expertise also tend to be coded masculine within dichotomous models of thought (Oakley 1992) and the absolutist/dualist discourses that inform contemporary foodways. Indeed, men draw upon hegemonic forms throughout their narratives, whether this refers to the acquisition of high culinary capital or the pleasures of food and its associations with sex/sexuality.

Another way for men to distance themselves from emphasised femininities (Connell 2005) is through a dedication to epicurean foodways. I therefore consider how men use epicurean foodways, as a means of positioning themselves outside of the domestic sphere. Indeed, despite the high cultural capital embedded in epicurean foodways, men still reference forms of hegemonic masculinities. Thus, whilst the intersectionalities of gender and class are performed within epicurean foodways, the predominant feature in men's accounts is the performance of a masculine subjectivity. Thus, men become skilled in cookery, acquainted with the best restaurants, the latest techniques, the fashionable chefs, because of a commitment to the pleasures of food play. When food play becomes work, it is similarly coded masculine, skilled, competitive and hard. There are 26 men who contributed to my study. Their ages ranged from 27 to 76, although they are mostly between the ages of 39 and 60. The most striking difference between these narratives and those from the women is the extent to which they are located within the public sphere and outward looking. In other words, their narratives are less to do with the domestic sphere, body management or the feminised practices of cooking as 'emotion' work (Hochschild 1979, Hochschild 1983, DeVault 1991) or 'love' labour (Lynch 2007) and more to do with how they develop 'epicurean' (Scholliers 2001) or 'elite' (Bourdieu 1984) tastes over time.

Definitions

I use the term 'epicurean' foodways, as opposed to gastronomic, gourmet, foodie or gourmand, because an epicure takes particular sensual pleasure in 'good' food and drink (Waley-Cohen 20017: 106). Gastronomy on the other hand 'according to Brillat-Savarin [1825] should bring together pleasure and good health' (Drouard 2007: 266). Indeed, in terms of the history of taste, according to Waley-Cohen (2007: 104) 'gastronomy is an intimate understanding of the properties of food and a quest to achieve perfect balance'. When considering male respondents' food narratives, balance and health are not significant concerns. Further, respondents practicing epicurean foodways can be considered 'gourmets', defined as 'a connoisseur of good food; a person with a discerning palate', or the more informal 'foodie', defined by Johnston and Baumann (2010) and Cairns et al. (2010) as an 'individual who is passionate about the pursuit of good food, with a long standing passion for eating and learning about food' (2010: 591). Further, Hollows (2003) argues that men engaged in domestic cookery do so as a creative leisure activity that distinguishes it from feminised domestic labour and as such it becomes 'a domestic culinary masculinity'

(Hollows 2003: 239). However, it is impossible to be a gourmet if this entails much more than a passing interest in 'good food' or what Warder et al. (2007) refer to as ordinary omnivorousness without committed engagement. For example, Ashley et al. (2004) illustrate how:

> *In the 'Official Foodie Handbook' for example, the foodie is contrasted with the gourmet. The latter was typically a rich male amateur to whom food was a passion. Foodies are typically an aspiring professional couple to whom food is a fashion. 'The' Fashion.*
>
> (Barr & Levy 1984: 7 as cited in Ashley et al. 2004: 149)

Hence, it is appropriate to make use of the terms gourmet and epicurean foodways. Generally, men who responded to my request for their auto/biographical food stories negotiated their male identities, by utilising hegemonic masculinities and/or epicurean foodways both within and beyond the domestic sphere. This is not to suggest that women cannot engage in epicurean foodways, just that the pressures on women who are mothers is such that it is almost impossible to engage in appropriate middle class maternal foodways and epicurean foodways at the same time. Throughout this chapter therefore I consider epicurean foodways as significant for male identity because this stresses the importance of pleasure and food play, as opposed to the emphasised femininities identified with food work (family/ maternal foodways) and the control of food (health/embodied foodways). Indeed, again according to Brillat-Savarin [1825] 'cuisine de ménage or domestic cooking; was woman's work, done everyday in the home kitchen, [and] lacking prestige' (Drouard 2007: 266). Of course, as with family and maternal foodways, epicurean foodways are concerned with the intersectionalities of gender and class as a means of performing, displaying and accruing high cultural capital.

Cultural omnivorousness

Freeman (2007: 7) notes in *The History of Taste* that there have been continuous shifts in gastronomic fashion associated with epicurean foodways since earliest times:

> *According to Greek classical and also Chinese tradition, barbarians eat raw or crudely cooked meat rather than observing the civilised practice of cooking, and this is an essential aspect of their barbarism.*

In contemporary epicurean foodways 'seemingly low class foods can be elevated to esteem with some tweaking ... [such as] street food and gourmet hamburgers' (Freeman 2007: 14). Indeed, cultural omnivorousness (enjoying a blend of high and low cultures) is a significant symbolic marker of culinary capital for gourmets as well as a 'desire to connect with a tradition of hearty authenticity' (Freeman 2007: 17). There are further divisions within epicurean foodways. For example, Naccarato and LeBesco (2012) differentiate between 'foodies' and 'chowhounds', within the key domains of cultural omnivorousness; aesthetic appreciation (taste), authenticity (participation) and knowledge acquisition. Chowhounds are less elitist in their trailblazing quests for authenticity and fully embrace cultural omnivorousness. Dave notes:

I do not consider myself a 'foodie snob' in that I believe that all sorts of establishments and types of food have their place. One of my favourite restaurants is Michael Caines Abode at the Royal Clarence Hotel, Exeter, where we have enjoyed sublime Michelin starred cuisine – I was also distraught on finding out that my favourite doner-kebab shop in Exeter had closed!

Here, Dave may be considered a 'chowhound' as he distinguishes himself by disavowing foodie elitism. Drew on the other hand writes:

My true food hero though has to be Anthony Bourdain, a food rebel, but I love his philosophy re food. When he travels he eats local not in 5 star restaurants and this is the only real way to get to experience the culture. When I went to Beijing my big ask was to try Peking Duck, it wasn't the Wall, it wasn't shopping, it was just to try proper local food. When I go to India it is Dosas for breakfast, not full English. It is those little apprehensive moments before trying something new that get me, that moment of discovery and the thought that I could replicate it for others who have never tried it.

Again, Drew is highlighting his quest for authentic cuisine. However, he admits to following Anthony Bourdain, his true food hero and rebel. In the culinary field, according to Naccarato and LeBesco (2012: 77), chowhounds are leaders; it is only foodies who mimic experts and follow culinary trends. Regardless of these seemingly arbitrary distinctions, both chowhound and foodie identities suppose high economic and cultural capital, 'only those with leisure time, culinary knowledge and economic resources dine out on a regular basis' and can fully engage in chowhound or foodie practices (Naccarato and LeBesco 2012: 83). These types of distinctions serve to highlight the elitism of 'culinary capital'. In the culinary field the drawing of internal boundaries between smaller groups serves to reinforce the significance of the wider field in which the actors position themselves. It is notable that Drew positions himself as a 'food adventurer' (Heldke 2003: xxiii) and a rebel, and these tend to be coded as masculine attributes.

Therefore, I consider epicurean foodways as part of a repertoire of hegemonic masculinities, a means of distancing the self from association with more traditional domestic or feminised foodways, as well as an elite culinary endeavour. There are only two women in the study who could be identified as gourmets, Paula, a food writer, and Dalia, who was interested in the aesthetics of food, gastronomy or the 'art of good eating' (Merriam Webster Dictionary 2014) as might be understood within gastronomic discourses (Freeman 2007, Johnston and Baumann 2010, Naccarato and LeBesco 2012, DeSolier 2013). Overall, respondents engaged in epicurean foodways are concerned with the sensual pleasures of food beyond the mundane everyday associations with family foodways.

Gourmets therefore tend to have relationships with food free from a fear of fatness, health concerns and guilt associated with indulgence. They differed from 'foodies' analysed in other studies and are 'hyper' gourmets not engaged in feminised aspects of caring/food work at all (Cairns et al. 2010, Johnston and Baumann 2010, Naccarato and LeBesco 2012, DeSolier 2013). Indeed, those who self-identify as gourmets are 'food adventurers' (Heldke 2003: xxiii) and use epicurean foodways as markers of elite cultural capital, focusing on elite practices, knowledge acquisition and cultural omnivorousness (Peterson and Kern 1996). Food shopping and cookery rather than being highly feminised domestic activities are part of a search for authentic or exotic cuisine and/or an expression of expert knowledge, 'taste' and distinction. This epicurean identity assumes high levels of economic, social and cultural capital and includes elements of high adventure and risk. Further, unlike gourmets identified elsewhere; respondents did not express concern with sustainability or ethical consumption (Cairns et al. 2010, Johnston and Baumann 2010, Naccarato and LeBesco 2012, DeSolier 2013). There was some reference to the humane treatment of animals and organic produce generally, but this did not extend to concern with the democratisation of food production or the human costs of this. What is significant is that epicurean foodways continue to be associated with legitimate cultural capital and coded masculine. More generally the dualistic gendering of everyday foodways means that men are forced to negotiate traditionally feminised culinary fields by resorting to hegemonic masculinities. What emerges is that notions of masculinity are connected to issues of taste, status, distinction, as well as notions of pleasure. It is the emphasis on foodways as pleasurable that marks them as distinct from feminised approaches to everyday foodways. Thus, epicurean foodways are about asserting class status and a gender identity associated with hegemonic masculinities. Indeed, female and male gourmet narratives are classed and narrated from a privileged white middle class perspective.

Epicurean educations

The route to adopting epicurean foodways is narrated in terms of acquiring a taste for high status foodways and neophilia (Falk 1991, Lupton 1996) or the distancing of the self from family foodways of the past in preference for all things new or exotic. Thus, appearing adventurous in seeking out new tastes is connected to the desire to reject foods from one's youth and/or family background as well as a means of marking cultural boundaries (Bourdieu 1984). Indeed, respondents are keen to demonstrate their status as gourmets and how this developed over the life course.

In the men's narratives epicurean foodways are heavily coded as masculine by reference to a range of hegemonic masculinities. In the women's, they chart a development of epicurean foodways due to relationships with men. This reinforces a dichotomous approach to foodways that naturalises a gendered division of labour, one that associates women with the mundane, low-skilled work of feeding the family (DeVault 1991), whilst men work and play in an exciting culinary field that centres on pleasure and success. Thus, there are intersectionalities of gender and class within epicurean foodways, which chart a development of food consciousness from a taste of necessity to a taste of luxury, from low to high status with regards to food and cultural distinctions (Bourdieu 1984). This includes outside or 'foreign' influences, as highlighted in Chapter 2; for example Ed, Simon and Charlie's epicurean tastes are influenced by childhood experiences living abroad. Indeed, these external influences are significant and include references to school, university, work, as well as significant 'others' who act as mentors or tutors in the culinary arts. Gerry (a 47-year-old solicitor, living with his partner) begins his epicurean narrative with a reference to his mother sieving his mushroom soup and boarding school. He notes:

> *I was a very fussy child. I didn't really like things, which had much in the way of texture. I made my Mum sieve tinned mushroom soup to get rid of the little black bits of mushroom. What next? – Boarding school. bleeeurgh. Tough meat. Custard. Limp salad. Over cooked veg. Only fish fingers and chips redeemed this dismal fare. Two good food memories of that time which I remember: firstly overcoming my aversion to the texture of mushrooms – along with the young matron who gave me the nickname of Billy – which then stuck with me until I was 18 – we went mushroom picking in the big field next to school. Not magic mushrooms I should add – they came later! Big fat field mushrooms. And then she chopped them up, cooked them in butter and made us all mushrooms on toast. I didn't want to, but I did and oh boy! How good did that taste?! I think this was a quantum taste leap for me – I guess I would have been about 11.*

School dinner references have been commented upon already (Chapter 2). However, Gerry distances himself from contamination from feminised associations with 'fussiness' by reference to 'magic mushrooms'. Indeed, drug taking is the kind of risky activity that is usually coded as male and Robertson (2007: 47) argues that men are 'risk takers' and 'at risk' due to having to conform to notions of hegemonic masculinities. Hence, taking drugs is a kind of edgework and a means of 'transcending the banality of every day existence' or 'living on the edge as a means of performing dominant masculinity' (Collinson 1996, Robertson 2007: 48-9). In Dalia's account of her development of epicurean foodways, she cites a French exchange trip as significant in her acquisition of gourmet 'tastes':

> *When I was thirteen years old I spent six weeks in France as part of a foreign exchange. This had the first profound effect on my culinary*

appreciation. My French exchange family was of the opinion that all English people ate roast beef and peas. My experience on a rural farm in the Loire Valley, was of eating baby birds fresh out of a nest, chicken's heads (brains and tongue), pieces of chocolate with bread for breakfast, baguettes (which seemed strange at the time), vegetables eaten separately to meat or fish and dessert eaten on the flip side of the plate having mopped up your main with bread. I drank Pastis diluted with water and wine.

Indeed, for all respondents actively engaged in epicurean foodways, an important aspect of elite culinary capital refers to the inculcation of legitimate tastes, along with knowledge and participation; here Dalia is learning traditions associated with French foodways, which have long been associated with high cultural capital and cultural omnivorousness (Peterson and Kern 1996, Warde et al. 2007). Indeed, many professional chefs are usually trained in the arts of French cookery (Freeman 2007). Thus, Dalia is positioning herself as aware of French culinary traditions as well as appreciating a cultural omnivorousness that values authentic cuisine. Indeed, Gerry similarly writes about a French exchange:

But the thing, which happened at that time which was far more significant, was a French exchange and a seismic shift in the area of my taste buds. I went with my mate Fred to stay with a Parisian family who had a place in Brittany. They were a single Mum and three kids. I can see now the first dinner. A huge bowl filled with nothing more than tomatoes – heavily dressed in vinaigrette. I hated tomatoes. Bread (fine) and huge slabs of coarse pate (Pate!!!). That was it. So I ate it – and was an instant convert. For two weeks we lived on that – plus huge bowls of lettuce and dressing, black pudding, moules, curds and whey for breakfast, crepes, hot chocolate with croissants and jam. My life was changed forever. I loved it all. I think that since then I have been up for eating anything (with the exception of my veggie intermission at college).

Thus, Gerry's cultural omnivorousness and new found 'tastes' are inculcated outside of his family in 1970s *France*, not only a different country, with a distinct food culture but within what would have been at that time a non-traditional family environment. He continues his epicurean adventure and writes (emoticon and confidential comments in original text):

> So – yes – college. Going to college meant having to 'cook' for ourselves and/or live off takeaways – I think this phase really lasted ten years … There was also a short right-on phase of vegetarianism. AKA living off Bulgarian red wine, chips, bean stews and buckwheat bakes. This suited an agenda of direct-action, peace protesting activism. And the chips and red wine (and some speed too) suited parties, discos, club-nights in town, and occasional forays to London. The other food discovery of this time was hash-cakes :) (Assume this is confidential) … Then I moved to London to work on the [organization], and into a shared house where they ate bacon and sausages. My politics were already getting more flexible. My vegetarianism lasted about two weeks.

It is notable that Gerry associates his vegetarianism with politics and the public sphere; it is not a domestic (feminised) concern. It is part of a lifestyle that incorporates more risky behaviour, such as drug taking and partying and activities usually associated with what Collinson (1996) refers to as edgework, or 'living on the edge as a means of performing dominant masculinity' (Robertson 2007: 48–9). In Gerry's account this is a phase and something he grows out of. This reinforces the association of femininity with vegetarianism and meat eating with masculinity that is well documented (Adams 1990, Fiddes 1991). Indeed, Bourdieu (2005: 75) argues that meat is 'the nourishing food par excellence, strong and strong-making, giving vigour, blood and health'. Certainly, men identify with this. For example, Lex (a 42-year-old managing director, married with four children) writes:

> … one of my favourite meals is steak and I think this is perhaps because I associate it with Dad as it was his special thing that he cooked. It still feels special to me now and I take charge of cooking it in our house.

In this account, meat is not just about its significance in terms of consumption, but its preparation requires special treatment and this is an important household role that he has learned from his father. Tom, as well has a strong 'need' for meat: 'I very rarely order or cook vegetarian. I tend to feel I need meat on my plate'. Adams (1990: 36–7) argues that there is a:

*Kind of symmetrical symbolism between meat and vegetable, mascu-
line and feminine ... men are active and consume foods imbued with
power ... women are passive and consume foods derived from inactive,
immobile forms of life.*

Of course this is an over simplified symmetry, but meat is expensive to produce and has long associations with high cultural capital
and elite status. The relationship between meat and masculinity
raises issues for men who are vegetarians 'as men who refrain from
meat eating may be regarded as repudiating or undermining conventional conceptions of masculinity' (Beardsworth and Keil 1997: 213).
Indeed, in Nath's (2011: 276) Australian study, 'meals without meat
are still widely considered by non-vegetarian men to be feminine
dietary choices, while meat and animal products are the superior
food for a "real" man'. She argues that vegetarian men are engaged
in negotiating their masculine identities within a context in which
meat is associated with sexuality and strength. Ian notes:

*Not keen on vegetarian food because it's a tad insipid unless it's Indian
and there I find a whole range of aromatic spicy tasty dishes. One of
the best was lentils, thick brown and juicy. Had those in Bombay with
fresh cooked coriander nan – fantastic!*

Ian is therefore explaining that if he doesn't have masculine food
(meat) then he has chunky fish (not food that requires picking) or
strong and spicy Indian food. It is notable that vegetarian food is
palatable if it is Indian. It demonstrates cultural omnivorousness, as
vegetarianism is common in Indian culture. The fact that Ian ate this
in Bombay contributes to his cultural capital and potential gourmet
identity. This is about authentic cuisine and 'gourmet' globetrotting,
key elements of epicurean foodways. In Drew's account, he writes
about how he learnt to cook:

*Moved away from home at 19 – that's when cooking became a neces-
sity, moving in with lads, cooking in was the cheapest option and the
deal was if you cooked you did not clean up – so this I think was what
swayed me. Moving to London opened my mind to a number of new
ingredients; Indian friends explained the herbs and that became my first
endeavour into enjoying cooking. People liked my food, so I would cook*

more, and then it became expected, the boys would wait for me to come home to eat, even if I was home late.

Thus, Drew positions himself as one of the lads (not feminine) and acquires additional status from his peers because of his cookery skills. Indeed, he was so good that the boys would wait for him to come home to taste his food. Simon on the other hand notes:

I found myself working in Dublin. It seems an odd place to have an epiphany about cooking, but the combination of the City (it was expensive), my salary as the junior working for an art dealer (meager) and the daughter of one of his clients (yummy), seemed to do the trick. She was pretty and posh; I was skint, but eager. So with a menu from a borrowed cookbook, I queued at the butcher and fishmonger looking for ingredients and advice...

Hence, Simon's route to culinary expertise began in an effort to impress a woman. Connor too notes:

When I was 17 and I left home. I had a girlfriend coming round for dinner and I wanted to do something. So I rang my Aunty and she told me to buy pasta, tinned tomatoes, onions, garlic and some Italian herbs and taught me to make a tomato sauce. I think I have only just understood how to make this sauce good (11 years later) but it was a great starting point as it showed me that you don't need to have magical hands for the kitchen. You just need to be able to follow instructions.

Indeed, Connor, Simon, and Drew position themselves as skilled, experimental experts. Their routes into cookery are almost accidental or contingent, they did not set out to become interested in cookery, it sort of happened, for Simon in order to impress a woman and for Drew he only became interested in a feminised domestic activity (cookery) so he didn't have to participate in another inferior domestic activity (washing up), as if it was a decision between the lesser of two evils. Simon continues:

But I enjoyed the company of chefs, not the provincial journeyman who did it because he couldn't do anything else, but the ones with swagger and a knowing braggadocio, who were in it because no other industry

could put up with them, who rated a person for their sauces, their sour-
dough or skills under pressure. And all the time I ate well, I picked up
knowledge about marbling in meat and rigor mortis in fish, about 'top
heat' and 'bottom lift'.

In Simon's narrative he suggests that although he took up cookery to
impress a woman, he enjoys the company of real 'chefs', or by implication real men, with manly traits such as fearlessness, confidence
and arrogance. Again these men (chefs like himself) are highly skilled,
knowledgeable experts and he is aligning himself with them. He also
ate well, or accrued the culinary capital associated with 'good' food.
His reference to 'bottom lift' also has sexual connotations, reaffirming his interest in the opposite sex. Henry equally draws on forms of
hegemonic masculinities (Connell 2005), but takes a slightly different
approach when writing about the origins of his epicurean foodways:

My mother used to encourage me to help with cooking. Early successes
at school cooking what I realise now were possibly pretty crappy cakes
but were not only enjoyed but I was given praise for even long after they
had been eaten. That encouraged me to take an interest in what was
being cooked and how it all fitted together. I was not much interested in
day-to-day food more the Nasi Goreng (Malay fried rice) and Singapore
curries. My parents had been based in Singapore during the middle
1960s. They had a Muslim Amah who taught my mother how to mix,
grind, choose and use spices.

Henry highlights how he enjoyed being praised for his cookery but
was not interested in feminine domestic practices; instead he demonstrates an early appreciation of the skills his mother acquired from
a Muslim Amah in Singapore. He is therefore indifferent to ordinary
(feminised) everyday foodways, but excited by authentic spices and
he continues:

But I did not really start to cook until I owned my own home and started
entertaining, so [I was] early 20's. Also the feeling of competitive macho
eating at curry houses possibly helped the use of chili. Rather like trying
stronger alcohol like putting Carlsberg extra strong larger in the freezer
so the water freezes and only leaves the alcohol. Why would anyone do
this? Yuk!! But we did.

Again, Henry positions himself as a male 'macho' cook, he draws on hegemonic forms of masculinities associated with beer drinking and hot spicy food (Connell 2005, Gough 2007). Then, when explaining why he started cooking, he adds:

Again possibly [my] competitive urge to produce something people not only liked but would also rave about. I think cookery books helped enormously. One of my earliest complicated dinner parties was wild boar stew with peaches poached in Masala wine, served with sweet chestnuts. This was in the late 1980's when Wild Boar was virtually unheard of and Masala wine almost had to be mail ordered. But it was a great evening and delicious food. All thanks to Keith Floyd. So perhaps TV helped first time cooks feel that they could do it?

There are several forms of hegemonic masculinities at work in Henry's narrative, his references to competition, success, and expertise. These intersect with markers of high cultural capital, such as access to unusual or hard to source ingredients. Henry also makes reference to Keith Floyd, a 'pioneer of modern food television' (Rousseau 2012: xvi) who was 'famous for his eccentricity and because he did what he liked' (Rousseau 2012: xvii). Thus, Henry like Simon aligns himself with the type of approach adopted by 'eccentric' and arrogant chefs. Indeed, working outside of the mainstream, challenging culinary boundaries and not complying with dietary guidelines are ways in which male cooks distance themselves from domestic foodways. Drew also makes reference to a celebrity chef and writes:

Then as I got older got my own place, Jamie became famous and food and cooking became trendy – I would say I was ahead of the curve though already experimenting.

However, whilst Drew aligns himself with Jamie Oliver whose first TV series aired in 1999 (Rousseau 2012), he also positions himself 'ahead' of the game; in the culinary field Drew is an expert and already engaged in appropriate epicurean foodways. Also, in both Drew and Henry's accounts, there is an association made between buying a home or 'getting my own place' and marking this transition by engaging in epicurean foodways. Of course, these are not domestic home-cooked family meals prepared from scratch (Parsons 2014a,

2014b), but experimental and complicated high-end cookery. Hence, for men engaged in epicurean foodways gender and class intersect, this consolidates boundaries and marks their foodways as distinct from everyday domestic and/or feminised foodways. It is notable that in Dave's account of his epicurean foodways, he intersects his education in cookery with his progress in the public sphere. Hence, he writes:

I left home at 18 and went to work and live in London. My first bedsit was in Any Town. I enjoyed food, but couldn't cook – other than fried eggs and beans on toast. After six months of this tedious diet I was rescued by a couple of recently graduated students moved into the bedsit next door. Pam took me under her wing and taught me how to cook – I was hooked and I have loved cooking ever since.

Therefore, Dave like other male gourmets did not necessarily set out to become interested in epicurean foodways, but did so in order to differentiate his cookery from associations with feminised domestic everyday foodways. Thus, Dave continues:

Leap forward to the early 80s I am working for a fashion company based in Any City and gaining a reputation for being a pretty good cook – I was the one at communal barbeques who would take the chicken breast marinated in yoghurt, garlic and lemon juice instead of the usual bangers and burgers (not that there is anything wrong with a good burger or sausage!)

Hence, Dave now has a reputation for being a good cook and fearlessly turning up with non-traditional food at barbeques. His comment about 'good' burgers and sausages is a nod to his cultural omnivorousness and lack of food snobbery. Later, Dave recalls:

A few more years see me working as a senior buyer with the Retail Company in London. This job involved extensive travel particularly to the Far East. I discovered authentic regional Chinese food in Hong Kong, was introduced to the delights of Japanese cuisine and bemused by the delightful presentation yet totally alien flavours of Korean food. However my most astonishing discovery was that of Thai food in Bangkok. I must point out that Thai food was unheard of in early to mid 80s Britain. My first taste was of a chicken, chilli, lemongrass and coconut milk soup garnished with pea aubergines and fresh coriander leaves (I had absolutely never seen or tasted this herb before). It was glorious. It took some time for me to track down a good Thai cookbook in order to delight friends back at home.

Again, Dave like Drew positions himself ahead of the game in terms of epicurean foodways. He is expanding his knowledge and culinary repertoire, travelling the world and developing his tastes. This is not about healthy home-cooked food, but an exploration of the exotic and unusual (Heldke 2003). It is also like all gourmets about the presentation of the self as an accomplished expert cook, well travelled and skilled. In none of these accounts or any of the other men's narratives are they interested in the obligations or responsibilities for feeding the family healthy home-cooked meals from scratch (Parsons 2014a, 2014b). Instead it is about taste, knowledge and participation (Warde et al. 2007), and epicurean foodways as leisure and pleasure and symbols of high cultural capital (Naccarato and LeBesco 2012). Connor similarly writes about his cookery skills and expertise:

Ever since I started cooking my family have been as excited as me. I have got several boxes full of cookbooks some good and some crap. I have developed a little hobby of searching second hand shops for retro cook books, some good, some crap ... but always good as a reference point. I'm sure lard and dripping does have its place (especially for Yorkshire puddings!). So, as I have grown up my cooking skills have developed. I have broadened my repertoire of recipes and recipes from different countries. My basics have improved, my béchamel sauce, how to get pasta al dente, getting the perfect amount of water for basmati rice to cook with the right texture without taking the lid off the pan (if I am honest I am still perfecting that), how to peel tomatoes, the most efficient way to chop garlic and how to pretend that cutting onions doesn't make me cry. (I'm getting better at that)

It is notable that whilst male gourmets are distinguishing their foodways from associations with feminised domesticity, the two women gourmets are inculcated into epicurean foodways through relationships with men, as Dalia notes:

I lived with my future husband on leaving University. He was the cook; I was usually working and would get home late. He introduced me to pasta Tagliatelle with a béchamel sauce, mushrooms and bacon with a breadcrumb topping. I loved his cooking. I began to eat out at restaurants (a very rare occasion when growing up). I remember eating muscles and drinking Chardonnay at about age 22, it felt very grown up.

Dalia makes a connection here between 'growing up' and learning appropriate epicurean foodways. This is also similar to Simon's account in the connections between the sensual pleasures of food and seduction. She continues:

The next big relationship in my life brought about my love affair with food. Again, it was not me who was the cook. My partner introduced/ seduced me with beef fillet cooked medium rare and encrusted with black pepper. We ate lobster and all kinds of fish that I had never tasted – skate, scallops, whitebait, red mullet, hake, and squid. I overdosed on snails and chips and mayo one afternoon and it took me a year to revisit them. My role was KP in the kitchen. I learnt how to make homemade mayonnaise and to make a tomato pasta sauce using my hands (the Italian way). My partner's four children lived with us and they grew up asking 'what is this Dad?' on tasting an oyster and steak pie.

Hence, Dalia positions herself as a pupil in the arts of gastronomy, her junior (inferior) status compared to that of Kitchen Porter (KP) in professional kitchens. Indeed, Dalia is laying the groundwork for her current epicurean status by reference to her rigorous training in the gastronomic arts by the men in her life. This reifies the doxic order that it is men who are experts and skilled in epicurean foodways. Similarly, Paula writes:

I met a gorgeous guy 6 years older, half French and obsessed with food. Started to eat out on regular basis in very good French bistros, would drive into Soho every Sunday morning just to buy pastries and croissants from Maison Bertaux. Started to shop on Berwick St market where even cultivated dandelion available for salads, bought coffee only from Algerian Coffee Stores, and pasta, parma, parmesan, etc. etc. from Fratelli Camisa. TOTAL TRANSFORMATION!!

It is notable that Paula also identifies the necessary French aspects of epicurean tutelage. This includes inculcation into the art of dining out and learning about authentic French and Italian cuisine. She continues:

> *Within the 6 years we were together I watched him cook, and loved the eating out. I swear that once you know what good food tastes like there is no going back. Now I was into red wine, Gitanes, Langan's Brasserie, Le Chef, La Poule au Pot, Café des Amis ... and a series of articles published by the Observer from Anne Willan's book 'La Varenne' started me off on pastry/yeast dough cookery that has caused me to make my own brioche ever since (and for the last 8 years or so, all my own bread). After splitting up with Tom I felt less self-conscious in the kitchen and started to cook in earnest, buying books, eating my way through the Good Food Guide. So by 28 I had gone from embarrassingly bad food habits/diet to ridiculously good ...*

Thus, Paula is thoroughly inculcated into epicurean foodways, from being tutored by her boyfriend to reading appropriate sources and cooking herself. She has developed a taste for fine dining, French and Italian cuisine and these are now part of her cultural habitus, naturalised (Bourdieu 1984). What is clear from Paula's and Dalia's accounts is that they became interested in epicurean foodways and high culinary capital because of their association with men engaged in epicurean foodways or men with access to high cultural capital. This reinforces a doxic order that codes high cultural capital and elite foodways as masculine and therefore domestic everyday foodways as feminine/inferior.

Pleasure and leisure

One of the biggest distinctions between epicurean and family/maternal foodways is the emphasis the gourmet places on leisure and pleasure. Indeed, 'feeding the family' (DeVault 1991) is not a key issue for gourmets in my study. This does not mean they are not interested in cooking for their loved ones, but this is not a domestic responsibility, as Dave claims:

> *Cooking continues to be a passion. It is my way of unwinding at the end of the working day. I almost always cook the evening meal for Ali (my*

partner) and myself. I love cooking for her, particularly her favourite,
Moules Marinières.

Simon too, explains that his everyday cooking decisions are based
on 'which food fad is currently being toyed with in our house'.
This implies that whilst he has a more measured and professional
approach to everyday foodways, his wife is more susceptible to fads
and fashions (Fischler 1980), which he accommodates under duress.
Again, this is about clearly defined gender differences in the home,
even though he is the cook. Drew writes:

Cooking is relaxing to me – if I am cooking for family, small group
or myself from my home kitchen ... I always cook to the audience –
nothing worse than food not being eaten, so if my parents are in town,
I tone down the food, for Angus (friend) no seafood, kids then I like to
have food they can play with dig into and enjoy.

In Ed's narrative his cooking is relaxed and exciting, but not everyday domestic cooking:

I enjoy cooking, but not to the extent that it is an ordeal and a worry.
The whole buzz for me is serving up something that's tasty, and a good
enough reason to get a bunch of my favourite people around the table.

So, for Ed, food is a social event and not a routinised everyday
activity. Generally, for gourmets, domestic, everyday cooking and
shopping is not their primary concern. Larry's response is typical, the
'routine shopping is handled by my wife', whilst he cooks:

Mostly for friends and family. I like to entertain and although Sunday
roast is a favourite, I try to challenge myself from time to time ... I have
recently bought a new full width range/oven and it is definitely getting
used. If I want to do something different, I cast my mind back to the
places I used to work and try to remember menu items.

Later Larry writes:

If I am cooking a dinner party then important choices for me are what
vegetables to serve to complement the main course. I like to include the

less commonly used such as parsnips or asparagus ... I always make my own stock – it's absolutely essential to being able to create a good sauce to go with the meat ... typically I use chicken backs roasted first and then boiled with onions and any vegetables you can no longer use. Often I boil it, cool it and reheat it several times over a couple of days before straining and storing it in jars in the freezer ...

Thus, Larry is detailing his expertise on how to make a good stock; both Simon and Ed notably sent recipes with their narratives, Simon a recipe for 'pumpkin, coconut and cardamom soup' and Ed a recipe for '*pasta con arrabiatta*', adding that 'every student, or indeed anyone on a tight budget should know this one'. It is notable that Larry refers to his recent purchase of a 'full width range/oven'; this is a high status domestic item. Hence, because cultural omnivorousness focuses on male activities and values outside of the domestic sphere, when gourmets bring their culinary practices into the home they are framed within different parameters that change the domestic space. Drew writes, for example:

In doing up my first house in Scotland there was only one concern – I wanted to have a say in the kitchen design – the cooker etc etc – the rest of the house could be bright pink, I did not care as long as the kitchen looked good. Then the final move to a house with a big kitchen such bliss ...

Hence, Drew is making his mark on the domestic space, it is his and not a feminine 'bright pink' space. Indeed, Gough (2006: 387) argues that 'cooking and enjoying diverse cuisine [are] no longer regarded as exclusively women's business', also that 'it is feasible that shopping, cooking and enjoying a greater range of foods have been absorbed into current definitions of masculinity' (Gough 2007: 2481). Thus, in Dave's epicurean narrative journey, he notes:

I proved to be a dab hand in the kitchen and was soon cooking the evening meal a couple of times a week. I not only enjoyed the preparation and cooking but also, much to the astonishment of male friends in the pub football team, the sourcing and buying of ingredients – food shopping in other words!

Hence, although food shopping is usually coded as highly feminised, he counters the potential contamination of this attribute by reference to 'sourcing and buying ingredients', which implies expertise and skill. He was also employed as a 'buyer'. This experience is also framed within the context of the pub and football, which are similarly coded masculine leisure pursuits.

Other gourmets whilst clearly interested in 'good food', did not, like Nick, engage in cooking much at all:

Sally is pretty much in charge of the kitchen so she plans what we eat really. When she's not around she tends to leave food / meal suggestions for me to do for the children. When I am here on my own I tend to revert to bachelordom ... cereal, or toast or fried eggs. Don't really cook for me.

Thus, Nick is reaffirming the cultural norm that divides domestic responsibilities in the home along gender lines. Similarly, Sam writes:

My wife Amelia generally decides what we are going to eat and this is governed by budget and time ... I like to cook but seldom do and I love fresh ingredients ... I am a great fan of fresh veg and my homemade hot chilli sauce is to die for. Nowadays I love to explore the tastes and textures of different foods and find myself very animated while cooking 'Potjiekos' on the fire. Potjiekos is a South African style of cooking in large cast iron pots over an open fire, very slow, all day stews, fabulous! As I have become more at one with food my cooking skills have got better and better, I still don't cook much but enjoy it when I do.

It is notable that Sam, like Henry, previously refers to 'hot' chilli sauce; indeed, spicy foods tend to be coded as masculine. Also, cooking outside of the kitchen on an open fire or a barbeque liberates men from association with domestic feminised cooking practices. Indeed, 'the barbecue seems to quarantine masculinity from conjecture and ridicule about men doing women's work' (Nath 2011: 269). Lex, for example, writes:

I love BBQs and again I think this is associated with being at the cottage and being happy there.

Further, Tom declares: 'when I decide to cook, I'm quite a good cook, but my repertoire is limited. They haven't changed much. Fry-ups and BBQs are my other specialties'. Tom's food references are noticeably fatty and meaty and not healthy or feminine. Cooking is clearly his decision and something he chooses to do outside of the domestic sphere. Walt (a 57-year-old manager, married with three grown up children) is a gourmet, who not only cooks on a BBQ but also claims that:

> *BBQs for 15 is normal for me, I enjoy the artistry of food, the planning, preparation, the balance the mix, colour, tastes, the variety of ingredients. I don't just do it for those who come, but also for the pleasure of the creation.*

So for Walt, the BBQ is an arena for demonstrating culinary skills and expertise, cooking in this way is an art and a performance. It is certainly not everyday domestic cooking. In Ian's account he writes:

> *Not much I won't eat really. Bit more on the meat than fish side. Find vegetarian (if not Indian a little dull). I am more meat than veg and the fish I prefer is white and chunky I also enjoy smoked fish ... Some times I like to cook, this could be a roast lunch, casserole, curry but that generally take the edge my appetite. I didn't find (learning to cook) it too hard. I could follow a cookbook; ring my mum or a pal (generally female). It was Ok to make mistakes. Yes family and relations, friends but not every day ... I would say not. But I find myself buying coriander, balsamic vinegar and virgin olive oil ...*

Ian therefore includes several references to traditionally coded masculine foodways such as preferences for spicy, meaty food. He has also experienced authentic global cuisines and is engaged in contemporary epicurean foodways with his reference to coriander, balsamic vinegar and olive oil. He can cook if he wants to and make mistakes. In Drew's narrative, he is similarly not engaged in everyday domestic foodways. He notes:

> *Some of my favourite food moments have been shared with another foodie friend in Any Village, marinating bits of pig and roasting them, in fact spending all day cooking them and then devouring it with a good*

bottle of wine. Then waking up and realizing you have left overs for breakfast – that has to be some of the best food moments. I love food and the best way to get to try this used to be cooking it. My wife laughs about me sneaking off to the summerhouse with a bottle of wine and my 'porn collection', which actually consists of one of my many, many, cookbooks – working out what to cook next and how to cook it. I miss that about Home country and having the facilities to do that. Guess I shouldn't complain about being cooked for, but cooking was my relaxation, my Saturday night in, my Sunday afternoon.

Thus, Drew's gourmet identity encompasses hegemonic masculinities, as well as sensual experiences that are part of an elite cultural habitus (Bourdieu 1984). It is about pleasure and sex, as evidenced in Simon's narrative when he claims he learned to cook in order to 'schmooze the ladies' and in Drew's with his reference to his cookery books as his 'porn collection'. That Drew feels compelled to describe his interest in cookery books in such a highly sexualised and macho way demonstrates the power of hetero-normative cultural scripts around everyday foodways. The reference to a 'porn collection' isn't 'food porn' (which is something else), but a collection of books about cookery. Instead of 'sneaking off' to look at pornography, which is articulated as almost acceptable within the boundaries of hetero-normative masculinity (his wife knows about it so its okay) he is taking a bottle of wine with him (which adds to the sense of this being a sexual or sensual encounter) to his shed to read his cookery books. So, Drew cannot admit to reading about food unless it is presented in terms of a highly sexualised male activity (Connell 2005). Indeed, gourmet narratives can be read in direct contrast to traditional feminised foodways examined in earlier research (Charles and Kerr 1988, DeVault 1991). It is difficult to imagine a woman discussing the week's family food menu in this way. The male gourmets in Cairn et al.'s (2010) study, as in mine did not engage in food work as care work, and the women in their study who self identified as foodies tended to engage in both.

External influences and eating out

High cultural capital is associated with a gourmet identity; thus, a feel for the game and playing in a culinary field is important

(Bourdieu 1984). This means engaging in debates and discussions or 'talk' about food, through blogs, specialised magazines, cookbooks and TV programmes. Hence, Dave notes:

Nigel Slater is number one for me. As well as wearing glasses he has a very unpretentious way about him, his recipes work and he likes simple everyday food as well as the more exotic. He is an advocate of good fresh ingredients without shoving the organic mantra down your throat! His recipe for a sausage sandwich can't be beat ... Jamie Oliver – good variety of recipes – everyone tried has worked – some have become staples in our house e.g. Sticky Chicken. Doesn't mess about too much with classic recipes (why change proven recipes?) ... Ainsley Harriot – exceptionally good barbecue recipe book – his pork spare ribs with maple syrup is THE default recipe! Nigella Lawson – Don't particularly like her TV shows, but her book on baking is fab. Hugh Fernley Fernley – some good recipes, however far too up his own backside with the organic mantra – who in their right mind would pay £22 (yes twenty two of your English pounds) for a medium sized organic chicken from his shop in Axminster? Delia – Hmmm ... Not a favourite. Messes about far too much with classic recipes in an attempt to make them her own (see Jamie Oliver above) and another thing! How can you trust a chef who doesn't taste their food as they go along to ensure flavour and seasonings are correct? Delia has never tasted the food prepared on her shows; in fact she completely disagrees with doing so.

Hence, Dave is keen to demonstrate his acquaintance with a range of popular TV chefs in keeping with his position as cultural omnivore. He expresses cultural hostility towards organic food and the chef that appeals to this sector; in keeping with a 'chowhound' identity he is asserting his breadth of knowledge and unwillingness to follow food trends (Naccarato and LeBesco 2012). Dalia on the other hand identifies herself with more of the high-end chefs/food writers:

It was my discovery of chef, David Everitt Matthius that really took me a stage further in my cooking and gave me a taste for wild food and foraging. I have had some favourite chefs – and some who I didn't get on with at all. Margarite Patten was my worst enemy. I blamed her recipes. Everything I cooked from one of her books was a disaster. This was at the beginning of my cooking, so I can't be sure that it was her fault.

I hated her none the less. Keith Floyd, Jamie Oliver, Rick Stein, Gordon Ramsey have been favourites. Now I covet my books by Pierre Gagnaire, Vineet Bhatia, Anthony Bourdain, David Everitt Matthius and Noma.

It is notable that men/experts in epicurean foodways have written the majority of the tomes that Dalia covets. Drew, as a cultural omnivore discusses his familiarity with both high-end restaurants and popular TV chefs:

Favorites to date are Roux at the Landau and Wishart at Cameron House ... But food is not just about the food it is about the experience, and if I could pick one restaurant to go back to it would be Monachly Mhor with chef Tom Lewis (small country farmhouse middle of nowhere, own grown veg's and raised animals) it is a all encompassing, relaxing food experience ... Other chefs I like but for different reasons, Glynn Purnell as he is in my home town of Birmingham not known for its food and putting it on the map (he is what I maybe could have been if I knew I enjoyed food at an earlier age) ... Jamie – as it was his simple recipes that really got me cooking although I have no real desire to eat at one of his restaurants ... Heston is a legend, I have a number of old cook books 1890s through to 1930s and what I see is that many recipes today are cyclical, reappearing and becoming fashionable, these are the classics and many chefs are good at preparing them or even adding a twist. But Heston has revolutionised how I think about food and challenged psychology around eating food – sadly I have never eaten at his restaurant but he does fascinate me.

Notably, Drew aligns himself with the Michelin starred chef Glynn Purnell, but distinguishes between popular TV chefs like Jamie Oliver with his mass appeal and Heston Blumenthal, who has revolutionised how he thinks about food. There are clearly further divisions and distinctions within culinary fields (Naccarato and LeBesco 2012, DeSolier 2013). Indeed, specialised knowledge and understanding is significant in building a gourmet identity.

Therefore, epicurean foodways includes 'gourmet globetrotting, as finding new and exciting cuisines earns a kind of social status' (Johnston and Baumann's 2010: 98–100). This underlines the extent to which a gourmet identity is linked to elite status and cultural capital. It is about confirming one's belonging to a group that is able to travel the world and to experience exotic cuisines first hand. Thus, 'cultural capital is required to appreciate foodie discourse and discern which features of exoticism are worth pursuing' (Johnston and Baumann 2010: 104). Hence, Fred writes:

> *I love Thai and Japanese and Indian and that modern English vibe. I love sashimi. I don't really eat potatoes or much pasta (or indeed carbs). Totally favourite specific food items would be soft shell crab tempura, a rib of beef for two (the best one ever is sold at the Anchor & Hope in Waterloo). I love almost all vegetables (especially raw). Some of the best food I've had at shacks (I remember salt cod fritters in Mexico and hawker food in Singapore). My two best restaurants in the world would be Gordon Ramsay, Hospital Road, Brompton and Tetsuya, Sydney, Australia. With both its as much about the experience as the exquisite food.*

Indeed, as noted earlier, the gourmets in my study have a lot in common with Heldke's (2003) 'foodie adventurers'. However, she claims that 'we like our exoticism somewhat familiar, recognisable, controllable' Heldke (2003: 19). Similarly, gourmets in Johnston and Baumann's (2010) study 'avoided norm breaking exotic food', so they 'concluded that the assumptions about gourmets interest in global cuisine is overstated and that whilst ... norm breaking foods generated foodie cachet, most of the gourmets ... are generally not interested in adhering to that standard' (Johnston and Baumann's 2010: 120–1). Of course, this may have been because of the number of female gourmets that they had in their sample who are also engaged in family foodways. The gourmets in my study are interested in the exotic. Perhaps the addition of hegemonic masculinities to the foodie mix increases the desire to impress in terms of strange and exotic food consumption. For example, Ed writes:

> *Whilst cruising down through the Windward Island chain in the Caribbean towards Trinidad, we stopped off on the French island of Martinique. It was a Sunday, and we decided we'd have a day ashore and a lunch ... After wandering around looking for an interesting place to eat that wasn't on the tourist track, we stopped at a slightly run down, though brightly painted looking place. There was no menu; just*

*what was being served that day – salad, chicken curry, and a selection
of tropical fruit. The salad appeared, a large plate laden with colourful
ingredients including avocado and shrimp, and what appeared to be
diced beetroot. Feeling pleased with the results of our determined search
for somewhere that didn't serve burgers, we toasted our good luck with
chilled beer. After a while we started talking about the odd taste of the
beetroot, and how it didn't taste cooked or pickled. Finally, it dawned on
[one of our companions] that she had heard of this dish years previously
when she was a student doing her year out in France. The 'beetroot' was
neither cooked nor pickled; it was finely diced cow's nose.*

Indeed, it is within the realm of eating offal that the test of a
true gourmet or food adventurer comes in to play, as 'when food
flagrantly violates social or culinary conventions, it creates a bold
spectacle of norm breaking exoticism and this is especially evident
in the gourmet focus on eating offal' (Johnston and Baumann 2010:
120). Offal is the foodstuff that elicited disgust for the majority of
respondents, as Henry comments:

*I never liked insides, so heart, liver, kidneys etc. I have always loathed. I
did try lamb hearts recently and realised why steak is so popular! I was
also once confused by a foreign menu and ordered calf's brain, sorry I
just had to go and be sick, and pride forced me to eat the lot. Not as
bad tasting, as you would think just a friable texture ... sorry had to be
sick again, which stuck in my mind.*

Henry's narrative is a gourmet journey of training, exploring his
palate and developing epicurean foodways, yet even for Henry some
foods are off limits and his distaste is so strong that he has to rush off
to be sick. Beyond the physiology of taste, this cultural and almost
universal 'distaste' is related to the concept of eating food associated
with 'insides' and 'waste' or what Douglas (1966) referred to as 'pollutants'. These pollutants are associated with feminine, 'unclean'
bodily fluids/parts, menstruation and so on (Fiddes 1991, Douglas
1966). The 'distaste' for offal also arises due to its use as a cheap
substitute for more expensive parts of the animal and a distancing
from foodways that used a lot of offal in the past. However, there
are 'gourmets' for whom eating offal is a sign of a true gourmet and

this intersects with notions of 'bravery' as a marker of hegemonic masculinity, as Drew writes:

> *Talking of Beijing – let me share my favourite restaurant story – I was in Beijing with an Australian and American colleague. Having found a good local restaurant and persuaded them to eat there. We sat and perused the menu. Peking duck was a must and we selected some other dishes. Then I saw Devilled Duck Hearts as side dish and asked the waiter for a small bowl, as I was fascinated. They appeared small purple and plump covered in chilli oil and I started to eat them. I was asked by my colleagues what I was eating and advised – 'duck hearts', 'no your not' was the response 'they are olives' – 'no they are duck hearts' I advised, although they did look like big olives. 'Shut up and give me an olive' was the response. Handing the bowl over they carefully selected an 'olive' each. And synchronised placed them in their mouths. Instant reaction, one swallowed and swore the other nearly threw up in a napkin. 'They are duck hearts – why didn't you tell me' – this was probably the first time I have been reprimanded for telling the truth. Gladly I finished the bowl myself.*

It is hardly surprising therefore when considering high levels of cultural capital amongst gourmets, that not only are they often from a high status elite group, but that they would engage in hegemonic masculinities.

Overall, a gourmet identity is not coded as feminine and gourmets are 'doing' epicurean foodways by reference to masculine cultural codes. These are not family or maternal foodways that centre on notions of obligation and responsibility. Gourmets are not preparing endless routinised meals for their families and they are not nurturing or feeding the family in De Vault's (1991) sense of the term. Neither do they express any interest in the 'healthiness' or otherwise of their foodways. Instead, they are building upon and adding to knowledge, status and expertise regarding all aspects of epicurean foodways.

Hence, male respondents engage in hegemonic masculinities and distance themselves from association with feminised activities such as vegetarianism, healthy eating or weight loss, with references to sex or alcohol or drugs or other risk-taking activities. Everyday masculine foodways are leisure activities freely chosen and not part of a heteronormative feminised approach. Further, men who participate in epicurean foodways and develop a gourmet identity also draw upon forms of hegemonic masculinities. The high cultural capital, elite status, cultural omnivorousness, knowledge and expertise associated with a gourmet identity though coded masculine is not far enough away from contemporary feminised domestic foodways.

Hence, shopping and cooking rather than being highly feminised domestic activities are also re-contextualised as part of a search for authentic or exotic cuisine, as well as an expression of expert knowledge, 'taste' and distinction. Thus, I argue a gourmet identity is a masculine one, that assumes high levels of economic, social, symbolic and cultural capital including elements of high adventure and risk-taking.

7
Reflections

This book clearly demonstrates the extent to which everyday food-ways are infused with the intersectionalities of gender and class. The focus has been on the intimacies and intricacies of relations within the domestic sphere. Respondent narratives highlight the interconnectedness of the self with 'other' as well as with wider socio-cultural and structural norms and values. When articulating one's identity it is difficult to avoid 'common vocabularies' (Mills 1959). In the telling of the self it is necessary to connect with recognisable cultural scripts. What it means to be a middle class woman or man in twenty-first century neo-liberal consumer capitalist societies is embedded in discourses of responsible individualism. However, despite a commitment to this ideology, identities are difficult to define beyond the meta-narratives of modernity and without recourse to dichotomous thinking (Oakley 1992) or the binary oppositions that help create/re-create gender and class. These Cartesian dualisms continue to draw and re-draw the boundaries between/within social groups, not least on the basis of gender and class. In contemporary neo-liberal westernised societies the atomised individual free from social obligations is coded male (Lewis 2007), as women continue to be judged in terms of a selfless, seemingly 'natural' feminine disposition. Thus, living one's own life, whilst being there for others is part of a contradictory, yet enduring cultural script of 'appropriate' middle class femininity.

Hence the symbolic violence (Bourdieu and Wacquant 2002) afforded to women, especially mothers who transgress the boundaries of 'appropriate' middle class mothering norms. This is most evident in the abiding symbol of the 'working class Mum' who feeds her 'kid' 'cheese and chips out of a Styrofoam container' (Parsons 2014a). Indeed, when considering the power of everyday foodways in contributing to a sense of self and belonging this imagery 'works' on several levels. Firstly, it positions women as primarily responsible for the nourishment and nurturing of children and therefore society, as part of a natural doxic order. Secondly, it suggests that there are identifiable cultural codes, rules and rituals around everyday foodways. Thirdly, that 'proper' foodways can be located in diametric opposition to the quick, cheap, mass-produced, instant gratification implied here. Thus, those that 'lack' access to cultural resources or fail to abide by public policy discourses on 'healthy' foodways are subject to moral approbation and stigma. This is not to assume that health or healthiness are easily definable, just that there is a persistent absolutist approach to 'good'/'bad' foodways and in a contemporary foodscape 'good' is associated with what is beneficial for health.

Of course, 'good' foodways as evidenced throughout this book are about health, yet for a small number of respondents references to health were noticeably absent. Instead for epicureans, everyday foodways are connected to the display of elite cultural practices that emphasise sensual pleasure (Waley-Cohen 2007) and leisure. Indeed, in the gendering of everyday foodways there are unremitting distinctions between food work and food play within the domestic sphere, with the former coded as feminine and the latter masculine. For example, feeding the family (DeVault 1991) is emotional work carried out in the home for the benefit of family members and a persistently feminised activity. Epicurean foodways on the other hand are highly individualised performances of elite cultural or culinary capital (Nacaratto and LeBesco 2012) in the pursuit of taste, knowledge and participation. Hence, there is a persistent gendered division of labour within the domestic sphere that ensures women are wholly responsible for food work, which has low cultural capital, whilst men play in a culinary field, which has higher cultural capital.

However, in a contemporary foodscape high cultural capital is also expressed through appropriate family foodways, a distaste of convenience/commercial foodways, preferences for healthy home-cooked food, authentic cuisine and cultural omnivorousness. Hence, respondents articulate a strong cultural hostility towards convenience/commercial foodways in favour of healthy home-cooked food prepared from scratch, home-baking (cakes and snacks) and home-grown produce. This represents a distinct shift away from the excessive industrialisation of food production (Mennell 1985) in favour of a glorification of feminine domesticity (Negra 2009) and a kind of 'noshtalgia' (Becket et al. 2002). There is also cultural hostility expressed towards what might be considered bodies out of control, that is those deemed to be too fat or too thin. Similarly, when negotiating boundaries around health foodways, respondents often (though not always) lapsed strict dietary regimes for the purposes of commensality or sociability, therefore recognising the importance of legitimate cultural capital and playing by the rules of the game in a culinary field. Thus, everyday foodways centre on distancing the self from association with commercial/convenience foodways, displaying responsible individualism, negotiating a middle ground (not being too thin or too fat) and/or participating in epicurean pleasures.

Indeed respondents' everyday foodways reflect current UK political concerns and public policies with regards to the role of the family, healthy eating, eating for health, eating disorders, 'fat' bodies and elite foodways. Hence, whilst individuals are supposedly free to make rational choices, it is apparent in respondents' narratives that gender and class bind them. An auto/biographical approach to foodways is therefore significant in highlighting the interconnectedness of the individual and the social (Morgan 1998), the micro and the macro, the private and the public. Generally, both men and women displayed cultural hostility towards convenience/commercial foodways, which are simultaneously lacking, in terms of a lack of care (time, money), and excessive, as mass-produced food for the masses. Thus, feeding the family healthy home-cooked food prepared from scratch is a means of performing, displaying and reproducing a middle class habitus and drawing distinctions within culinary fields (Parsons 2014a, 2014b). Further, having time for taste, participation and knowledge of contemporary family, maternal, health, embodied and/or epicurean foodways demonstrates a cultural omnivorousness, which is a significant aspect of high cultural capital.

The original aim of the research on which this book is based centred on a misplaced notion that individuals make food choices free from wider structural constraints. This was set against a background of public policy debates in the UK tasked with educating families to make appropriate healthy food choices (DOH 2010, 2011). However, there is a lack of fit between public policy initiatives that emphasise individual choice and the lived reality in which there is often no choice. Indeed, 'choice' is part of an individual affective practice (Wetherell 2012) that sediments over time rather than a rational and deliberate act. It is bound by a middle class cultural habitus that values neo-liberal politics and responsible individualism. Indeed, individuals articulate everyday foodways with a 'common vocabulary' (Mills 1959), they utilise specific forms of social, symbolic and cultural capital (Bourdieu 1984) further embedded in cultural scripts of hetero-normative femininities and masculinities, particularly in terms of cultural practices and values in the fields of mothering and gastronomy.

Thus, notions of 'choice' continue to be influenced by the inter-sectionalities of gender and class. In effect they are hardly choices at all. For example, in the field of culinary arts an epicurean represents a particular gendered habitus in which femininity rarely operates as symbolic capital. Also, when feeding the family, aspects associated with intensive mothering (Hays 1996) are significant and respondents adhere to traditional gender roles in pursuit of a glorified feminised domesticity (Negra 2009). There is little evidence of a negotiated family model (Beck and Beck-Gernsheim 2002). Hence, whilst women make inroads into the public sphere and despite the blurring of boundaries between work/home (Hochschild 1997, Hochschild and Machung 2003), most women are excluded from cultural fields of play where 'foodies' and 'chowhounds' roam (Naccarato and LeBesco 2012), particularly if they have responsibility for feeding the family (DeVault 1991). Today in an era of 'yummy mummies' (Allen and Osgood 2009, Littler 2013) and public health discourses, there is the added pressure of feeding the family healthy home-cooked meals from scratch (Pollan 2013), which functions as a symbolic reification and valorisation of a middle class maternal identity. When women engage in intensive mothering (Hays 1996) how can they have time to be epicureans? Similarly, a concern with health and weight counters the unbounded pleasures of sensual eating (epicurean foodways).

Further, when considering maternal identities, what it means to be a mother is not answered internally, but is addressed by a reflexive awareness of what other 'good' mothers do (Dawson 2012). Neo-liberal policies and discourses conceptualise 'good' mothering as a consumer choice that requires economic capital. In effect, middle class mothering practices are presented as the norm and others pathologised. Hence, the intersectionalities of gender and class determine access to resources – education, employment, health – and these remain significant in providing a sense of ontological security (Dawson 2012: 311).

Indeed, respondents' everyday foodways are embedded in family and kinship relations, with family practices (Morgan 1996) considered a source of social, symbolic and cultural capital. Certainly, whilst respondents are indignant at not being treated as individuals within the families of their childhoods, there are limits to the 'right to a life of one's own' (Beck and Beck-Gernsheim 2002: xxii). Women especially, found negotiating an individualist agenda when responsible for others health and welfare, problematic. Hence, the gendered division of labour persists and continues to marginalise and exclude those engaged in family food work from the field of culinary cultural capital.

The epicurean field is elitist and geared towards those with time and/or money. Indeed in 'foodie' studies (Cairns et al. 2010, Johnston and Baumann 2010), taste is contextualised as an essential element of a consumer activity that centres on leisure time or time for leisure. This supposes a clear distinction between work and leisure, which is not the case for many women (Hochschild 1997, Hochschild and Machung 2003). It is pertinent that in this study an epicurean identity is predominantly male. Indeed, many markers of cultural capital are associated with what might be considered traditionally male leisure activities. It is men who have time to play.

Hence, as noted throughout the book, the 'micro-politics of food revolve around gender' (Morgan 1996: 158) and exploring gender is therefore vital when looking to understand relationships with food over the life course. Women conform to cultural scripts of heteronormative femininity when examining their attitudes to food, the body, health, emotion, mothering and relationships. Women develop a sense of 'lipoliteracy' (reading bodies, from Graham 2005) and engage in 'fat talk' (Ambjörnsson 2005) as a means of doing gender (West and Zimmerman 1987). Men resort to forms of hegemonic masculinities (Connell 2005) when distancing themselves from traditionally feminised practices, such as healthy eating and dieting. Even when espousing an epicurean identity, men differentiate their interest in foodways, such as food shopping and cooking from the feminised domestic practices associated with feeding the family (DeVault 1991). These gendered identities are classed and associated with social, symbolic and cultural capital. Hence, an epicurean identity is predominantly (though not exclusively) male and associated with elite cultural status. Maternal identity is similarly associated with distinction. Feeding the family healthy home-cooked food from scratch is an element of intensive mothering (Hays 1996) and as such, is used to demonstrate engagement with middle class cultural norms and values.

It was anticipated that health discourses would impact on foodways and that weight loss and dietary management would be a concern for women. Indeed, the impact of health discourses on foodways is strongest within the women's narratives. The public and media discourses regarding a perceived obesity epidemic (Gard 2009) fed directly into the role of women as the guardians of health, both their own and other people's. Indeed, women's narratives are infused with concerns regarding health and healthiness. This is occasionally related to weight management. However, health is not a major consideration in men's narratives. If health is mentioned it tends to be couched in terms of a 'hum' in the background or because a girlfriend was interested to see if eating healthily made any difference. It did not. The feminisation of health and the notion that being concerned about one's health is feminine has implications in terms of health policy. The problem of hegemonic masculinities in relation to health behaviour has been well documented in research elsewhere (Gough 2006, 2007, 2009). The continued government focus on families to change their behaviour belies the fact that it is women who are charged with this task within families/society. Yet, unless health foodways are considered masculine or coded elite, they are likely to continue to be marginalised as feminine concerns and/ or associated with 'other' foodways.

When dietary regimes are used as CAM, men and women use food as a means of treating certain conditions, the avoidance of dairy, for example, as a route to treating childhood eczema. However, as already noted, being concerned with health is part of a cultural script of femininity. Hence, it is mainly women who practice CAM. Thus, specific dietary management practices were used to treat conditions, notably IBS, food intolerances and drug resistant epilepsy in childhood. Some food culture scholars argue that strict dietary regimes represent a means of imposing restraint in the face of increased nor-mlessness around eating. Fischler (1980, 1988, 2011), for example, has long insisted on a kind of gastro-anomy at work, with a decline in the social rules and rituals associated with commensality (eating together). Respondents practising health foodways highlight some of the problems associated with negotiating social aspects of every-day foodways, and this valorises its continued significance. Hence, in terms of public policy a focus on individual choice neglects the myriad ways in which individuals negotiate their social identities and these are important.

Overall, the intersectionalities of gender and class remain signifi-cant when documenting relationships with food over the life course. These gendered identities are classed and respondents are concerned to position themselves with high cultural capital, whether they are epicureans, or engaged in aspirational mothering practices or health conscious. The extent to which class and gender continue to influence everyday foodways is important. This has implica-tions for implementing and developing policies that look to change individual eating/lifestyle behaviours, especially those policy initia-tives that focus on individual choice without acknowledging wider structural inequalities. Of course, this persistence of gender and class might be related to the ages of respondents in my study – there were none between the ages of 18–25. This may be worth considering in terms of future research. Further, those with negative working class experiences as children were keen to distance themselves from the food of their childhoods, a form of neophilia (Lupton 1996) and mat-rophobia (Rich 1986). This is also part of displaying a middle class habitus, as cultural hostility is an expression of disgust towards poor nutrition, poor food and therefore poverty itself. Yet, not everyone escapes a poor background. This has consequences for those trapped in poverty and reinforces the extent to which everyday foodways are embedded in class identities. It reifies distinctions between those who lack on many levels, including lack of access to resources, taste and cultural capital.

Indeed, taste on many levels is associated with social stratifica-tion and respondents engage in positioning themselves within a hierarchy of middle class values. Thus, the impact of individualist discourses on foodways is limited by the intersectionalities of gender and class. Far from a cacophony of individual tastes and experiences, individuals are constrained by desire. This manifests itself in a longing to belong. Thus, respondents comply with a gendered middle class habitus that values health and self-care or responsible individualism. For epicureans, this is expressed through cultural omnivorousness and food adventurism. Indeed, the individual is embedded in a particular social and cultural milieu and this impacts upon identity. In the current foodscape everyday foodways can be used as a means of demonstrating elite status and power. Cultural hostility persists and reinforces boundaries between social groups around what might be considered appropriate food and foodways. Generally, respondents did not express an interest in ethical concerns regarding everyday foodways. Instead, they provided everyday glimpses into the intimacies of domestic life.

In the final analysis, an auto/biographical approach makes a unique contribution in the field of food studies, as it provides in-depth, rich data on individual foodways over the life course. These include common vocabularies and are relational. In this book the focus is on foodways from women *and* men. This is deliberate in order to counter the recent upsurge of interest in men/masculinities in the domestic sphere, whether this is a focus on the male role in 'families' (Jackson et al. 2009) or in the kitchen (Cairns et al. 2010) or as 'food adventurers' (Heldke 2003). Notably, despite differences in how these interests are framed, men/masculine identities are not tasked with the responsibility for feeding the family as part of a cultural script of what it means to be a 'good' middle class mother. Hence, the emphasis on men in the domestic sphere negates the impact of responsible individualism and middle class cultural norms on the performance of femininity; it is women who are considered wholly 'responsible' for feeding (socialising) the family and therefore inculcating appropriate cultural norms and values. This reifies a doxic order that it is natural/normal and therefore unworthy of comment for women to work at feeding the family or indeed any other selfless care work activity. Thus, women are written out of the domestic foodscape, their contributions so naturalised, so taken for granted that they no longer need to be mentioned or researched. This has implications beyond everyday domestic foodways, as men and women negotiate their positions infused with the intersectionalities of gender and class. This book therefore goes some way to redressing this imbalance.

Appendix: Respondent demographics

Name	A	Occupation	Quals	Living arrangements	N
				Female respondents	
Alison	49	Teacher	Degree	Co-habiting	GB
Annie	50	Life Coach	A' level	Divorced +2 +3 G/U	GB
Beth	57	Housewife	P/G Dip	Married +2 children	GB
Bryony	33	PhD Student	P/G	Co-habiting	BM
Carly	46	Consultant	Degree	Co-habiting	GB
Celia	85	Retired farmer's wife	SRN	Married +4 G/U	GB
Chloe	46	Occ. Health Advisor	Degree	Co-habiting +2 +1 G/U	GB
Daisy	73	Social Worker	Degree	Married +3 G/U	GB
Dalia	50	Painter	Degree	Co-habiting	GB
Edith	54	Arts Coordinator	Degree	Divorced +1 +2 G/U	GB
Ellen	61	Dance Teacher	A 'level	Divorced	GB
Faith	30	TA	P/G	Married +2 children	ZB
Faye	46	Secretary	GCSE*	Married +1 child	GB
Gaby	51	Architect Designer	Degree	Married +2 G/U	GB
Harriet	64	Housewife	Life/SRN	Married +3 G/U	GB
Hannah	43	Secretary	GCSE*	Married +2 G/U	GB
Helen	54	Publisher	Diploma	Married +2 + 1 G/U	GB
Ida	54	Midwife	Degree	Married +2 G/U	GB
Imogen	36	Housekeeper	NVQ	Married +4 children	GB
Jade	37	Architect	P/G	Single	NL
Jocelyn	44	Shop Manager	GCSE*	Married +3 children	GB
Katrina	43	Pre-School teacher	Degree	Married +2 +1 G/U	GB
Kelly	30	PhD Student	P/G	Single	BG
Laura	35	Teaching Assistant	A 'level	Married +2 children	GB
Linda	67	Housewife	Diploma	Divorced +3 G/U	GB
Lola	40	PhD Student	P/G	Married +3 children	GB
Magenta	38	Academic	PhD	Single	GB
Melissa	46	Viola Player	GCSE*	Married +2 children	GB
Molly	45	Housewife	GCSE*	Co-habiting +4 children	GB
Nadia	40	Artist	Degree	Co-habiting +1 child	AU
Noreen	40	Housewife	GCSE*	Co-Habiting +2 children	GB
Olivia	37	PR Manager	Degree	Co-habiting	GB

(*continued*)

Appendix: continued

Name	A	Occupation	Quals	Living arrangements	N
Ophelia	53	Author	GCSE*	Married + 2 children	GB
Otaline	32	PhD Student	P/G	Co-habiting +1 child	GB
Paloma	47	Lecturer	P/G	Married +1 +1 G/U	GB
Paula	55	Food Writer	Degree	Married +2 G/U	GB
Queenie	62	Retired Hairdresser	GCSE*	Married	GB
Regan	48	Housewife	GCSE*	Married +2 children	GB
Ruth	47	MD	Degree	Married +2 children	GB
Sasha	50	Academic	PhD	Single	US
Steph	39	Housewife	Degree	Co-habiting +2 children	GB
Tammy	63	Guest House Owner	GCSE*	Married	GB
Tilda	53	Nurse	Degree	Single	GB
Ulrika	46	Property Developer	Degree	Single	GB
Ursula	52	Housewife	A' level	Married +2 +1 G/U	GB
Valerie	46	Website Manager	A' level	Single +1 child	GB
Vera	59	Shop Assistant	Degree	Divorced +2 G/U	GB
Willow	55	Senior Lecturer	Degree	Single +1 G/U	GB
Zoe	44	Recruiter	Degree	Married +2 children	GB

Male respondents

Name	A	Occupation	Quals	Living arrangements	N
Charlie	49	Consultant	GCSE*	Co-habiting	GB
Connor	27	Musician	BTEC	Single	GB
Dave	59	Consultant	GCSE*	Co-habiting	GB
Drew	42	Senior Manager	P/G	Married +1 child	GB
Ed	55	Carpenter	GCSE*	Co-habiting +1 S/C	GB
Fred	39	Solicitor	P/G	Single	GB
Gerry	47	Solicitor	P/G	Co-habiting	GB
Henry	42	Director	GCSE*	Married +2 S/C	GB
Ian	64	Management Trainer	GCSE*	Married +3 children	GB
Jake	48	MD	P/G	Married +1 +1 G/U	GB
James	68	PLC Director	Degree	Married +3 G/U	GB
Kevin	47	Consultant	Degree	Co-habiting + 2 children	GB
Larry	48	MD	GCSE*	Married +2 children	GB
Lex	42	MD	GCSE*	Married +4 children	GB
Mark	45	Consultant	Degree	Married +3 children	GB
Nick	51	Consultant	Degree	Married +2 children	GB
Ollie	44	Teacher	Degree	Married +2 children	GB
Paul	67	Guest House Owner	GCSE*	Married +3 G/U	GB
Quentin	60	Sales Rep	A' level	Married	GB
Richard	76	Retired Academic	P/G	Married +3 G/U	GB

(continued)

Appendix: continued

Name	A	Occupation	Quals	Living arrangements	N
			Male respondents		
Roger	55	Writer	HND	Single	GB
Sam	50	Yachtsman	HND	Married +1 child	GB
Simon	55	Private Cook	GCSE*	Married +1 child	GB
Stephen	53	General Practitioner	Degree	Married +2 G/U	GB
Tom	37	Occupational Therapist	Degree	Married +1 child	GB
Walt	57	Management	Diploma	Married +3 G/U	IT

Key:

A = Age

TA = Teaching Assistant

SRN = State Registered Nurse

MD = Managing Director

Quals = Highest Qualification

P/G = Post Graduate

P/G Dip = Post Gradate Diploma

GCSE* = GCSE Equivalent

+1/2/3 = Number of children currently living in the family home

G/U = Grown up children, no longer living in the family home

S/C = step children

N = Nationality

References

Adams, C. (1990) *The Sexual Politics of Meat: A Feminist Vegetarian Critical Theory*, New York: Continuum.

Adkins, L. (2004) Introduction: Feminism, Bourdieu and After, in Adkins, L. and Skeggs, B. (eds) *Feminism After Bourdieu*, Oxford: Blackwell, pp. 1–3.

Adkins, L. (2011) Practice as Temporalisation: Bourdieu and Economic Crisis, in Susen, S. and Turner, B. (eds) *The Legacy of Pierre Bourdieu: Critical Essays*, London: Anthem Press, pp. 347–366.

Adkins, L. and Jokinen, E. (2008) Introduction: Gender, living and the fourth shift, *Nordic Journal of Feminist and Gender Research*, 16: 3, 138–149.

Adkins, L. and Lury, C. (1999) The labour of identity: Performing identities, performing economies, *Economy and Society*, 28, 598–614.

Adkins, L. and Skeggs, B. (2004) *Feminism After Bourdieu*, Oxford: Blackwell.

Allen, K. and Osgood, J. (2009) Young women negotiating maternal subjectivities: The significance of social class, *Studies in the Maternal*, 1: 2, unpaginated. http://www.mamsie.bbk.ac.uk/documents/allen-osgood.pdf.

Allen, P. and Sachs, C. (2007) Women and food chains: The gendered politics of food, *International Journal of Sociology of Food and Agriculture*, 15: 1, 1–23.

Ambjörnsson, F. (2005) Talk, in Kulick, D. and Meneley, A. (eds), *Fat the Anthropology of an Obsession*, New York: Jeremy P. Tarcher/Penguin, pp. 109–120.

Andreou, A. (2013) Jamie Oliver, you haven't tasted real poverty, Cut out the tutting, *The Guardian*, Tuesday 27th August, accessed 28/August/2013 http://www.theguardian.com/commentisfree/2013/aug/27/jamie-oliver-poverty-ready-meals-tv.

Aphramor, L. (2010) Validity of claims in weight management: A review of dietetic literature, *Nutrition Journal*, 9: 30, 1–9, http://www.nutritionj.com/content/pdf/1475-2891-9-30.pdf.

Arendt, H. ([1929] 1996) *Love and Saint Augustine*, Chicago and London: The University of Chicago Press.

Armstrong, D. (1995) The rise of surveillance medicine, *Sociology of Health & Illness*, 17, 393–404.

Ashley, B., Hollows, J., Jones, S. and Taylor, B. (2004) *Food and Cultural Studies*, London: Routledge.

Baarts, C. and Kryger Pedersen, I. (2009) Derivative benefits: Exploring the body through complementary and alternative medicine, *Sociology of Health and Illness*, 31: 5, 719–733.

Bahr Buge, A. and Almas, R. (2006) Domestic dinner representations and practices of a proper meal among young suburban mothers, *Journal of Consumer Culture*, 6, 203–227.

Balfe, M (2007) Diets and discipline: The narratives of practice of university students with type 1 diabetes, *Sociology of Health and Illness*, 29: 1, 136–153.

Barthel, D. (1989) Modernism and marketing: The chocolate box revisited, *Theory, Culture and Society*, 6: 3, 429–438.

Baxter, J., Hewitt, B. and Haynes M. (2008) Life course transitions and housework: Marriage, parenthood, and time on housework, *Journal of Marriage and Family*, 70, 259–272.

Beagan, B. and Saunders, S. (2005) Occupations of masculinity: Producing gender through what men do and don't do, *Journal of Occupational Science*, 12: 3, 161–169.

Beagan, B., Chapman, G. E., D'Sylva, A. and Bassett, B. R. (2008) 'It's just easier for me to do It': Rationalizing the family division of foodwork, *Sociology*, 42: 4, 653–671.

Beardsworth, A. and Keil, T (1997) *Sociology on the Menu. An Invitation to the Study of Food and Society*, London: Routledge.

Beck, U. (1992) *Risk Society: Towards a New Modernity*, London: Sage.

Beck, U. (2002) The cosmopolitan society and its enemies, *Theory Culture Society*, 19: 1–2, 17–44.

Beck, U. and Beck-Gernsheim, E. (2002) *Individualization, Institutionalized Individualism and its Social and Political Consequences*, London: Sage.

Becker, A. E., Burwell, R. A., Gilman, S. E., Herzog, D. B. and Hamburg, P. (2002) Eating behaviours and attitudes following prolonged exposure to television among ethnic Fijian adolescent girls, *British Journal of Psychiatry*, 180, 509–514.

Becker A. E., Fay, K., Gilman, S. and Stiegel-Moore, R. (2007) Facets of acculturation and their diverse relations to body shape concern in Fiji, *International Journal of Eating Disorders*, 40: 1, 42–50.

Beckett, F., Blythman, J., Ehrlich, R., Fort, M., Gluck, M., and Protz, R. (2002) Noshtalgia, *The Guardian*, 29th June 2002, accessed 5/February/2015 http://www.theguardian.com/lifeandstyle/2002/jun/29/foodanddrink.shopping1.

Bendelow, G. (2009) *Health, Emotion and the Body*, Cambridge: Polity Press.

Bennett, T., Savage, M., Silva, E., Warde, A., Gayo-Cal, Modesto, and Wright, D. (2009) *Culture, Class, Distinction*, London: Routledge.

Belasco, W. (2008) *Food, the Key Concepts*, Oxford: Berg.

Bergman, S. (2009) Part-Time Fatso. Sometimes I'm Fat and Sometimes I'm Not, in Rothblum, W. and Solovay, S. (eds) *The Fat Studies Reader*, New York: New York University Press, pp. 139–142.

Billig, M. (1995) *Banal Nationalism*, London: Sage.

Bordo, S, (2003) *Reading the Slender Body, Body Politics: Women and the Discourses of Science*, (2nd Ed), London: Routledge.

Bourdieu, P. (1984) *Distinction, A Social Critique of the Judgement of Taste*, London: Routledge.

Bourdieu, P. (1986) The Forms of Capital, in J. (ed) *Handbook of Theory and Research for the Sociology of Education*, New York: Greenwood, pp. 241–258.

Bourdieu, P. (1996 [1992]) *The Rules of Art: Genesis and Structure of the Literary Field*, Cambridge: Polity.

Bourdieu, P. (2005) Taste of Luxury, Taste of Necessity, in Korsmyer, C. (ed) *The Taste Culture Reader: Experiencing Food and Drink*, New York: Berg, pp. 72–79.

Bourdieu, P. and Wacquant, L. (2002 [1992]) *An Invitation to Reflexive Sociology*, Cambridge: Polity.

Bradley, H. (1996) *Fractured Identities: Changing Patterns of Inequality*, Cambridge: Polity Press.

Bradley, H. (2007) *Gender*, Cambridge: Polity Press.

Bradley, H. (2014) Class descriptors or class relations? Thoughts towards a critique of Savage et al. *Sociology*, June 2014, 48: 3, 429–436.

Brillat-Savarin, J. A. (1970 [1825]) *The Physiology of Taste*, London: Penguin.

Budgeon, S. (2014) The dynamics of gender hegemony: Femininities, masculinities and social change, *Sociology*, 48: 2, 317–334.

Burns, M. (2009) Bodies as (Im)material? Bulimia and Body Image Discourse, in Malson, H. and Burns, M. (eds) *Critical Feminist Approaches to Eating Dis/Orders*, London and New York: Routledge, pp. 124–134.

Bury, M. R. (1982) Chronic illness as biographical disruption, *Sociology of Health and Illness*, 4: 2, 167–182.

Bury, M. R. (2001) Illness narratives: Fact or fiction?, *Sociology of Health and Illness*, 23: 3, 263–285.

Butler, J. (1999) *Gender Trouble*, New York: Routledge.

Cairns, K., Johnston, J. and Baumann, S (2010) Caring about food: Doing gender in the foodie kitchen, *Gender and Society*, 24: 5, 591–615.

Cairns, K. and Johnston, J. (in press) *Food and Femininitites*, London: Bloomsbury.

Caplan, P. (ed) (1997) *Food, Health and Identity*, London: Routledge.

Carolan, M. (2011) *Embodied Food Politics*, Farnham: Ashgate.

Carrigan, M., Szmigin, I. and Leek, S. (2006) Managing routine food choices in UK families: The role of convenience consumption, *Appetite*, 47, 372–383.

Celnik, D., Gillespie, L. and Lean M. E. J. (2012) Time-scarcity, ready-meals, ill-health and the obesity epidemic, *Trends in Food Science and Technology*, 27, 4–11.

Charles, N. and Kerr, M. (1988) *Women, Food and Families*, Manchester: Manchester University Press.

Charmaz, K. (2006) *Constructing Grounded Theory*, London: Sage.

Chernin, K. (1981) *Womanize: The Tyranny of Slenderness*, London: Women's Press.

Christakis, N. A. and Fowler, J. H. (2007) The spread of obesity in a large scale network over 32 years, *The New England Journal of Medicine*, 357: 4, 370–379.

Clough, P. T. (ed) (2007) *The Affective Turn: Theorizing the Social*, Durham, NC: Duke University Press.

Cohen, S. ([1972] (2011) *Folk Devils and Moral Panics: The Creation of the Mods and the Rockers*, Abingdon: Routledge Classics.

Collinson, M. (1996) In search of the high life: Drugs, crime, masculinities and consumption, *British Journal of Criminology*, 36: 3, 428–444.

Connell, R. W. (1995) *Masculinities*, Oxford: Polity Press.

Connell, R. W. (2005) *Masculinities* (2nd Ed), Cambridge: Polity Press.

Counihan, M. (1999) *The Anthropology of Food and Body, Gender, Meaning and Power*, London: Routledge.

Coveney, J. (2006) *Food, Morals and Meaning* (2nd Ed), London: Routledge.

Coveney, J. (2014) *Food*, London and New York: Routledge.

Coveney, J. and Bunton, R. (2003) In pursuit of the study of pleasure: Implications for health research and practice, *Health*, 7: 2, 161–179.

Crawford, R. (1980) Healthism and the medicalisation of everyday life, *International Journal of Health Services*, 10, 365–388.

Crawford, R. (2000) The ritual of health promotion, in Williams, S., Gabe J. and Calnan, M. (eds) *Health, Medicine and Society. Key Theories, Future Agendas*, London: Routledge, pp. 219–236.

Dalley, S. E., Pollet, T. V. and Vidal, J. (2013), Body size and body esteem in women: The mediating role of possible self expectancy, *Body Image*, 10: 3, 411–414.

Davis, K. (2008) Intersectionality as buzzword: A sociology of science perspective on what make a feminist theory successful, *Feminist Theory*, 9: 1, 67–85.

Dawson, M. (2012) Reviewing the critique of individualization: The disembedded and embedded theses, *Acta Sociologica*, 55: 4, 305–319.

Deans, J. (2013) Jamie Oliver bemoans chips, cheese and giant TVs of modern-day poverty, *The Guardian*, Tuesday 27th August 2013, Page 3.

Deleuze, G. and Guattari, F. (1998) *A Thousand Plateaus*, London: Athlone Press.

DeSolier, I. (2013) *Food and the Self: Consumption, Production and material Culture*, London: Bloomsbury Academic.

DeVault, M. l. (1991) *Feeding the Family*, London: University of Chicago Press.

Dixon, J. and Banwell, C. (2004) Heading the table: Parenting and the junior consumer, *British Food Journal*, 105: 3, 182–193.

DOH, (2010) Healthy lives, healthy people: Our strategy for public health in England, *HM Government White Paper*, accessed 03/August/2013 https://www.gov.uk/government/uploads/system/uploads/attachment_data/file/216096/dh_127424.pdf.

DOH, (2011) Healthy lives, healthy people: A call to action on obesity in England, *HM Government*, accessed 03/August/2013 https://www.gov.uk/government/uploads/system/uploads/attachment_data/file/213720/dh_130487.pdf.

Doucet, A. (2009) Can men mother – or is mothering essentially female? The Vanier institute of the family, *Transitions*, spring, accessed 06/June/2013, http://www.andreadoucet.com/wp-content/uploads/2011/05/Gender-Equality-and-Gender-Differences.pdf.

Douglas, M. (1966) *Purity and Danger, An Analysis of Pollution and Taboo*, London: Routledge.

Douglas, M. and Nicod, M. (1974) Taking the biscuit, the structure of British meals, *New Sociology*, 19, 744–747.

Douglas, S. J. and Michaels, M. (2004) *The Mommy Myth: The Idealisation of Motherhood and How it has Undermined All Women*, New York: Free Press.

Drouard, A. (2007) Chefs, Gourmets and Gourmands, in Freeman, P (eds) *Food: The History of Taste*, London: Thames & Hudson, pp. 263–301.

Duncan, S. and Edwards, R. (1999) *Lone Mothers, Paid Work and Gendered Moral Rationalities*. London: MacMillan.

Earle, S.E. (2003) Bums and boobs: Fatness and women's experiences of pregnancy, *Women's' Studies International Forum*, 26: 3, 245–252.

Eckerman, L. (2009) Theorising Self-Starvation. Beyond Risk, Governmentality and the Normalizing Gaze, in Malson, H. and Burns, M. (eds) *Critical Feminist Approaches to Eating Dis/Orders*, London and New York: Routledge, pp. 9–21.

Elias, N. (1978) *The History of Manners. The Civilising Process: Volume 1*, New York: Pantheon Books.

Erickson, R. J. (2005) Why emotion work matters: Sex, gender and the division of household labour, *Journal of Marriage and the Family*, 67: 2, 337–351.

Falk, P. (1991), The Sweetness of Forbidden Fruit, Towards an Anthropology of Taste, in Fürst, E. L., Prättälä, R., Ekström, M., Holm, L. and Kjaernes, U. (eds), *Palatable Worlds: Sociocultural Food Studies*, Oslo: Solum Forlag, pp. 221–234.

Fawcett Society (2010), http://www.fawcettsociety.org.uk/index.asp?PageID= 37, accessed 03/December/2010).

Fiddes, N. (1991) *Meat a Natural Symbol*, London: Routledge.

Finch, J. (1984) It's Good to have Someone to Talk to: The Ethics and The Politics of Interviewing Women, in Bell, C. and Roberts, H. (eds) *Social Researching*, London: Routledge and Kegan Paul.

Finch, J. (2007) Displaying families, *Sociology*, 41: 1, 65–81.

Fischler, C. (1980) Commensality, food habits, social change and the nature/ culture dilemma, *Social Science Information*, 19: 6, 937–953.

Fischler, C. (1988) Food, self and identity, *Social Science Information*, 27: 2, 275–292.

Fischler, C. (2011) Commensality, society and culture, *Social Science Information*, 50: 3–4, 528–548.

Foucault, M. (1973) *The Birth of the Clinic: An Archaeology of Medical Perception*, London: Tavistock.

Foucault, M. (1977) *Discipline and Punish, The Birth of The Prison*, London: Penguin.

Foucault, M. (1979) *The History of Sexuality: Volume 1, An Introduction*, London: Penguin.

Foucault, M. (1988) Technologies of the Self, in Martin, L. H., Gutman, H. and Hutton, P.H. (eds) *Technologies of the Self: A Seminar with Michael Foucault*, London: Tavistock, pp. 16–49.

Foucault, M. (1991) Governmentality, in Burchell, G., Gordon, C. and Miller, P. (eds) *The Foucault Effect: Studies in Governmentality*, Hemel Hempstead: Harverter Wheatsheaf, pp. 87–104.

Francis, A. A. (2012) The dynamics of family trouble: Middle-class parents whose children have problems, *Journal of Contemporary Ethnography*, 41: 4, 371–401.

Frank, A. W. (1995) *The Wounded Storyteller: Body, Illness and Ethics*, Chicago: Chicago University Press.

Freeman, P (eds) (2007) *Food: The History of Taste*, London: Thames & Hudson.

Friedman, S. (2011) The cultural currency of a 'good' sense of humour: British comedy and new forms of distinction, *British Journal of Sociology*, 62: 2, 347–370.

Frost, L. (2001) *Young Women and the Body, A Feminist Sociology*, Basingstoke: Palgrave MacMillan.

Gard, M. (2009) Understanding Obesity by Understanding Desire, in Malson, H. and Burns, M. (eds) *Critical Feminist Approaches to Eating Dis/Orders*, London and New York: Routledge, pp. 35–45.

Germov, J. and Williams, L. (2004) *Sociology of Food and Nutrition: The Social Appetite* (2nd Ed), Oxford: OUP.

Gerson, K. (2002) Moral dilemmas, moral strategies, and the transformation of gender: Lessons from two generations of work and family change. *Gender and Society*, 16, 8–28.

Giddens, A. (1991) *Modernity and Self Identity, Self and Society in the Late Modern Age*, Cambridge: Polity Press.

Giddens, A. (1992) *The Transformation of Intimacy: Sexuality, Love and Eroticism in Modern Societies*, Cambridge: Polity.

Gillis, J. (1997) *A World of Their Own Making, Myth, Ritual and the Quest for Family Values*, Cambridge, MA: Harvard University Press.

Giovanelli, D. and Ostertag, S. (2009) Controlling the Body, Media Representations, Body Size and Self Discipline, in Rothblum, E. and Solovay, S. (eds) *The Fat Studies Reader*, New York: New York University Press.

Goffman, E. (1959) *The Presentation of the Self in Every Day Life*, London: Penguin.

Goffman, E. (1963) *Stigma, Notes on the Management of a Spoiled Identity*, London: Penguin.

Gough, B. and Conor, M. T. (2006) Barriers to healthy eating amongst men: A qualitative analysis, *Social Science and Medicine*, 62: 2, 387–395.

Gough, B. (2006) Try to be healthy, but don't forgo your masculinity: Deconstructing men's health discourse in the media, *Social Science and Medicine* 63: 9, 2476–2488.

Gough, B. (2007) Real Men don't diet: An analysis of contemporary newspaper representations of men, food and health, *Social Science and Medicine*, 64: 2, 326–337.

Gough, B. (2009) The Stubborn Resistance of Hegemonic Masculinities within Discourses of Men's Health and Embodiment, in Biricik, A. and Hearn, J. (eds) *GEXcel Work in Progress Report*, vol. 6. *Proceedings from GEXcel Theme 2*.

Graham, M. (2005) Chaos, in Kulik, D. and Meneley, A. (eds), *Fat: The Anthropology of an Obsession* New York: London: Tarcher; Penguin.

Grignon, C. (2001) Commensality and Social Morphology: An Essay, in Typology, from Scholliers, P. (ed), *Food, Drink & Identity, Cooking, Eating & Drinking in Europe since the Middle Ages*, Oxford: Berg, pp. 23–36.

Hays, S. (1996) *The Cultural Contradictions of Motherhood*, New Haven, CT: Yale University Press.

Heldke, L. (2003) *Exotic Appetites, Ruminations of a Food Adventurer*, London: Routledge.

Herzlich, C. (1973) *Health and Illness*, London: Academic Press.

Hey, V. and Bradford, S. (2006) Re-engineering motherhood? Surestart in the community, *Contemporary Issues in Early Childhood*, 7: 1, 53–67.

Hickman, M. (2012) End to calorie confusion as standardised food labelling system is announced for supermarkets, *The Independent*, 24/October/ 2012, accessed 31/October/2013 http://www.independent.co.uk/life-style/ food-and-drink/news/end-to-calorie-confusion-as-standardised-food-label- ling-system-is-announced-for-supermarkets-8223798.html.

Hochschild, A. R. (1979) Emotion work, feeling rules and social structure, *American Journal of Sociology*, 85: 3, 551–575.

Hochschild, A. R. (1983) *The Managed Heart: Commercialization of Human Feeling*, Berkeley: University of California Press.

Hochschild, A. (1997) *The Time Bind. When Work Becomes Home and Home Becomes Work*, New York: Metropolitan.

Hochschild, A. R. and Machung, A. (2003) *The Second Shift*, (2nd Ed) London: Penguin Books.

Hollows, J. (2003) Oliver's twist, leisure, labour and domestic masculinity in The Naked Chef, *International Journal of Cultural Studies*, 6: 2, 229–248.

Hollows, J. and Jones, S. (2010) At least he's doing something: Moral entrepreneurship and individual; responsibility in Jamie's Ministry of Food, *European Journal of Cultural Studies*, 13, 307–322.

Howson, A. (2004) *The Body in Society: An Introduction*, Cambridge: Polity Press.

Huppatz, K. (2009) Reworking Bourdieu's 'Capital': Feminine and female capitals in the field of paid caring work, *Sociology*, 43: 1, 45–66.

Inckle, K. (2007) *Writing on the Body? Thinking through Gendered Embodiment of the Marked Flesh*, Newcastle: Cambridge Scholars Publishing.

Jabs, J. and Devine, C. (2006) Time-scarcity and food-choices: An overview, *Appetite*, 47: 2, 196–204.

Jackson, P. (eds) (2009) *Changing Families, Changing Food*, London: Palgrave MacMillan.

Jallinoja, P., Pajari, P. and Absetz, P. (2010) Negotiated pleasures in health-seeking lifestyles of participants of a health promoting intervention, *Health (London)*, 14: 2, 115–130.

Jallinoja, R. and Widmer, E. D. (eds) (2011) *Families and Kinship in Contemporary Europe: Rules and Practices of Relatedness*. Basingstoke: Palgrave Macmillan.

James, A. (2010) Children's Food: Reflections on Politics, Policy and Practices, BSA Food Studies Conference, London, accessed 3/December/2013. http://www.britsoc.co.uk/media/24962/AllisonJames.ppt.

James, A., Curtis, P. and Ellis, K. (2009a) Negotiating Family, Negotiating Food: Children as Family Participants?, in James, A., Trine Kjorholt, A. and Tingstad, V. (eds) *Children, Food and Identity in Everyday Life*, London: Palgrave MacMillan, pp. 35–52.

James, A. Trine Kjorholt, and A. Tingstad, V. (eds) (2009b) *Children, Food and Identity in Everyday Life*, London: Palgrave MacMillan.

Jarvis, A-A. (2011), How Britain Fell Back in Love with Baking, Independent4/October/2011, accessed 23/January/14 http://www.independent.co.uk/life-style/food-and-drink/features/how-britain-fell-back-in-love-with-baking-2365082.html.

Johansson, B, Ossiansson, E., Dreas, J. A. and Märild, S, (2013) Proper food and a tight budget, German and Swedish parents reflecting on children, *Food and Health, Food, Culture and Society*, 16: 3, 457–477.

Johnston, J. and Baumann, S. (2010) *Foodies, Democracy and Distinction in the Gourmet Kitchen*, London: Routledge.

Jutel, A. (2005) Weighing health: The moral burden of obesity, *Social Semiotics*, 15: 2, 113–125.

Kauffman, J. C, (2010) *The Meaning of Cooking*, Cambridge: Polity Press.

Kemmer, D. (2000) Tradition and change in domestic roles and food preparation, *Sociology*, 34: 2, 323–333.

Kennedy, P. and Kennedy, C.A. (2010) *Using Theory to Explore Health, Medicine and Society*, Bristol: Polity Press.

Kolata, G. (2007) *Rethinking Thin. The New Science of Weight Loss – and the Myths and Realities of Dieting*, New York: Farrar, Strauss and Giroux.

Kozinets, R. V. (2010) *Netnography, Doing Ethnographic Research Online*, London: Sage.

Kulik, D. and Meneley, A. (2005) *Fat The Anthropology of an Obsession*, New York: Jeremy P. Tarcher/Penguin.

Lareau, A. (2003) *Unequal Childhoods: Class, Race and Family Life*, Berkeley, CA: University of California Press.

Lawler, S. (2008) *Identity: Sociological Perspectives*, Cambridge: Polity Press.

LeBesco, K. (2001) Queering Fat Bodies/Politics, in Braziel, J. E. and LeBesco, K. (eds) *Bodies Out Of Bounds, Fatness and Transgression*, London: University of California Press, pp. 74–90.

LeBesco, K. (2009) Weight Management, Good Health and the Will to Normality, in Malson, H. and Burns, M. (eds) *Critical Feminist Approaches to Eating Dis/Orders*, London and New York: Routledge, pp. 146–156.

Letherby, G. (2003) *Feminist Research in Theory and Practice*, Buckingham: Open University Press.

Letherby, G. and Zdrodowski, D. (1995) 'Dear researcher', the use of correspondence as a method within feminist qualitative research, *Gender and Society*, 9: 5, 576–593.

Levi-Strauss, C. (1969) *The Raw and the Cooked*, London: Jonathan Cape.

Lewis, J. (2007) Gender ageing and the 'new social settlement': The importance of developing a holistic approach to care politics, *Current Sociology*, 55: 2, 271–286.

Little, J., Llbery, B. and Watts, D. (2009) Gender, consumption and the relocalisation of food: A research agenda, *Sociolgia Ruralis*, 49: 3, 201–217.

Littler, J. (2013) The rise of the 'Yummy Mummy': Popular conservatism and the neoliberal maternal in contemporary British culture, *Communication, Culture & Critique*, 6: 2, 227–243.

Lowenberg, J. and Davis, F. (1994) Beyond medicalisation-demedicalisation: The case of holistic health, *Sociology of Health & Illness*, 16: 5, 579–599.

Luke ([1611], 2013) King James Bible, 'Authorized Version', Cambridge Edition, accessed 03/11/2013, http://www.kingjamesbibleonline.org/Luke-12-19/.

Lupton, D. (1996) *Food, the Body and the Self*, London: Sage.

Lupton, D. (1998) *The Emotional Self*, London: Sage.

Lupton, D. (2000) The heart of the meal: Food preferences amongst rural Australian couples, *Sociology of Health and Illness*, 22:1, 94–109.

Lupton, D. (2003) *Medicine as Culture: Illness, Disease, and the Body in Western Societies*, London: Sage.

Lupton, D. (2005) Lay Discourses and beliefs related to food risks: An Australian perspective, *Sociology of Health and Illness*, 27: 4, 448–467.

Lupton, D. (2013) *Fat*, Abingdon: Routledge.

Lynch, K. (2007) Love labour as a distinct form of non-comodifiable form of labour care, *The Sociological Review*, 55: 3, 550–570.

Malson, H. (1998) *The Thin Woman: Feminism, Post-Structuralism and the Social Psychology of Anorexia Nervosa*, London: Routledge.

Malson, H. (2007) Deconstructing Un/Healthy Body-Weight and Weight Management, in Riley, S. Burns, M., Frith, H., Wiggins, S. and Markula, P. (eds) *Critical Bodies: Representations, Identities and Practices of Weight Management*, Basingstoke: Palgrave MacMillan.

Malson, H. and Burns, M. (eds) (2009) *Critical Feminist Approaches to Eating Dis/Orders*, London and New York: Routledge.

Malson, H., Schmidt, U. and Humfress, S. (2006) Between paternalism and neo-liberalism regulation: Producing motivated clients of psychotherapy, *International Journal of Critical Psychology*, 18: 4, 107–135.MarketLine (2013) United Kingdom, Ready Meals, The Grocer, accessed 06/August/2013, http://www.thegrocer.co.uk/reports/third-party-reports/united-kingdom-ready-meals/348106.article.

Marmot, M. and Bell, R. (2012) Fair society, healthy lives, *Public Health* 126, S4–S10.

Mauss, M. ([1922]1990) *The Gift: Forms And Functions Of Exchange in Archaic Societies*, London: Routledge.

Meadow, M. and Weiss, L. (1992) *Women's Conflicts about Eating and Sexuality: The Relationship between Food and Sex*, New York: The Haworth Press.

McKie, L., Gregory, S. and Bowlby, S. (2002) Shadow times: The temporal and spatial frameworks and experiences of caring and working, *Sociology*, 36: 4, 897–924.

McIntosh, W. A. and Zey, M. (1989) Women as gatekeepers of food consumption: A sociological critique, *Food and Foodways*, 3: 4, 317–332.

McRobbie, A. (2008) *Gender Culture and Social Change: In the Aftermath of Feminism*. London: Sage.

Meah, A. and Jackson, P. (2013) Crowded kitchens: The 'democratisation' of domesticity?, *Gender, Place and Culture: A Journal of Feminist Geography*, 20: 3, 578–596.

Meah, A. and Watson, W. (2011) Saints and slackers: Challenging discourses about the decline of domestic cooking, *Sociological Research Online*, 16: 2, unpaginated, http://www.socresonline.org.uk/16/2/6.html.

Meah, A. and Watson, W. (2013) Cooking up consumer anxieties about 'Provenance' and 'Ethics' in *Food, Culture and Society*, 16: 3, 495–513.

Mennell, S. (1985) *All Manners of Food*, Blackwell: Oxford.

Mills, C. W. (1959) *The Sociological Imagination*, London: Penguin.

Mintz, S. (1985) *Sweetness and Power*, United States: Viking Penguin.

Miriam Webster Dictionary (2014) Miriam Webster Dictionary online, accessed 10/November/2014) http://www.thefreedictionary.com/gastronomy.

Moore, S. E. H. (2010) Is the healthy body gendered? Toward a feminist critique of the new paradigm of health, *Body and Society*, 16: 2, 95–118.

Monaghan, L. F. (2007) McDonaldizing men's bodies? Slimming, associated (ir)rationalities and resistances, *Body and Society*, 7: 13, 67–93.

Moran, C. (2011) *How to be a Woman*, Croydon: Ebury Press, Random House.

Morgan, D. (1996) *An Introduction to Family Studies*, Cambridge: Polity Press.

Morgan, D. (1998) Sociological Imaginations and imagining sociologies: Bodies, auto/biographies and other mysteries, *Sociology*, 32: 4, 647–663.

Morgan, D. (2011) *Rethinking Family Practices*, Basingstoke: Palgrave MacMillan.

Mosio, R., Arnould, E. and Price, L. (2004) Between mothers and markets, constructing family identity through homemade food, *Journal of Consumer Culture*, 4: 2, 361–384.

Murcott, A. (1982) On the social significance of the cooked dinner in South Wales, *Social Science Information*, 21: 4, 677–696.

Murcott, A. (1983) It's a Pleasure to Cook for Him…: Food, Mealtimes and Gender in some South Wales Households, in Gamarnikow, E., Morgan, D., Purvis, J. and Taylorson, D. (eds) *The Public and the Private*, London: Heineman, pp. 962–77.

Murcott, A. (1995) Raw, Cooked and Proper Meals at Home, in Marshall, D. (ed) *Food Choice And The Consumer*, Glasgow: Blackie Academic Publications, pp. 219–234.

Murcott, A. (1997) Family Meals, a Thing of the Past, in Caplan, P. (ed) *Food, Health and Identity*, London: Routledge, pp. 32–49.

Murcott, A. (eds) (1998), *The Nation's Diet, the Social Science of Food Choice*, Harlow: Longman.

Murray, S. (2008) *The 'Fat' Female Body*, Basingstoke: Palgrave MacMillan.

Naccarato, P. and LeBesco, K. (2012) *Culinary Capital*, London: Berg.

Nash, J. C. (2008) Re-thinking intersectionality, *Feminist Review*, 89, 1–15.

Nath, J. (2011) Gendered fare?: A qualitative investigation of alternative food and masculinities, *Journal of Sociology*, 47: 3, 261–278.

Negra, D. (2009). *What a Girl Wants? Reclamation of the Self in Post-Feminism*, London, England: Routledge.

Nettleton, S. (2006) *The Sociology of Health And Illness* (2nd Edition), Cambridge: Polity Press.

Nettleton, S., Woods, B., Burrows, R. and Kerr, A. (2010) Experiencing food allergy and food intolerance, an analysis of lay accounts, *Sociology*, 44: 2, 289–305.

Oakley, A. (1981) Interviewing Women: A Contradiction in Terms, in Roberts, H. (ed) *Doing Feminist Research*, London: Routledge, pp. 30–62.

Oakley, A. (1992) *Social Support and Motherhood*, Oxford: Blackwell.

O'Brien Hallstein, L. (2010) *White Feminists and Contemporary Maternity: Purging Matrophobia*, New York: Palgrave MacMillan.

O'Reilly, A. (2004) *Mother Outlaws: Theories and Practices of Empowered Mothering*, Toronto: Canada Women's Press.

Orbach, (1982) *Fat is a Feminist Issue II*, London: Arrow Books.

Pajari, P., Jallinoja P. and Absetz, P. (2006) Negotiating over self-control and activity: An analysis of balancing in the repertoires of Finnish healthy lifestyle. *Social Science and Medicine*, 62: 10, 2601–2611.

Parsons, J. M. (2014a) Cheese and chips out of styrofoam containers: An exploration of taste and cultural symbols of appropriate family foodways, *A Journal of Media and Culture*, 17 – 'taste', http://journal.media-culture.org.au/index.php/mcjournal/article/viewArticle/766.

Parsons, J. M. (2014b) When convenience is inconvenient, 'healthy' family foodways and the persistent intersectionalities of gender and class, *Journal of Gender Studies*, published online 20 December, pp. 1–16, http://dx.doi.org/10.1080/09589236.2014.987656.

Parsons, T. ([1951], 1991) *The Social System*, London: Routledge.

Petersen, A. (2007) *The Body in Question, A Socio-Cultural Approach*, London: Routledge.

Petersen, A. and Bunton, R. (1997) *Foucault, Health and Medicine*, Abingdon: Routlege.

Peterson, R. A. and Kern, R. M. (1996) Changing highbrow taste: From snob to omnivore, *American Sociological Review*, 61: 5, 900–909.

Pollan, M. (2013) *Cooked, a Natural History of Transformation*, New York: Penguin.

Poulain J-P (2002) The contemporary diet in France: 'De-structuration' or from commensalism to 'vagabond feeding', *Appetite*, 39: 1, 43–55.

Puwar, N. (2004) *Space Invaders: Race, Gender and Bodies Out of Place*, Oxford and NewYork: Berg.

Ratna, A. (2013) 'Intersectional plays of identity: The experiences of British Asian female footballers', *Sociological Research Online*, 18: 1, unpaginated (Online Journal).

Reay, D. (2004) Gendering Bourdieu's Concept of Capitals? Emotional Capital, Women and Social Class, in Adkins, L. and Skeggs, B. (eds) *Feminism After Bourdieu*, Oxford: Blackwell, pp. 57–76.

Reckwitz, A. (2002) The status of the 'Material' in theories of culture: From 'Social Structure' to 'Artefacts', *Journal for the Theory of Social Behaviour*, 32: 2, 195–217.

Rich, A. (1986) *Of Woman Born: Motherhood as Experience and Institution*, (2nd Edition), New York: Norton.

Richardson, L. (1997) *Fields of Play, Constructing an Academic Life*, New Brunswick, New Jersey: Rutgers University Press.

Riley, S., Burns, M., Frith, H., Wiggins, S. and Markula, P. (2007) (eds) *Critical Bodies: Representations, Identities and Practices of Weight Management*, Basingstoke: Palgrave MacMillan.

Ringrose, J. and Walkerdine. V. (2008) Regulating the abject, *Feminist Media Studies*, 8: 3, 227–246.

Risman, B. J. (2004). Gender as social structure: Theory wrestling with activism, *Gender and Society*, 18, 429–450.

Robertson, S. (2007) *Understanding Men and Health*, OUP: Maidenhead.

Robinson, B. K. and Hunter, E. (2008), Is mom still doing it ll? Re-examining Depictions of Family Work in Popular dvertising, *Journal of Family Issues*, 29: 4, 465–486.

Rothblum, E. D. and Solovay, S. (eds) (2009) *The Fat Studies Reader*, New York: New York University Press.

Rousseau, S. (2012) *Food Media, Celebrity Chefs and the Politics of Everyday Interference*, London: Berg.

Ruppel-Shell, E. (2002) *Fatwars: The Inside Story of the Obesity Industry*, London, Atlantic Books.

Saguy, A. C. (2013) *What's Wrong with Fat?*, New York: Oxford University Press.

Sassatelli, R. (2001) Tamed Hedonism: Choice, Desires and Deviant Pleasure, in Gronow, J. and Warde, A. (eds) *Ordinary Consumption*. London: Routledge, pp. 93–106.

Savage, M., Devine, F., Cunningham, N., Taylor, M., Li, Y., Hjellbrekke, J., Le Roux, B., Friedman, S. and Miles, A. (2013) A New Model of Social Class? Findings from the BBC's Great British Class Survey Experiment. *Sociology*, 47: 2, 219–250.

Schippers, M. (2007) Recovering the feminine other; Masculinity, femininity and gender hegemony, *Theoretical Sociology*, 36: 1, 85–102.

Scholliers, P. (ed) (2001) *Food, Drink and Identity, Cooking, Eating and Drinking in Europe since the Middle Ages*, Oxford: Berg.

Scott, S. (2009) *Making Sense of Everyday Life*, Cambridge: Polity Press.

Senn, M. and Elhardt, C. (2014) Bourdieu and the bomb: Power, language and the doxic battle over the value of nuclear weapons, *European Journal of International Relations*, 20: 2, 316–340.

Seymour, R. (2013) 'Austerity cooking' has been hijacked by the moralisers, *The Guardian.com*, published online 28th August 2013, accessed 28/August/2013 http://www.theguardian.com/commentisfree/2013/aug/28/austerity-cooking-jack-monroe-hijacked-moralisers.

Shirani, F., Henwood, K. and Coltart C. (2012) Meeting the challenges of intensive parenting culture: Gender, risk, management and the moral parent, *Sociology*, 46: 1, 25–40.

Short, F. (2006) *Kitchen Secrets: The Meaning of Cooking in Everyday Life*, Oxford: Berg.

Singh-Manoux, A. Marmot, M. (2005) Role of socialization in explaining social inequalities in health, *Social Science and Medicine*, 60: 9, 2129–2133.

Skeggs, B. (1997) *Formations of Class and Gender*, London: Sage.

Skeggs, B. (2004a) *Class, Self and Culture*, London: Routledge.

Skeggs, B. (2004b) Introducing Pierre Bourdieu's Analysis of Class, Gender and Sexuality, in Adkins, L. and Skeggs, B. (eds) *Feminism after Bourdieu*, Oxford: Blackwell, pp. 19–35.

Skeggs, B. (2005) The Making of class and gender through visualizing moral subject formation, *Sociology*, 39: 5, 965–982.

Slater, D. and Ritzer, G. (2001) Interview with Ulrich Beck, *Journal of Consumer Culture*, 1: 2, 261–277.

Squire, S. (2002) The personal and the political: Writing the theorist's body, *Australian Journal of Feminist Studies*, 17: 37, 55–64.

Stanley, L. (2004) The epistolarium: On theorising letters and correspondences', *Auto/Biography*, 12: 1, 216–250.

Stanley, L. and Morgan, D. (1993) On auto/biography in sociology, *Sociology*, 27: 1, 41–52.

Sutton, D. (2001) *Remembrance of Repasts: An Anthropology of Food and Memory*, Oxford: Berg.

Szabo, M. (2013) Foodwork or foodplay? Men's domestic cooking, privilege and leisure, *Sociology*, 47: 4, 623–638.

Tamboukou, M. (2010) *In the Fold between Power and Desire: Women Artists' Narratives*, Newcastle Upon Tyne: Cambridge Scholars Publishing.

Taylor, Y. (2012) *Fitting into Place? Class and Gender Geographies and Temporalities*, Farnham: Ashgate.

Turner, B. S. (1987) *Medical Power and Social Knowledge*, London: Sage.

Turner, B. S. (2008) *The Body and Society*, (3rd Edition), London: Sage.

Tyler, I. (2008) 'Chav mum, Chav scum': Class disgust in contemporary Britain, *Feminist Media Studies*, 8: 2, 17–34.

Vincent C. and Ball, S. J. (2007) 'Making up' the middle-class child: Families, activities and class dispositions, *Sociology*, 41: 6, 1061–1077.

Visser, M. (1991) *The Rituals of Dinner*, New York: Penguin.

Walby, S. (1990) *Theorising Patriarchy*, Oxford: Blackwell Press.

Waley-Cohen, J. (2007) The Quest for Perfect Balance, in Freeman, P (eds) *Food: The History of Taste*, London: Thames & Hudson, pp. 99–135.

Wann, M. (2009) Foreward, Fat Studies: An Invitation to Revolution, in Rothblum, W. and Solovay, S. (eds) *The Fat Studies Reader*, New York: New York University Press, pp. xi–xxvi.

Warde, A. (1997) *Consumption, Food and Taste*, London: Sage.

Warde, A. (2011) Cultural hostility re-considered, *Cultural Sociology*, 5: 3, 341–366.

Warde, A., Cheng S., Olsen W. and Southerton, D. (2007b) Changes in the practice of eating: A comparative analysis of time-use, *Acta Sociologica*, 50: 4, 363–385.

Warde, A., Wright, D. and Gayo-Cal, M. (2007), Understanding cultural omnivorousness: Or the myth of the cultural omnivore, *Cultural Sociology*, 1: 2, 143–164.

Wardrop, M. (2009) 'Kate moss: Nothing tastes as good as skinny feels', *Telegraph*, 19/November/2009, accessed 23/January/2013 http://www.telegraph.co.uk/news/celebritynews/6602430/Kate-Moss-Nothing-tastes-as-good-as-skinny-feels.html.

Warin, M., Turner, K., Moore, V. and Davies, M. (2008) Bodies, mothers and identities: Rethinking obesity and the BMI, *Sociology of Health and Illness*, 30: 1, 97–111.

Weir, A. (2010) *The Real Me is Thin*, London, Fourth Estate.

West, C. and. Zimmerman D. H. (1987) Doing ender, *Gender and Society*, 1: 2, 125–151.

West, C. and Zimmerman, D. H. (2009) Accounting for doing gender, *Gender and Society* 23: 1: 112–122.

Wetherell, M. (2012) *Affect And Emotion, A New Social Science Understanding*, London: Sage.

Whitehead, S. (2002) *Men and Masculinities*, Cambridge: Polity.

Wills, W., Backett-Milburn, K., Lawton, J. and Roberts M. L. (2009) Consuming Fast Food: The Perceptions and Practices of Middle Class Teenagers, in James, A., Trine Kjorholt, A. and Tingstad, V. (eds) *Children, Food and Identity in Everyday Life*, London, Palgrave MacMillan, pp. 52–68.

Winterman, D. (2013) The Rise of the Ready Meal, *BBC News Magazine*, 16/February/2013, accessed 23/January/2015 http://www.bbc.co.uk/news/magazine-21443166).

Index

Printed by Printforce, United Kingdom